NFT For Beginners

The Ultimate Guide To Understand Non-Fungible Tokens And To Profit From Investing In Them. Learn To Create, Buy And Sell Crypto Art To Make Money | + Bonus 5-Step Guide To Sell NFTs

MAX BANCROFT

TABLE OF CONTENTS

INTRODUCTION

In the real world, fiat currency acts as a store of value and a medium of exchange, allowing you to buy and sell whatever you desire. But how do you suppose you'll pay for your painting, land, and Taylor Swift concert in a smooth, immediate manner in your virtual world? Crypto is the answer.

It isn't easy to see the metaverse, the alternate reality, functioning without cryptocurrency.

Without cryptocurrencies, it isn't easy to imagine the metaverse, or parallel reality, functioning. Crypto has become a must rather than an option inside a society where security, speed, and transparency are nearly required. At its foundation, cryptocurrency is the suitable medium of exchange for this quickly evolving hybrid society.

Take time to think about that. To begin with, rapid, swift, and frequent transactions, such as selling your antique and purchasing a new one right away, or even gaining that NFT, demand decentralization and transparency, in which the ability to authorize and authenticate your desired transactions resides with everyone in the network collectively, rather than with a single centralized authority or hub, making it more democratic, accessible, and quick! You do not place your trust in just one individual.

Secondly, given cryptocurrencies like bitcoin depend on advanced cryptographic technology for encryption and fund security, you can be sure that your acquisitions are safe if you're using a public ledger like blockchain, where each transaction is irreversible, traceable, and secure.

The enviable lightning-fast speed would surely be the third pillar of the metaverse and a gap filled admirably by cryptocurrencies' scalability promise or their ability to process or complete a more significant number of transactions per second! So go ahead and enter the metaverse, a parallel universe that is just as real and probably even more expansive than the one we live in! Crypto is the way to go because it solidifies the concept of interoperability, which includes the ability to work across several blockchain systems, quick value transfer, and digital, permanent proof of ownership in the metaverse. And the simplest way to get started with cryptocurrencies and take the plunge is to use reputable cryptocurrency exchanges and trading platforms such as CoinSwitch Kuber.

Like some other game-changing technology applications such as artificial intelligence (AI) and the internet of things (IoT), the metaverse and blockchain are not isolated notions. Because they all contain a variety of traits and functions that complement one another, allowing them to diverge in ways that make them more excellent than the sum of their parts! When they're used together, they'll reach their full potential.

Cryptocurrencies are a type of virtual currency.

Let's begin with some of the most prominent applications of blockchain technology in the metaverse: money! The metaverse has the potential to create a virtual world like "Ready Player One," in which we can play, work, and mingle with our friends in immersive environs without ever leaving our homes. And, of course, anyone who understands anything regarding human nature can forecast one of the most prominent activities people will want to do while shopping and buying goods!

It's already possible to buy virtual real estate plots inside the Decentraland online environment using the cryptocurrency Mana – in fact, someone recently made headlines for doing so for $2.4 million. Aside from land, we'll be able to buy digital representations of everything and anything we can acquire in the actual world, as well as a lot of things we can't! Governments are also getting in on the game, with Barbados recently opening the world's first metaverse embassy utilizing Decentraland.

On the other hand, buying stuff is likely to be just the start of blockchain-based currency in the metaverse. Decentralized finance (De-Fi) is a fast-growing field that is well-suited to operate within virtual worlds and surroundings. We should expect to see more metaverse-based financing, borrowing, trading, and investing.

WHAT IS AN NFT

NFTs, also known as Nyfties, are digital assets on a blockchain. They have unique qualities that stop them from being interchangeable. That means that they are difficult to forge, so it guarantees the authenticity of the purchased item.

NFTs had helped solve the problem artists worldwide have been having when it came to getting their well-earned royalties. As technology grew, so did the ease of making forgeries, duplicating work, and so forth that have been costing artists their well-earned pay for decades. NFT ownership is recorded on the blockchain, thus preventing illegal copies from being made. That ensures that artists get paid for their work.

Hence, the different types of NFTs spring up, including music, artwork, event tickets, domain names, physical asset ownership, and collectibles. At the moment, these are sold at auctions in a similar style to how artwork is sold at a live auction. The only difference is that it is all done online.

How Does It Work?

NFTs are mostly found on the Ethereum blockchain, and Ethereum-based tokens are used to authenticate ownership of the NFT. That's because the item or asset is attached to the token so that you can copy the file from someone else's NFT, but it won't be the original, and that can be traced. Whoever owns the token owns the NFT. Each copy or reproduction is verified as not being the foremost. The token contains the ownership information, a certificate of authenticity, and copyright information.

The blockchain is the public register for ownership of a particular digital item because it can't be hacked or overwritten. A ledger entry is created the same way as with any blockchain cryptocurrency. This entry contains the address to the file, which establishes the NFT. When the NFT is sold, that token code is also transferred and noted as a ledger entry. That is how ownership is tracked on the blockchain.

The NFT owner can add metadata to the character of their new NFT. This additional information would describe whether it is art, music, and so forth and what format it is in: for example, jpeg—video, and so on.

Tokens don't have any value on their own; they are based on the media attached to them. Think of an award-winning piece of art. The artist's talent and reputation give the painting its value, which it gets priced for an auction. Value is based on market demand. It is also based on rarity or scarcity because the NFT creator can decide if they want to make copies and, if so, how many.

Something essential to bear in mind is that the artist still owns the copyright, which they use to claim their royalties.

Therefore, ensure that you know what happens to the asset should these things occur to protect your purchase.

Why Is It Popular Now?

The amount that several digital items have been sold for has turned heads. And the industry has exploded purely because cryptocurrency is on the rise, and the COVID-19 pandemic has pushed a lot of items online. People can't physically watch a concert, so they purchase a whole album online and watch it there.

People were also not spending as much money because they were stuck indoors, didn't have to drive to work, and couldn't travel, so they now had the extra cash to spend. Plus, cryptocurrencies have surged in popularity, so one could say that the stars have aligned for NFT trading.

Its popularity has also helped create several companies that facilitate the buying and selling of NFTs, called NFT Marketplaces.

Many investors are paying high rates to promote NFTs based on their belief that they will only increase profitability.

Trade is an easy process that doesn't require extra financial backing or platforms. For example, if you create a piece of digital art, you have to sell it on a marketplace. There is no need to market it, spend money on promoting it, or punt potential buyers. With all this backing, it's no wonder more people are interested.

Is It A Crypto Fad?

I have mentioned a few times that NFTs are not new and have been around for at least a decade. An example of this is CryptoKitties, digital kittens that were collectibles and very popular among those involved in cryptocurrency when they were created in 2017. Despite all the celebrity hype, NFTs aren't a fad based on how high the trading volume is and is still growing.

NFTs have been linked to a technological revolution that taps into us wanting to own rare items of high value without the worry of illegal copies. That is fantastic in an age where everything online can and is copied. NFTs, bring back value to items with security and traceability.

Even though there were record-making sales in the news, NFT prices have dropped but are staying constant even as the hype dies down, making it a much more stable market in which to invest. It's also innovative and new, which can be a pushback to many presented with something that appears too fine to be true.

But not everyone is skeptical. NFTs have been likened to the dot-com bubble when people thought the internet was a fad. In reality, it was just overly priced early projects that had caused all the excitement. That is why there are problems that the NFT market could crash and bring down investors with it.

At this point, there is a ton of hype, so prices are high, but they will drop and stabilize. That is a pleasing item because it signifies that NFT trading is here long term.

What Are Speculative Investments?

You need to research any investment, so it's essential to cover all three types of assets: saving, investing, and speculating.

You will thank me later.

Save

The first way to invest is to save by putting money aside. For example, you can put your money into a savings account to keep for a specific item. Although you have the item's value, that can change but not rapidly, and you are saving towards it. The process is slow, with very little growth in terms of interest, but your money is safe because you won't lose any in the process.

That method can be used for short-term usage if you're saving for something specific and don't want to pay the penalty for an early withdrawal from an IRA. But most retirement funds for long-term usage are included in these types of investments.

Invest

Investing your money means that you are taking on a slight risk as your money starts growing, based on where it is supported. That is a long-term process with a minimum of 3 years so that any losses can be offset when the profits increase. Anything shorter, and you won't see a good trade-off. That's because your money will rise and fall as markets do but not at an alarming rate, and by the end, you would have weathered the ups and downs and realized a good profit.

That can be done by owning a successful business because you expect its success to mean more significant returns for you. Most people will invest with companies specializing in this and put the money to grow.

Speculate

With speculation, you are looking at quick profits over brief periods. The risk is significantly higher as you hope you don't lose your money and make a high return. An example of this is day trading.

Speculation has been likened to gambling one's money, but there is an art to belief, and when done right, the rewards are fantastic. The key is to maintain an eye on the markets to determine what will bring in the most profit.

That isn't a new concept, as it is used for art, collectibles, stocks, and other tangible items. The only difference now is that the things are digital, not physical, and you can trace their authenticity in a secure environment.

NFTs fall under speculative investment because their value fluctuates, depending on popularity. It's essential to understand this concept well as you begin your journey into NFT trading because the risks are high.

What Are The Most Expensive Nfts To Date?

As the list is continuously changing, I will not list the top 10 most expensive NFTs to date but list some of the most notable NFTs based on their price, rarity, and originality.

Beeple With Every day: The First 5,000 Days

That piece of NFT art was sold at Christie's for $69 million and, to date, is the enormous amount anyone has paid for an NFT, as well as the most expensive work of art by a living artist. It comprises 500 pieces of art that were created in May 2007.

The artwork was bought by Vignesh Sundaresan, also known as MetaKovan, who has displayed it in a digital art museum in the Metaverse, a virtual space shared.

Edward Snowden with Stay Free (Edward Snowden 2021)

This piece of art depicts Edward Snowden's portrait over the court documents showing that the National Security Agency in the United States illegally masses surveyed individuals. That was a piece of charity art that benefited a company called Freedom of the Press Foundation by being sold for over $5.4 million.

Mad Dog Jones with Replicator

This artist is currently the most-expensively selling living Canadian artist because of this piece of art. It is also unique because new NFTs will come from it every 28 days, each with its resale value. That is quite a return on investment for the buyer, who could own up to 220 unique NFTs that they can sell. It's well worth the cost of $4.1 million if you can get so much more out of it.

Kevin McCoy with Quantum

That is an exceptionally unique NFT, as it is the first-ever created as far back as 2014. The artist created the token on Namecoin in May 2014 using technology he made with the coder Anil Dash. They presented this to an audience at the New Museum in New York, but they laughed.

But as the phrase goes, "Who's laughing now?" I would say $1.4 million is undoubtedly having the two creators laughing all the way to the bank.

Pak with the Switch

That artwork gives the owner the option of changing the painting to a new unknown image. That part of the artist's way of representing art is evolving digitally. However, once the new owner decides to trigger the switch, it can't be changed back.

It was sold as part of a collection of seven digital art pieces at Sotheby's for $17 million, so I can see why the owner would be hesitant to change the piece.

3LAU with Gunky's Uprising

This piece combines animated artwork and a music video to celebrate the disc jockey (DJ) and electronic musician's third anniversary of his album Ultraviolet. For $1.3 million, it's no wonder he has a couple more art pieces for sale.

These unreleased feature music with the option for the buyer to name the songs when purchased.

Don Diablo With Destination Hexagonia

This Dutch DJ, record producer, musician, and songwriter is known for his electronic music created this full-length, 1-hour concert.

Based on a Sci-Fi theme, the owner received a hard drive containing the only copy of the file. That makes it a rare collectible and worth roughly $1.2 million costs.

Don Diablo is now creating NFT comic books.

HISTORY OF NON-FUNGIBLE TOKENS

L et's delve into the history of non-fungible tokens, where we understand their functions and uses and deepen our understanding of how they are used in trade. Non-fungible tokens have been around since the start of blockchain technology. The first cryptocurrency ever established, Bitcoin, produced a digital asset entirely controlled by its developers. These assets were referred to as "bitcoins," giving their owners a particular level of importance. The coins could be possessed by a user and used to purchase or sell real-world assets (mainly BTC) via the Bitcoin network. That meant that these assets could be used to create fiat money on the blockchain, which was unprecedented at the time. That gave Bitcoin early adopters an edge over others looking to purchase cryptocurrencies because there was a straightforward way of using them to buy real-world goods. Some of the first NFT games were made with Bitcoin in mind. For example, Spells of Genesis (SoG) and CryptoKitties make it feasible to spend their cryptocurrencies in a match.

The popularity of NFTs started to expand significantly in 2017 and 2018. That was primarily because of the advanced awareness and usage of cryptocurrencies on the blockchain—games focused mainly on creating a digital asset traded for real-world assets (fiat). However, more and more users were becoming curious about using NFTs and other blockchain tools to create progressive game experiences. That resulted in the creation of CryptoKitties, which became an instant hit. By the end of 2017, it obtained more than $12 million in funds from investors. That was huge at the time, particularly for a blockchain-based game. The cost of a CryptoKitty was reportedly so high that a digital cat went for $110,000. That means it was on par with the price of a work of art! That shows just how valuable NFTs can be. They can be operated to build assets that have real-world significance, not just game value. It was after the triumph of CryptoKitties that the ERC-721 prototype was created. One of the leading causes of this standard is CryptoKitties and the point that it presented NFTs to an even larger audience. That indicated that people who had never heard about blockchain technology now comprehended what they were, how they functioned, and how they could be utilized in a game. Around this time, blockchain technology began to become additional mainstream, which also helped increase the number of developers who noticed the value in NFTs and other blockchain tools.

Today, any game can use non-fungible tokens because they are effortless to build and integrate. The popularity of NFTs has directed to many other chances for games that were formerly thought unimaginable. It's also worth mentioning that many games are now designed to increase the value of NFTs. As we believe earlier, NFTs are more beneficial and have more roles than classic digital assets. For example, CryptoKitties follows the total number of cats that have been made and even allows users to collect and trade them.

Shortly, we will start to see a lot of games that use non-fungible tokens as their core currency. That will permit players to use NFTs to purchase things, services, and other investments within the game. These assets can be of any sort, including weapons and vehicles.

Non-Fungible Tokens Myths

Several myths surround NFTs and non-fungible tokens. That is understandable, considering that most of these myths have existed for years. Here's a checklist of some of the more typical myths:

1. Myth: "Ethereum has thousands of pending transactions" is one of the most common misconceptions about Ethereum. It reveals a misconception about how blockchains work and how they process data. The number of pending transactions has nothing to do with the number of people using the network or its popularity. It only means that there are many uncertain transactions in this block, which is good because many developers and users use Ethereum. The more additional people who use Ethereum, the more beneficial it becomes. That is true in some markets, but it is not the case in most cases.

2. Myth: "NFTs are a scam" is another common misconception about NFTs. A few years ago, this was right because people were unfamiliar with the idea of non-fungible tokens. Nevertheless, as time went on and more people comprehended what they were, this myth died out. Today, many experienced traders who understand NFTs and blockchain technology's advantages start to view them as investments rather than scams. That was delivered by nine percent of all NFTs traded on the Ethereum network during 2018.

3. Myth: "NFTs are too volatile" is another typical misinterpretation about non-fungible tokens. The cost of an NFT will go up and down, just like any other coin or token. That is because it is not connected to a particular item and can be used in any number of games. That is why it can be exchanged for games and real-world assets.

4. Myth: "NFTs are too pricey" – This is not true at all. The price of NFTs alters, but the average cost is identical to that of other cryptocurrencies, which are already inexpensive compared to standard currencies. That implies you can get as many NFTs as you want for a fraction of the cost of conventional money.

5. Myth: "NFTs are too complex and hard to make" – This is not true, either. It all relies on the game developer and which blockchain platform they are using. Since there are many additional types of blockchain platforms, developers will use whichever one they prefer.

However, if they use Ethereum, they can use NFT-Crowdfund to create their own NFT token. That means they can rely on a protocol to create their NFT without learning a different programming language or building their smart contracts. They will only need some details about Ethereum and how it works.

6. Myth: "NFTs don't bring significance to the gaming industry" – This is another typical misinterpretation about non-fungible tokens. There are a lot of games that allow you to collect NFTs. That means that these components can increase the value of an NFT. After all, NFTs can be used in many different forms, including virtual items in games such as CryptoKitties and Spells of Genesis.

Problems Or Controversies

When you tear off the first layer of NFTs, some overlapping problems arise: environmental, logistical, ethical, etc.

Numerous have pointed out the effect (extreme ecological impact) of NFT formation and trade explosions on planets already destroyed by climate change (climate change-related disasters, environment, racism, inequality). What is the relationship between NFTs and climate change? Ethereum is a platform that hosts a fixed blockchain with many of these NFTs. Put, a lot of energy is used along with the process of issuing NFTs, adding tokens to the blockchain, and the wave of transactions (bidding, resale, etc.). Multiplying that by a considerable market driven by greed, we are initiating new forms of environmental destruction. That promised to transform the system into a carbon-depleting form so much that it kept it working safely, but this hasn't happened yet. The timing of this switch is still unknown.

From fairness and ethical standpoint, the choice to sell a particular art as an NFT may not have the right opportunity it has. Digital artist RJ Palmer recently warned that accounts extract art by minting tweets from fellow artists and artists and selling them as NFTs. The work of a budding artist can be severely abused if not properly enforced or investigated whether the person writing the NFT is the real artist, the actual creator, or the copyright holder. It has created an environment where the relative anonymity of cryptocurrency transactions can be exploited, stolen, and harmed.

Make Enlightened Business Decisions.

Transitioning the practice of art into cryptographic art requires careful planning as a business decision and the selection of art dealers and galleries. The crypto art industry is now valued at $445 million, with Nifty Gateway leading sales volume. Because the competition is intense, it's critical to grasp the terminology, choose the right platform, and seek out well-informed professionals for guidance. Do not focus on stable or fast profit yet. It is advisable not to allocate funds from the sale of cryptographic arts to pay the rent. Thus, it won't be different from the "old" art market.

Studies show that, given the environmental impact of Ether mining, the footprint a computer needs to create a single board NFT is the same as the total electricity usage of EU residents in a month. In comparison, for 2020, Louvre Museum consumed the same amount of electricity as 677,224 households in Paris. It would be good to invest some of the income earned from the art of cryptography to fund Jason Bailey's Green NFT grants and other attempts to decrease NFT consumption of energy.

Just as you would experiment with a new medium, experiment with one piece at a time. It's a good idea to complete, embed, or create activated encrypted art by playing it back in media, such as playing it as an animation in .mp4 or .gif format, adding sound, or converting a picture into interactive digital art. You can also create an NFTonly series to see which works are the most popular. We experiment and research what's best for your target collector and you while staying true to your values and trademark community.

Therefore, as long as the legal consequences are understood, NFT can provide an attractive alternative to the usual art market, the choice of the market and the detailed artwork to be sold result from careful consideration of commercial, practical, and legal aspects.

TYPES OF NFTS

The concept of what constitutes an NFT is still somewhat ambiguous, with the result that essentially anything may be classified as an NFT. Here is a list of the most general and reasonable NFTs currently available on the market.

Understanding The Different Types Of Non-Financial Transactions

Creating one-of-a-kind digital assets based on blockchain technology has gained considerable popularity in recent years. Non-fungible tokens, often known as NFTs, are prominent subjects that will get significant attention in 2021. Consequently, there has been a substantial increase in interest in learning more about the numerous kinds of nonlinear optical fibers.

Besides being intrigued by the potentially lucrative economic possibilities connected with NFTs, people are also intrigued by the prospect of altering traditional asset management. The progressive expansion seen in non-fungible tokens might result in a plethora of options for NFT developers and investors. As a result, having a firm understanding of the various sorts of non-fungible tickets will assist you in making smarter choices along your NFT journey.

- Art

The most often practiced type of NFT is an artistic expression. The creation of NFTs provided an excellent chance for artists to sell their greatest works online in the same way they would sell them in a physical store. At the moment, many of the costliest nonlinear optical transducers are pieces of art. "EVERYDAY'S: THE FIRST 5000 DAYS," by well-known artist Beeple, is the most value NFT ever sold, according to Luno, making it the most expensive NFT ever sold. An incredible $69 million was paid for this painting. There are additionally very costly non-financial transactions (NFTs) that are destroying the financial accounts of billionaires.

That holds for works of video art as well. Short films and even spirited GIFs have been selling like hotcakes for millions of dollars. Notably, a looping 10-second film called "Crossroad," which depicts a nude Donald Trump sprawled on the ground, went for $6.6 million and was the most expensive video ever sold on eBay. This one was created by Beeple as well.

- Music

Music is also a prominent component of the NFT spectrum. Music has been a fungible product for decades, having been produced and delivered on various media, including records, cassettes, CDs, and now digitally over the internet. NFTs, on the other hand, have become more popular with artists and DJs, resulting in some of them earning millions of dollars in a matter of hours.

Because of cutbacks made by streaming platforms and record labels, musicians often only get a percentage of the revenue generated by their work. When it comes to non-financial transactions, artists may retain around 100 percent of the money, which is why so many musicians are turning this way.

- Video Game Items

With video games, we have reached another frontier in the NFT domain. Companies are not selling whole games as non-transferable tokens. Instead, they'll sell in-game material such as skins, characters, and other accessories. At the moment, users may purchase millions of copies of DLC assets. An NFT item, on the other hand, will be unique and exclusive to a single customer. NFT allows developers to sell ordinary DLC while also selling a limited edition version of that DLC on the NFT marketplace.

- Trading Cards/Collectible Items

NFTs may be compared to digital trading cards in several ways. It is common knowledge that limited edition baseball cards can sell for thousands of dollars, and the NFT market is no exception. It is possible to purchase and exchange virtual replicas of trading cards on the market, and they may be kept in the same way that genuine trading cards are supported. And, much like the real thing, some of these replicas fetch more than a million dollars in price.

Businesses can sell various sorts of collecting things, not simply trading cards, on the NFT market. If anything is considered collectible, it can be sold on the open market.

- Big Sports Moments

NFTs provide something that cannot be replicated in the physical world: a recollection of unforgettable sporting occasions. These are brief videos of historical events in sports, such as game-changing slam dunks or game-changing touchdowns, that are worth seeing. Although these recordings may be as short as 10 seconds in length, they can fetch upwards of $200,000.

- Memes

If you were beneath the appearance that the internet couldn't get any more entertaining, the NFT market now allows you to buy and sell memes. A unique feature is that in certain circumstances, the person shown in the meme is the person who is selling the item. Several of the most well-known memes, including Nyan Cat, Bad Luck Brian, Disaster Girl, and others, appear on the list, with earnings ranging from $30,000 to $770,000 per meme. The Doge meme, the most valuable meme to date, was sold for a whopping $4 million at a recent auction.

- Domain Names

NFT fever has expanded to domain names, which are not immune to the disease. It is possible to register a domain name and then sell it on the NFT market, and this has several advantages over other options. You will often be required to pay a third-party business to administer your occupation title. If you buy one on the NFT demand, you will be capable of claiming sole ownership of the word, therefore eliminating the need for a third-party intermediary.

- Virtual Fashion

Everything purchased and sold on the NFT market has been done virtually, so why should fashion be an exception? You may pay a lot of money for a great bikini, but you won't be able to wear it properly. Instead of dressing up their real-life avatars, those who purchase fashion NFTs will do it online.

That may appear ridiculous, but keep in mind that someone paid $4 million to own the Doge meme somewhere in this world. Being the proud owner of a virtual purse or jewelry is reserved for the more lavish and fashion-forward. These, of course, will all be one-of-a-kind creations with a limited number available.

- Miscellaneous Online Items

The other elements on this list were straightforward to describe, but the NFT market is somewhat of a wild west of online business, as seen by the NFT market meltdown that occurred a few months ago. As formerly indicated, Jack Dorsey essentially sold a single tweet. That opens the door for anyone to sell whatever they want on the NFT market, which is indeed what it is for. Whether it is tweeted, Facebook statuses, articles, Snapchat Stories, or TikToks, the sky is the limit when it comes to what people may sell on the internet.

NFT - KEY CONCEPTS

NFTs have reached such a level of fame due to the celebrities who participated in creating, buying and selling them and due to something intrinsic to NFTs themselves: their ability to create value. To fully understand what NFTs are, you don't just need to know about the technology they are based on; you need to understand a few key concepts. This knowledge will reveal the beauty of NFTs, and you will be amazed at their impact on everyone's lives and their future direction.

To better understand the topic, we will start with the basics and evaluation each essential term thoroughly.

Objective Value Versus Subjective Value

People attach value to many things, including objects, activities, goals, careers, and more. If you were to question a group of people what a valuable experience or something is to them, you would receive a wide range of answers, perhaps including a luxury sports car, a nice walk on a dream beach, being with friends, listening to good music, etc. The common thread that runs through these items is desire. What tends to be considered valuable is thought of that way because of the intrinsic desire to achieve or satisfy it. We don't desire objects, experiences, or anything else because of the feeling these create, but because of the passion, they profit. And desire creates subjective value.

The concept of value is intimately tied to preferences, which tend to be arbitrary and depend on what a given person believes, desires, or perceives. Through desires, the reasons for pursuing pleasure are perpetuated. Moreover, the more desires are satisfied, the more value is produced. Subjective value, therefore, is the value that each individual is willing to assign to a good. Thus, it is arbitrary and temporary. Try to think about it: an urgent necessity can exponentially increase the value of a good concerning what might be considered regular or average.

Trying to define objective value is not as simple. Although we can speak of the temporary and not arbitrary objectivity of prices (where a central power does not fix the price of a good), there is no reasonable way to determine value objectively. Thus, were not coercive by an authority, all matter is exclusively subjective: the market price is generated by subjective evaluations.

Therefore, the value is not something intrinsic to the product. It is not one of its properties, but simply the importance that we attribute to the satisfaction of our needs about our life and our well-being.

The Market

The correlation between subjective value and market prices is one of the most invisible aspects of modern economics. It is the correlation between personal value and objective monetary prices. When referring to the subjective matter, there is no single unit of measurement.

Through the attribution of value, people estimate and classify goods according to their preferences. The concept of value creation plays a central role in management theory.

The term "marketplace" has two possible meanings. First, it is a physical place where people go to sell, buy, or trade a product or good—for example, a supermarket, a shopping mall, or a car dealership; it can also be digital, including platforms such as Amazon, eBay, Alibaba, Shopify, and many others. Second, the term "market" or "marketplace" can also describe the existence of people who desire to buy, sell, or exchange a particular type of product. There is a market in that a specific product can elicit desire and be adjusted to consumers' tastes or preferences.

A market is organized according to the following different approaches:

- Free competition occurs when the price is formed by the encounter between goods or services offered by competing firms, and consumers have the freedom to choose between different offers.

- Oligopoly occurs when a small number makes the offer of operators.

- Monopoly: occurs when there is no choice but to accept the price imposed by the offer.

The advent of the free market has produced many benefits for community life. Consumers' needs and value on goods or services are always brought to the forefront within market research and marketing. This understanding of the term is much more abstract: a market exists when many people are curious about buying or selling a specific product, service, information, or currency.

For all physical assets, the market value is determined by supply and demand and, therefore, by the relationship between the number of goods available and the order. In physical assets, we talk about the concept of scarcity of support, which has not been part of the digital world for a long time. For example, an asset that is highly sought after but scarce acquires value due to the competition between those who want it, while a purchase that is available in large quantities or total, even if highly sought after, does not acquire value because those who seek to possess it can quickly obtain it.

A market test is a tool that companies use to identify the types of people interested in a product about to be put on the market. This test helps companies determine how much money people are willing to spend to get their products. The results show that different people are interested in various products and are eager to pay a specific amount for a particular product. Today's companies listen to the needs of consumers and respond to them. Classical economics has always been based on scarcity, which often defines prices and focuses on those products that satisfy 80% of the population. Thanks to the internet, the possibilities have increased exponentially. Our web offers greater market possibilities because it reaches a global audience, meaning that practically every product or good finds its market of reference. Chris Anderson's dream was with "the long tail" strategy, a retail plan based on statistical analysis. It is preferred to sell many unique items in relatively small quantities rather than a small number of popular items in large amounts.

The web market is very often devoid of intermediaries. Thus, trust and word-of-mouth opinions are critical and represent the most current marketing methods online.

Fungible Versus Non-Fungible Assets

To better understand the difference between fungible and non-fungible, it is essential to learn about (or brush up on) the concepts of assets, tokens, tokenization, and Blockchain.

What is an asset?

The asset is a term used in finance that refers to anything assigned a monetary value and can be helpful or desirable. It can be physical, digital, abstract, or that helps generate earnings. A fungible asset is interchangeable because it possesses the same value as another. For example, a bitcoin is a fungible asset because one bitcoin has the same value as another bitcoin. Fungibility is an alluring property for a currency because it allows free exchange when there is no way to know the history of each unit. However, fungibility is not a valuable property of collectibles.

A non-fungible asset is something that is not interchangeable or even divisible. A non-fungible investment is, for example, a house, a used car, or a unique football card. These cannot be divided because they would not have the same value. A token is nothing more than the digital representation, which can be anything, as long as it has recognizable and certifiable properties.

In the world of blockchain technology, a token is a virtual token whose value is issued by an organization. Tokens are value units; they represent a digital asset (a cryptocurrency, a physical product or object, etc.).

In a broad sense, a token is an object with a particular value only within a specific context.

How about an example? Casino chips. These chips are just pieces of plastic worth nothing outside the casino's walls. In this context, their value is agreed upon, and they become the representation of an asset.

Historically, tokens have created coins with value within a given context. Therefore, the value of a token is what its creator decides to provide it.

The moment when a token is assigned that property and value are called tokenization and occurs within blockchain technology. The Blockchain is a technology that can be equated to a database that collects classified data within computers and networks. Blockchain technology is supported by three pillars: decentralization, transparency, and immutability. Blockchain allows for a decentralized model where one computer does not control the entire network. A decentralized system allows for greater clarity: every movement is recorded within the Blockchain, and everyone can maintain the log of activities and transactions. It is almost impossible in physical reality to find a model with such a level of transparency, where everything is recorded and can be seen by everyone. Moreover, this data cannot be altered in any way, and, for this reason, it is immutable.

The tokenization of a digital asset within blockchain technology can create a non-fungible token: an NFT is the unique representation of a natural or digital asset that cannot be exchanged for an equivalent because an equivalent does not exist. There is no NFT equal to another in the world. People can accomplish with NFTs is endless. The application possibilities cover all sectors, including art, online gaming, music, collectibles of various kinds, exclusive luxury goods, virtual properties, and much more. Blockchain technology adds unique properties to digital assets by providing people with ownership and management of that token and the ability to transfer it to a decentralized, transparent, and immutable platform.

What Is Blockchain?

Blockchain is a shared and immutable data chain structure. It is a digital ledger containing data grouped into blocks concatenated together in chronological order whose integrity and credibility are ensured by cryptography. Moreover, the content cannot be modified or deleted once inside it unless the entire structure is invalidated. This technology is included in the family of distributed ledgers. The blockchain system is distributed across multiple nodes, and there is no single control center. Every transaction is thus recorded. That reinforces the integrity of the process itself. The whole thing is based on a set of properties that represents the foundation of the entire system, and that can be defined as the three fundamental pillars of the Blockchain:

1. Decentralization offers the possibility of transferring assets without a unified administration; for example, it allows for the transfer of money without the intervention of a banking institution. Within a distributed system, power does not lie solely with a single authority. In the Blockchain, there are no intermediaries between actions.

2. Transparency allows people to see how simple and secure the system is. Anyone can view transactions on the Blockchain but not individual data. That allows a transparent system that will enable owners to control their data and all associated movements. In this way, users' privacy is protected.

3. Immutability can be defined as the ability of a blockchain to remain unchanged and unalterable. No data can be modified, and the database cannot be manipulated in any way because each block is uniquely identified by a value called a hash.

WHY NFT IS BECOMING SO POPULAR

NFT marketplace development is a new industry that serves as a massive income structure for tech-savvy and talented developers and artists. It encourages the development of new, one-of-a-kind technological solutions. The significance of NFTs in art and games has led to the introduction of augmented reality and virtual reality in various services.

For many, NFT marketplace development is a once-in-a-lifetime opportunity to demonstrate individual talent and creativity, creative collectibles, and display those products to facilitate effective digital asset management.

The Best Evidence Of Nft Market Growth And A Promising Future

NFT marketplace development is a fantastic trend and a promising source of income due to the following factors. We'll show that NFT marketplaces development is a lucrative business. To begin with, its market capitalization is increasing rapidly, rising from $141.56 million in 2019 to $338.04 million in 2020. Making money in this manner is not challenging.

Benefits of an NFT marketplace:

- Transactions are settled instantly

NFT developers will easily take cryptos as payment and payout options, enabling cryptocurrency owners and new mainstream users to earn and settle transactions fast and without a hitch!

- Increased participation and support

The adoption of NFT technology in NFT marketplace development makes NFT minting and trades by promoting increased participation, marketplace expansion, and support for content creators worldwide.

- A seamless user experience for participants

An NFT marketplace, created on the solid design of a blockchain network, provides a smooth user experience to both participants. Each step of the process, such as tokenization, storage, and marketplace usage, is simple to grasp.

- Future of technology and art

NFT platforms are developing a set of features targeted at providing various solutions and services. Today, the emphasis is on bringing the uniqueness of NFT to every industry imaginable, not only traditional art! NFT, presently, is the start of a fantastic collaboration between technology and art.

Solutions offered by NFT marketplace

- An NFT marketplace powered by blockchain network and the colossal power of bitcoin that eliminates any third-party intervention in the whole process of selling, purchasing, and trading NFTs.

- Blockchain network creates permanent records of authenticity and provenance, minimizing the chances of fraud and counterfeits while remaining legally compliant.

- Collectibles may be bought and sold directly on the site without any license.

- Payments are made instantaneously in the marketplace's native coin.

- A marketplace is being created to provide direct access to collectors for artists without exorbitant fees or third parties.

- Accessibility to a worldwide audience that is not limited by geography.

- A platform where artists can find out all they need to know regarding the resale of their work.

- All transactions and exchanges are carried out transparently on the forum.

Tech Stack For Nft Marketplace Development

After you've decided on all of the elements you'd like to see in your NFT marketplace, it's time to determine the tech stack you'll need to put the project into action. You'll have to decide on a blockchain network, a storage system, front-end development architecture, and the NFT standard that your platform supports.

Blockchain Network

You'll require a blockchain network to run your NFT marketplace, as it'll be the backbone of the platform. Since records and token information are publicly verifiable, Ethereum is the traditional option of NFT marketplace developers, providing extra security to NFT activities. NFT holders may readily transfer their tokens using the standard backend of all Ethereum-supported NFT markets. NFT creators use Flow because of its simple, user-friendly Cadence programming language for creating digital assets, games, and apps. Tezos is another famous option since its FA2 NFT contracts are ideal for the NFT marketplace development goal. Finally, the Cardano platform is highly secure and long-lasting.

Storage Systems

You must select where NFTs will be held whenever you plan on an NFT marketplace development. The IPFS hypermedia protocol or the decentralized Filecoin hold system will be perfect fits for this reason. Pinata is also a viable option because it is IPFS compatible and provides safe, verifiable NFT storage.

NFT Standards

ERC-721, ERC-1155, FA2, dGoods, and TRC-721 are the current NFT-bases standards. Individually of this has its collection of technological challenges, so you'll need to work with your design team to develop a suitable solution.

Front-end

Vue, Angular, and React are the most preferred front-end development frameworks for the NFT platform. They're all essential and coder-friendly, with sleek, easy-to-navigate interfaces that provide rapid results.

Elements That Distinguish NFT Marketplace

Certain essential qualities characterize, define, and explain NFTs marketplace. From the video industry to collectibles and other digital items, it's possible to base this idea on many things. Nonfungible token developers can come to develop an unlimited volume of coins. The following are the primary characteristics of NFTs marketplace that entice business runners:

- Unified tokens

- Unique tokens

- Rarity

- More power to ownership

- Clearness

- Compatibility

You have many reasons to participate in the NFT marketplace development business when you blend trustworthiness, ease of transfer, and indivisibility.

NFT Marketplace User Flow

For nonfungible token sites, the user flow appears to be the same. Visitors to the website must create an account by filling out all required information. They must either create a cryptocurrency wallet or connect a current one to keep all their tokens in one place. The development of NFTs is the next step. Those who scaled through registration must tender digital assets that reflect their work. They can make complete collections and sell individual pieces at a defined price, or they may set up a bidding scheme in which the highest bidder receives the desired item. No items will appear on the site unless checked and validated. Moderation is essential. Once the system allows NFTs, users will see them ready for sales/bidding. The auction starts afterward. You can select the crypto you want to use for your transactions. When the items are sold, both parties are informed. Finally, the service maintains track of all trades and item movements.

That is how an actual user flow works. While participating in the development of the NFT marketplace, bear this in mind.

Launching NFT Marketplace as a Business

Do you want to begin a business with an NFT marketplace? Note, you must target your audience before launching the product. Furthermore, you must identify challenges that you intend to address. The issues determine these difficulties that your potential customers are facing.

After that, make a list of the essential components of the NFT marketplace, so you don't forget anything. Select the best NFT marketplace development approach and guidelines. If you consider building an exclusive NFT marketplace from the ground up, keep the following stages in mind:

Target Niche

Specialists advise betting on a vertical market rather than a horizontal market. The first implies that its members seek to offer goods/services that meet the needs and demands of a specific customer segment. Amazon and eBay are not the most excellent examples because, as horizontal suppliers, they provide everything to everyone.

Propose User Roles

There are not usually many possibilities but consider deeply. Will they be buyers, artists, or admins?

Structure Your Platform and Design

The marketplace development process starts with project documentation. It is a routine, and you risk spending substantial time if you do not document. In-house employees do not need the same level of documentation as offshore professionals.

Move to Development

It's now time to put your design idea into action once you've finished it. Choose the structure that you think best fits your objectives. Many people may consider employing a pro-NFT developer to ensure high performance and credibility. They help you save time and money.

Integrate Smart Contract Token Generator

Back-end development takes on a different appearance during an NFT marketplace. On the blockchain network, the vast majority of information is verified. Pass internal logic to the decentralized aspect if you plan to make an application decentralized.

Examine and Implement

Testing and deployment are the final but not least essential stages. It's all about spotting and avoiding potential pitfalls. Software testing guarantees that your project is running smoothly. Post-launch support is also necessary to keep bugs at bay and ensure the system's quality of service. Please do not remove the service until you have thoroughly tested its features. Is the finished product up to par with your expectations? Consider how users would receive it. This stage is crucial for establishing a reputation and delivering outstanding results.

Keep in mind the key features that the NFT marketplace platform must have before you begin to work on it.

Essential Features of the NFT Marketplace

NFT marketplace's essential features are the characteristics that distinguish the platform as unique and appealing to both buyers and sellers.

Before going over the remaining features, consider the following principal reasons why NFTs and NFT marketplaces in general pique the public interest. Blockchain technology makes it possible to formalize rights and create digital assets much easier to work with. NFTs can also be freely traded. What's more, blockchain technology assures users that they'll get what they need. Other important characteristics include:

Storefront

It is an essential feature. It should include information like bids, glimpse, holders, and price records, among other things.

Advanced Token Search

A user must obtain reliable information on products they require quickly and with minimal effort. All products in an NFT marketplace should be classified by specific features (for instance, books, articles, videos, art). Quick searches improve customer satisfaction.

Filters

This feature is similar to the former one in that the goal is to help users fast and efficiently determine the appropriate product. Split all products into several classes that impact the buyer's decision in most cases. Prices, new items, hot deals, best-sellers, and other factors can all be considered. Users will select items they require more quickly, increasing purchasing them.

Listing Creation

Users should have the ability to create and transfer collectibles. Ascertain that they can do so quickly and without difficulty. Create a page where consumers may upload a file and type in precise item information. Title, tags, and description are all required.

Listing Status

This alternative should assist those who provide items and satisfy item verification requirements. It enables you to see how long the confirmation process is. This functionality comes in handy when it comes to implementing collectible verification.

Bidding Option

Every e-commerce platform needs to allow users to buy and bid on products. It draws more users since some people like flexible pricing and doesn't want to pay the total price for collectibles. Bidding is usually entertaining. If you're using an auction function, don't forget to provide an expiration date. Users who have enrolled should view information about the present state of their bids. It will assist them in deciding whether to purchase or continue to place new bids. Another essential feature is the auction watch list.

Wallet

Users require a secure environment in which to hold and keep nonfungible tokens. Not all alternatives are appropriate since some may pose a risk to the security of assets. That is why the

NFT marketplace service should have an initial wallet installed so that tokens may be safely saved and submitted. Rather than requiring the customers to sign up for other online wallets, create and provide a linked, "native" wallet. First and foremost, consider their comfort. It would help if you did not make a wallet from the ground up.

UNDERSTANDING THE DIFFERENT TYPES OF NFTS

O ne of the prominent topics in 2022 is Non-fungible tokens or NFTs. Blockchain technology is based on unique digital assets which have gained popularity in recent times. As a result, the interest in comprehending the different types of NFT has been growing recently.

Apart from a vision for altering predictable asset management, people are fascinated by the promising economic potential associated with NFTs. The endless opportunities for NFT creators and investors can be guaranteed by the steady growth visible in the domain of NFTs. Therefore, for making better decisions in your NFT journey, a deep impression of the different types of non-fungible tokens could help significantly.

Digital tokens are not something innovative in the world of technology. Once the digital artist Beeple auctioned off his artwork at a Christie's auction in March, the NFTs started to catch the world's attention. Favorable opinions have been expressed regarding the NFTs by famous names such as Twitter chief Jack Dorsey and Elon Musk. Interestingly, only six years after minting the first NFT in 2014, the NFT market cap reached nearly $2 Billion, only in the first quarter of 2021. In 2020, the total value of sales reached nearly $250 million. NFTs are digital or cryptographic tokens you can find on a blockchain that can preserve exclusivity. NFTs could be tokenized alternatives of valuable assets or native digital assets.

However, one of the protruding aspects which can confuse many beginners in NFT is the association of NFTs with art. NFTs are not limited only to the field of art. Different types of NFTs with exclusive traits and specific use cases can be found.

The primary cataloging of types of NFTs mentions the general categories. The three common types of NFTs are:

- Original or copy of work that is accepted on a blockchain network or DLT

- Digitally inherent NFTs that own rights to an artwork that account for NFTs

- NFT metadata comprises the NFT that provides a demonstration of ownership for metadata files

The usual types of non-fungible tokens propose a comprehensive description of the standards used in NFT classification. The original NFTs are created on the blockchain network, and they remain there. Digitally native NFTs involve issuing NFTs to numerous people with asset ownership rights. A significant way to classify the non-fungible tokens is the NFT metadata, as it fundamentally has a link that leads to the metadata for the NFT. Consequently, you don't get ownership of the NFT and just the rights for using it.

What Are The Different Types Of Nfts?

Important discussion topics involve the different conjectures regarding the NFT potential and the value and risks associated with them. NFTs could explain the true origin of an asset with the functionalities of blockchain. Holding, limiting, or rejecting access to the rights of a person could be helped by NFTs, thereby guaranteeing exclusiveness.

The applications of NFTs could be nurtured in various sectors by developing the infrastructure and an increased opportunity for novelty in the NFTs space. Therefore, new types of NFTs can be reasonably expected to emerge. You can look at some of the notable NFT types popular in present times.

The protuberant records in a non-fungible tokens list would include the following,

- Artwork
- Event tickets
- Music and media
- Virtual items
- Real-world assets
- Identity
- Memes
- Domain names

To understand their significance, an overview of these different non-fungible tokens or NFT variants is given below.

Collectibles

With the development of Cryptokitties, the leading example of NFTs, the collectibles emerged. As a point of fact, The first occurrence of people using NFTs are crypto kitties. Cryptokitties became popular enough in 2017 to congest the Ethereum network as a matter of interest. One of the conspicuous accompaniments to the non-fungible tokens list in the class of digital collectibles is crypto kitties. They are fundamentally digital kittens with discrete traits that make them prevalent and promising than others.

Artwork

Another projecting contender for NFTs is the artwork. The usual non-fungible tokens in this area mention programmable art, containing an exceptional blend of creativity and technology. As of now, many limited edition artwork pieces are in circulation with the scope for programmability under certain conditions. To create images represented on blockchain networks, oracles and smart contracts could be used by artists, which could help immensely. NFTs have also stimulated participation from the legacy arts industry.

The adoption of NFTs could be encouraged by the tokenization of real-world assets. The exciting prospects for scanning a code or sticker on purchases could be offered by the possibilities of combining blockchain and IoT. The NFT types in artwork could certify that ownership of real-world artwork on a blockchain network could be quickly registered. Successively, the complete history of a painting, such as former ownerships and the prices for which they were sold in the past, could be found by users,

Event Tickets

Event tickets are another promising addition among the types of NFTs. Attending events like music festivals and concerts are allowed to verify their identity and tickets by using such types of NFTs. A specific number of NFT tickets could be mined on a selected blockchain platform by the event managers. Customers could buy the tickets through an auction, and those tickets could be stored in their wallets, easily accessible through mobile devices.

Music and Media

The domain of music and media leads to another category of NFTs due to the experiments they are trying to carry out with NFTs. Music and media files could be linked to NFTs, enabling an individual to access the files with a valid ownership claim. The two noticeable platforms helping artists mint their songs as NFTs include Rarible and Mintbase.

One of the leading reasons for infusing traits of vintage vinyl records is the intellect of uniqueness in purchasing NFT music. The listeners get a quality experience, while the artists benefit from reaching out directly to their followers and new audience. Consistent projections for addressing the concerns of music piracy and intermediaries could be offered by the growth of music NFTs in the non-fungible tokens list.

Gaming

In gaming, the common types of non-fungible tokens are principally fixated on in-game items. Profound levels of interest have been aroused among game developers by NFTs. The functionality of ownership records for in-game items could be offered by NFTs, thus driving the progress of in-game economies. Most importantly, NFTs in the gaming segment also focus on announcing a comprehensive display of benefits for players.

While in-game collectibles were mutual necessities for a better gaming experience, NFTs have the prospective for changing their value Money could be quickly recovered by in-game items as NFTs by selling it outside the game. On the flip side, game developers or the creators allotting NFTs could receive a royalty for every sale of items in the open marketplace.

Real-world Assets

Many NFT types could not be found serving as tokens for real-world items; it could be possible due to the progress in the NFT domain. For instance, many NFT projects are concentrating on the tokenization of real estate alongside luxury goods. NFTs are fundamentally deeds that can familiarize the flexibility for buying a car or home with an NFT deed. Consequently, NFTs demonstrating real-world assets can capitalize on the prospects with cryptographic proof of ownership.

Identity

Non-fungible tokens have a critical trait, and that is a rarity. Every NFT is unique and cannot be substituted with any other token. The working of identity NFTs is similar to that of event tickets NFTs. They can function as unique identifiers, hence aiding as trustworthy sustenance for the identity management systems.

The commonly used applications of identity-based NFTs are unmistakable in certifications and licensing. The identity management sector for proving and verifying records of an individual could be changed by minting certificates and licenses and NFTs. Furthermore, identity-based NFTs could also ensure that individuals could store proof of their identity without risking losing it.

Memes

The most noteworthy development in the domain of NFTs recently is the sale of memes as NFTs. While being a fragment of widespread culture and a favorite among internet users, memes have also been related to NFTs. They are selling the memes as NFTS displays the prospective for unique meme creators to participate in a progressing revolutionary ecosystem.

Domain Names

Domain names are another category of NFTs which have become popular recently. The top examples of domain name NFTs are Decentralized Domain Name Services such as Unstoppable

Domains and the Ethereum Name Service (ENS). ENS aids in translating long and complex user addresses to a flexible and friendly experience for users with easier onboarding.

The prevailing admittances in the non-fungible tokens list portray the NFT ecosystem's potential. Firstly, you can have an original NFT created and stored on the blockchain. It is a new class of digital or tokenized assets; NFTs are altering the predictable concepts of asset usage and ownership. Consequently, you can find the common types of non-fungible tokens concentrating on what you get with an NFT.

The second type of NFTs denotes digital natives in which numerous NFTs serve as parts of ownership rights to specific assets. The third category of NFTs only proposes access to NFT metadata, permitting you to use the NFT rather than distribute ownership. The various kinds of NFTs that are being distributed, such as artwork, music, media, domain names, memes, also demonstrate capable prospects for the future of NFTs.

CAUSES FOR CONCERN

It's not all wine and roses. There are causes to be hesitant, even if you are well-informed and see the potential. Everything has downsides, and NFTs and cryptocurrencies are no exception to this rule. There is a lot of alarmism and exaggeration about the dangers of crypto markets. Most are overblown, but even the overstated ones have their merits. It's necessary to address these because problems aren't solved until they are acknowledged.

Energy And Pollution

Lately, a ton of recent attention has been paid to the amount of energy used to maintain blockchains. Blockchain is very clever and valuable technology, but it is energy inefficient. Whereas two banks can send a tiny bit of data to one another, the blockchain requires a lot of powerful computers using a tremendous amount of power to compete with each other.

If you've read news headlines recently, this issue probably seems noncontroversial. News makes money by eliciting clicks with enticing headlines, and nuanced discussions don't generate the same traffic as doom and gloom stories. That said, the facts of pollution are not a consensus. There is a vigorous debate on this topic, with both sides of the issue making solid points that need to be considered.

Most of this news comes from one source, an academic article in the journal Nature Climate Change. This 2018 article raised alarms that Bitcoin alone could raise the global temperature by 2 degrees Celsius within the next 30 to 60 years, enough to begin raising the ocean to catastrophic levels (Dittmar & Praktiknjo, 2019).

Because the authors are experts on climate science and not computer science, they make some assumptions that aren't reliable. For one, the authors assume that the exponential adoption of crypto will continue indefinitely. That is far from a certainty. Few things grow exponentially forever, unabated. Almost all growth has peaks and valleys and periods of flattening.

The article also makes a significant mistake in saying that the Bitcoin network processes 1 billion processes, which is several times more than what Bitcoin can do. It also assumes that each transaction equals one block. As we consider earlier, a single block contains many trades, as many as 3,000 per block for Bitcoin.

The article claims that a single Bitcoin transaction requires more electricity than 750,000 credit card swipes. That is true, but electronic banking transactions are a lot more than just signals sent by swipes at retailers. Banks and credit card companies have an infrastructure. They have offices; they have company cars, ATMs, customer service systems, and many other things that use energy but aren't factored into the calculations.

The numbers also assume that Bitcoin energy comes exclusively from fossil fuels. Many crypto mining operations use coal as their primary energy source for a considerable amount of their work. Without a doubt, that is troubling and needs to be phased out, but it isn't particular to computing. The point is that the numbers require that ALL energy is spent this way, which isn't true.

Miners are incentivized to reduce the cost of mining by reducing energy. At a certain point, if energy expenses are too high, mining profits are at a net loss, and mining would end. The energy efficiency of mining equipment has been improving, though the paper doesn't address this.

According to Cambridge, their best guess is about 130TWh (CBECI, 2021), the same as the energy spent mining gold every year.

There are also some exciting ideas about making crypto greener. Computer farms of the sort that miners use produce a considerable amount of heat from their electricity. These miners are already developing ways to use that heart as a form of energy.

Renewable energy has a lot of promise, but at this time, they have a technological chokepoint that stops them from becoming the standard. Solar and wind power can pull tremendous amounts of energy if the sun is shining and the wind is blowing, much more than is needed on the electrical grid all at once. It produces nothing when the sun isn't shining, and the wind isn't blowing. At this time, we don't have the technology to store vast amounts of energy. That amount of battery storage necessary isn't feasible yet. During those peak times, that excess energy could be directed specifically to mining, and the crypto produced could be invested back into the energy company towards expanding renewables.

Don't take this to mean that crypto has no impact on the environment. That isn't true at all. There are legitimate concerns about this issue, but it is not likely the climate doomsday scenario that news headlines imply.

Bubbles

Crypto is not regulated like banks are. We are at the later stages of a Wild West crypto economy. The market has a lot of natural volatility and can be manipulated by governments and private citizens with the money to throw their weight around.

Tweets sent by people like Elon Musk can spike or tank the crypto market by enormous margins (Kau, 2021). That can be accidental or deliberate. One way to manipulate the market for profit is for a "whale," a well-financed person or institution, to purchase a lot of cryptos. They need a lot of money to make this happen, but the price will spike if coins are being bought up quickly and in large quantities. It creates a shortage and reinforces people's confidence in the asset's value, and more people want to get in on the action, increasing the weight. The whale's portfolio will go up. When they see it leveling off, the whale can dump their portfolio for a lot of money, which tanks the price. People see it going down, and panic sells. Now that the price is low again, the whale can buy it cheaply. They can repeat this process forever. It would be naive to assume governments aren't participating.

Bubbles are an unavoidable feature of any market, but crypto especially. That is a very new thing, and it is unregulated and still in its infancy. The traditional legacy banking system has put enormous resources into learning how to calculate risk, hedge it, maximize profits, and develop a massive library of financial instruments to maximize profit and keep the market stable enough that they feel secure to operate in it with minimal risk. Crypto is not quite so mature. It is more like a young person kicking in the door and claiming that the older adults don't know what they are speaking about and trying to change everything all at once. The crypto culture is right about many things, and they're also probably wrong about a lot of things. A specific amount of time needs to go by, and learning is necessary before this thing works itself out.

Legal Grey Area

During times of great economic crisis, people are often eager to find alternatives to the financial system in crisis. During the great depression and stock market crash in America in the 1930s, there was a fear that government policies and spending would lead to hyperinflation of the kind experienced in Germany. To protect themselves from poor government monetary policy, people with the means to do so attempted to turn their cash into commodities, particularly gold. Even if the cash value is devalued, the relative price of other assets like land and gold rises by the same amount, protecting the person from having their entire savings withered away by central banks.

The value of any currency is dependent on people's trust and faith in it. Cash is similar to any other asset. It has a supply and demand curve just like anything else. When people lose faith in the solvency and profitability of a corporation, the stock value plummets. When people lose faith in the solvency and future of a country, the value of its money vanishes. If people begin to jettison cash, that country's cash value diminishes.

The United States government was not naive to this fact. In their mind, if no one had a means of exiting the United States dollar, the value of it couldn't be destabilized quite so easily. For that

, they wanted to get ahead of the curve and decided that they had the right and responsibility to confiscate gold. They also instituted many financial regulations, some sensible, some crazy, to protect the United States dollar.

Make no mistake. If the United States dollar seems threatened by cryptocurrency, governments will intervene and shut it down. That includes NFTs. A problem with regulating digital assets is that the regulators don't know anything about computers. The middle age in the United States is 64 years old (Cillizza, 2021). Almost all of them have backgrounds in the military or law. There are few politicians with a strong experience in technology, except perhaps the 2020 presidential candidate, Andrew Yang, who is not an elected official at the time of this writing.

Without warning or a deep understanding of what is happening, other countries have begun to crack down on digital assets. In a recent case, India has outlawed cryptocurrencies entirely. That is a response to a technology that they fear the consequences and implications of, and they view banning these currencies as getting a head start on it before it gets out of their control. China has simultaneously begun to develop its cryptocurrency, outlaw competing currencies, and invest in current cryptocurrencies that are already popular and proven and in circulation. That is a sign that China has a good sense of the implications of what crypto is and wants to get a lockdown on it and control it.

There's no reason to think that United States governments or any governments in the West will not also begin investigating and regulating these things. On account of the general ignorance of these issues by the governments and by the voters, we can expect that whenever regulation does come our way will be guided by established institutions with deep pockets which have a reason to be concerned about a fledgling upstart that plans on putting them out of business through obsolescence. That is something that everyone needs to consider before going deeply into investment in NFTs or crypto. There's a lot of instability in these markets intrinsically because it is a new technology that people are still figuring out and constantly reinventing. Still, there's an additional layer of flux in the unpredictable reactions from the government. Government tends to operate at two speeds: "Do nothing" and "overreact." If senators aren't placed into a state of panic in a hurry, they usually don't do anything. When they do act, you can expect an overreaction.

Copyright And Illegal Content

Making an NFT doesn't automatically give you a copyright to the art. Likewise, tokenizing Disney's Snow White and the Seven Dwarves into a video NFT doesn't mean you have the right to it, either. There isn't much to stop people from tokenizing material they have no right to and spreading it.

DIGITAL ART AND DIGITAL CREATORS

Paints and brushes are tools that some painters utilize to produce their artwork. However, many others use contemporary creativity methods, such as video technology, television, and computers, to further their interests. Digital art is the term used to describe this kind of artwork.

Digital art is any work created or presented using digital technology, whether or not it was created using digital technology. Image types that fall under this category include pictures made entirely on a computer and hand-drawn drawings scanned into a computer and completed using software such as Adobe Illustrator. It is also possible to create digital art via animation and 3D virtual sculpting representations and projects that use many different technologies. Some digital art is created by manipulating video pictures in some way.

The phrase "digital art" was initially used in the 1980s to refer to a computer painting software developed. To be clear, this was far back when they weren't even called applications! It may potentially be seen in many different ways, including on television and the Internet, on desktops, and various social media platforms, making it a technique of art-making that lends itself to multimedia presentation. In a nutshell, digital art is a kind of fusion of the arts and technologies in specific ways. It opens them to a plethora of new possibilities for artistic expression.

Historical Development

In 1965, artist Frieder Nake used an ER 56 computer (about the size of a standard room in a home) to apply an algorithm to analyze a Paul Klee picture. That is considered to be the "beginning of digital art." The artist produced many versions of "Highroads Byroads," and he called the one that, in his opinion, was the most effective Hommage à Paul Klee. Several artists and computer scientists collaborated over the same period to develop computer-generated artworks, and the emphasis shifted to programming throughout the 1970s, allowing art to be made rather than merely copied or translated. The invention of the stylus enabled artists to use their inherent skills on computers. It distinguished work that was computer-generated from work that was computer-aided in the production of the work. As a generation of artists started to alter video, music, and graphics in the 1980s, digital media saw rapid development. By the early 2000s, the rapid expansion of computer usage has enabled artists to broaden their audience via digital technology.

What Do Digital Artists Do For A Living?

Digital artists have several different professional options from which to select. These jobs include creating visual effects and animated visuals for various media, such as videos and computer games, among others. Digital artists may find employment in multiple industries, including film production, advertising, video game development, and software creation. You will utilize computer software to bring your work to life, whether a painting or a sculpture, in any position involving digital artists. Depending on your profession, they may subsequently be transformed into 3D interactive graphics for websites or visual characters for animation. Specializations include game design, web design, multimedia, and energy, to name a few areas of interest. Whatever field you choose to work in, the ability to think creatively is essential.

How To Become A Digital Artist

Digital artists must have creative ability and a bachelor's degree in visual or commercial art, or a related area, to succeed in their careers. Even though a degree is not required, this is a competitive profession, and it is essential to include formal training in both your CV and your portfolio to stand out. It would be okay if you also maintained up with the latest creative and animation technologies developments. If you cannot transfer your creative abilities from a pen and paper to a drawing tablet, entering the digital art industry may be challenging. The opportunity to do an internship in your chosen profession is a fantastic way to acquire practical experience, develop your abilities, and network with others in the industry.

What Software Does Digital Artists Use?

Digital artists utilize a wide variety of software tools to create their works. These may vary depending on your area of expertise, but the most popular are found inside the Adobe Creative Cloud. You may use Adobe InDesign to plan up print projects such as brochures, ebooks, posters, and magazines, as well as digital projects such as websites. Photoshop is one of the most popular photo-editing applications, and it may be used to enhance the appearance of your artwork. On the other hand, Adobe Illustrator is essential for 2D art. That is the stage at which you sketch and create your designs. If you work in Maya, animation and Harmony, which are not part of the Adobe Creative Cloud, are utilized for 2D and 3D animation. Harmony and Maya are not part of the Adobe Creative Cloud. Similar to how your duties vary with your sector, so does the software you need.

What Is The Distinction Between A Digital Artist And A Graphic Designer?

It is essential to note significant distinctions between digital artists and graphic designers. A digital artist is concerned first and foremost with art. In contrast, a graphic designer is concerned first and foremost with conveying a message, which may include the use of various fonts, graphics, pictures, and sound in certain instances. Design graphic designers work in advertising or companies to develop layouts for advertisements, print projects, newsletters, and social media campaigns while keeping the target audience in mind. Being aware of your target audience impacts your decisions about color, style, and images to utilize in the project.

ARE NFTS A PASSIVE WAY OF INCOME?

NFTs allow us to come up with new financial applications that can then issue tokens that may represent anything from stocks and bonds to cars and real estate. It's all that you can think of.

The basis of the NFT technology is on Ethereum blockchain technology. The Ethereum blockchain is time and again termed as programmable money. Now, what is that? It means that it can let anyone come up with and create their tokens or NFTs using the Ethereum protocol.

Essentially there are two types of NFTs:

- Restricted NFTs

- Unrestricted NFTs

NFTs that allow you to claim ownership in buying and selling the asset is known as unrestricted NFTs.

NFTs that do not support such claims and transferability are termed restricted NFTs.

If you see, you will notice that money cannot be generated from the NFTs in their basic form. What happens is that these NFTs are used to create tokens, and then those tokens are made a part of the decentralized finance landscape.

Nft Vaults & Staking

It needs maintaining funds in a bitcoin wallet to retain the security and functionality of a blockchain network. To earn incentives from securing your assets, the process is known as staking. If you compare mining and staking, you will conclude that staking is a less resource-intensive substitute to mining.

The staking process has been implemented by various cryptocurrencies, including VeChain, Tezos, Decred, Navcoin, among others. Most NFT projects are expected to start staking as revenue of generating passive income from their platform as a result.

NFTs are the only ones that have the staking ability. It has become mandatory to acquire obligatory utility out of the NFT tokens.

NFTs can be stored in storage facilities called vaults. Issuers of vToken offer access to the token holders for their assets that are locked. Vaults are used for this purpose.

If you have an Ethereum address, you will generate a vault for any of your NFT assets. Everybody has the right to credit the eligible NFTs into the vault to create a fungible NFT-backed cryptocurrency called a "vToken."

vTokens make use of NFTs as a security to be held in escrow during a secure, peer-to-peer lending system. Decentralized exchanges assist this lending system. In a nutshell, one party leaves an asset locked up as security, and the other receives a loan from that asset at a cheap interest rate.

The person who creates the vTokens can specify the number of primary assets in a vault. He will also be able to plan the mechanism for pricing. It should be linked directly to the price of the primary asset or basket of assets. The vToken protocol has been executed on Ethereum.

A vToken allows you to generate income from any primary asset. It is a financial instrument that can generate revenue from the investment it represents. This revenue generated may be due to interest, dividends, or coupons.

If you are trying to create decentralized applications, you have to keep in mind that vTokens are crucial. VTokens allows the users to make protocol fees, trade fees as a liquidity provider, and farm as loan collateral. These can compete with the rivals with centralized counterparts in speed, efficiency, and scalability.

Protocols Designed For Passive Income

A new standard for transferring and settlement of tokens has been established. That is because the skating protocols allow better distribution and increased transparency in the delivery. The reach of those platforms will increase multiple folds that use these distribution protocols that may result from adoption.

New content may be rapidly used to generate liquid markets for virtual assets, which will get the most out of their utility.

Several skating protocols may be of use if you consider the gains of decentralization of finance.

Lending protocols provide permissions for forming financial assets that can be used as security on a decentralized lending platform.

The Peer-to-Peer lending market has great potential, but unfortunately, it is pretty under-serviced. The conditions required to progress the lending into blockchain will come from the introduction of next-generation credit scoring and asset tokenization.

Lending backed by assets could provide the borrowers with significant liquidity, low margin rates, fast compensation timeframes, and efficient risk management protocols.

An alternative class of asset tokenization that can signify the payment means and store the value for fiat currency on the Ethereum main net is collateralized stable coins.

In general, NFTs are comparatively illiquid and hard to price. Taking chances in the NFT market is more accessible due to the skating protocols. Another gain it provides to these platforms is to sell their NFTs faster. That also helps in providing the customers with an enhanced user experience.

Transaction costs are highly reduced and allow for near-instant transaction speeds.

If you consider the flexibility of the NFTs, you will notice that they are a flexible class of digital assets. It has numerous applications in art, gaming, finance, and more. Decentralized applications will be controlling their governance protocols, which will be made possible by this technology. Also, it will not be cutting down on its transparency and decentralization. A good way of passively generating revenue from digital properties is to monetize NFTs.

The collateralized stablecoins operated on the Ethereum mainnet are tremendously helpful by the businesses. Stablecoin that is used as collateral can help protect businesses from high fluctuations in the price and increase their ability to transact with customers in a quicker and well-organized way.

To create a standard of the next-gen decentralized finance applications or the DeFi, the next-gen protocols need to set the tokenization of assets as their primary objective.

FUNDAMENTAL ANALYSIS FOR NFT INVESTING

NFTs have progressed from specialist blockchain communities to everyday commercial sectors. The future potential of NFTs is far beyond imagination at this point.

The advances in blockchain technology have resulted in a revolution in the economic environment. In many ways, the arrival of cryptocurrencies such as Bitcoin, Ethereum, and Tether has disrupted the established financial industry.

Alternative assets, such as artworks or collections, are often sold through dealers or traditional auction platforms. Alternative asset classes in NFT markets, on the other hand, differ from existing markets in many ways. NFT markets are peer-to-peer auction markets driven by blockchain technology (e.g., OpenSea or Rarible).

There are no central bodies or trade intermediaries in NFT markets, allowing NFT owners or collectors to interact directly with their counterparts. Both parties can trade at an agreed price at any time if they have an Ethereum wallet (e.g., MetaMask), expanding public access to NFTs and lowering deadweight loss in illiquid asset markets.

Nft Marketplace

The use of NFTs in collectibles has brought NFTs to the forefront of the media. The market capitalization of the top 100 significant NFTs collections is roughly $14,492,390 as of this writing in July 2021. CryptoPunk and Crypto-Kitties created history in NFT technology in 2017 — the former because some of them were sold for millions of dollars, and the latter because the enormous volume of transactions initiated by their exchange rendered the Ethereum network useless for a few days. The HashMasks, Meebits, and Bored Ape Yacht Clubs are some of the most recent NFT collections from 202. They're all made up of a small number of assets with varying rarities.

Each collection is backed by a solid and cohesive community that communicates through social media channels like Twitter and Discord. Property is another potential application for NFTs. This notion has yet to be fully realized in the real world, but it has proven to be quite successful in the metaverse, where video game players may buy and sell collectible virtual universes. Even if NFTs can become a powerful example of digital personal property recognized by a decentralized body in the following years, the technology is still in its early stages.

Due to the lack of systematic summaries and the number of hype cycles, newcomers may become lost in its frantic evolution. Furthermore, logical analogies between NFT transaction networks and graphs characterize social media user interactions. It can disguise the characteristics of an engaging environment in which objects can be traded for extremely high prices, perhaps hundreds or thousands of ETH.

NFTs, like any other financial asset, can theoretically be traded on blockchain-based platforms. Although NFT marketplaces do not provide a low- or high-price estimate, anybody can evaluation historical transactions for a certain NFT, including bids, offers, sales prices, trading dates, ownership changes, and even information on the parties involved. With such trackable records, determining whether an NFT is a duplicate or an original work with such trackable records. These capabilities also allow us to investigate NFTs at the transaction level.

Transformation Of Assets

According to specific estimates, most investable assets available in private and public markets are non-fungible. For example, the estimated value of real estate, which is non-fungible, vastly outnumbers the capitalizations of both the global bond and equities markets. Perhaps more importantly, derivatives, the world's largest asset class with a notional value of $580 trillion, are also non-fungible. They can't be moved between multiple exchanges or trading platforms. Art and collectibles are non-fungible items, albeit with a far lesser value (about $2 trillion).

Because of the preceding discussion and current technological advancements, all non-fungible assets can be represented as NFTs. For a range of reasons, it is crucial to investigate this option. NFTs, for starters, boost market liquidity and price discovery. Trading assets are more efficient if ownership can be instantly proved and transferred swiftly and securely for a low charge. As a result, NFTs improve asset openness, transparency, and financial globalization. It results in increased trading volumes and market expansion on its own.

Second, NFTs do away with the functions of delayed clearing and settlement. Settlement times are currently measured in days. NFTs reduce the time it takes to decide a dispute from days to seconds. Furthermore, physical clearing is still used by some market participants. NFTs, on the other hand, rely on fraud-proof blockchains, which allow information to be validated and recorded in real-time. Third, collateral management necessitates openness, which can be severely harmed in the current financial system, as in the recent instance of Archegos9. Again, the NFT presents a clear-cut solution, removing any potential for market players to hide self-serving behavior.

Nft Liquidity Mining And Farming

NFT liquidity mining and NFT farming are two very similar concepts. NFT liquidity mining is an investing activity that entails locking an NFT in a smart contract with two primary goals, depending on the market side:

- Making NFT deposits (providing liquidity) on the NFT platform, and

- Making a return for the NFT investor who made the NFT deposit.

NFT liquidity mining, like a simple buy-and-hold method, entails making or purchasing an NFT and transferring it to a smart contract (akin to gambling activity in the PoS blockchain). Investors receive interest in exchange for providing NFT liquidity. Interest is usually paid in the network's native currency, dependent on NFT liquidity mining for survival. It's worth noting that if NFTs are fractionalized and hence directly interchangeable, mining algorithms could potentially acquire more liquidity.

Dego Finance (DEGO), for example, is an NFT-related project that focuses on NFT mining, auctioning, trading, farming, and other NFT-related applications10. Dego compensates NFT holders for converting their NFTs into the native Dego token, including voting and dividend rights. The mining efficiency and power value assigned to each NFT11 affect the staking yield. NFT farming, on the other hand, entails staking a blockchain native token in exchange for a native NFT, which can subsequently be stored, sold, or used as collateral. On some of the NFT-dedicated blockchains, NFT farming is now active (e.g., Ethernity, SuperFarm). The sealed native token can be un-farmed at any moment.

Nft Fractionalization

Unlike accredited investors and investment funds, retail clients have restricted capital access, limiting their investing options. Due to their excessive price levels, several asset classes, on the other hand, have insufficient liquidity and unbalanced markets. The preceding issues are addressed by blockchain technology, which allows for asset fractionalization or the division of an enormous asset into smaller pieces. This notion has been considered in the literature in artwork and is known as securitization.

Investors can buy a portion of the NFT through fractionalization. As a result, it is an opportunity to gain exposure to premium and well-known NFT at high absolute prices. For example, an NFT by modern artist Mike Winkelmann (aka Beeple) sold for 69($mil) at Christie's recently — an auction price beyond reaches for retail investors, admirers, and tiny collectors. Fractionalization also ensures a higher degree of variety. As a result, a piece of NFT can boost portfolio efficiency, or alpha, for a given level of threat.

Art creation can be called NFT, but once it has been divided into several parts, each of these parts may be represented by a fungible token, a token that can be used interchangeably with other parts of the same NFT. An NFT, on the other hand, can be fractionalized into several NFTs with different distinguishing properties and hence valuations while being non-fungible. A collector might be wanting to pay more for a shard of Mona Lisa's lips than for a fragment of the same painting's backdrop landscape. In any event, several different collectors can now own identical pieces of art, which has never happened before in history.

A further endowment of fractional NFT is possible. Owners of fractional NFTs could pool their assets to form a decentralized autonomous organization (DAO) and issue shares backed by that endowment. The example demonstrates that tokenizing unique assets open up a world of possibilities.

Nft Minting, Trading, And Auctioning

Artwork and in-game items are currently the most common use cases for NFT. It seems to be the case because NFT architecture eliminates the middleman between the artist and the audience, improving product reach, profit margins, and sales potential. It is commonly known that gatekeepers still exist in the art industry, limiting producers' access to the market. Exclusive locations, privileged organizations, and rent-collecting intermediaries are among them. The NFTs make it possible to bypass the art world's usual gatekeepers.

Notably, producers can use current online marketplaces (e.g., OpenSea, Rarible) or decentralized applications that directly connect them to the appropriate network to generate (mint) the NFT of their art piece or complete art collection on the blockchain. To mint, an NFT, a technique that reduces entrance barriers to the primary and secondary art markets, one does not need to be an expert. Further, it appears that minting an NFT is synonymous with marketing an NFT, whether at a fixed price or through various auction procedures.

A related problem is the rights sold in conjunction with the NFT. Existing standards are still adaptable. The present owner of the most expensive NFT to date, Beeple's "Everyday: The First 500 Days," which sold 69.3 million dollars, acquired the license to exhibit the NFT but not the copyrights. On the other hand, proprietors of the Hashmasks NFTs (16,384) get limitless rights to use, copy, and display the NFT. Surprisingly, the NFT of the tungsten cube sold on OpenSea only allows its owner "one visit to see/photograph/touch the cube each calendar year."

One may undertake systematic analysis and construct metrics that help determine how the wallets participating in this ecosystem interact by filtering publicly available information on the blockchain and organizing it in a graph model.

NFT AND BLOCKCHAIN

6 Key Properties

Blockchain-based NFTs allow users to own digital assets. However, this ownership of digital assets is different than physical ownership because these types of assets only exist within specific, purpose-built contexts, such as marketplaces, games, and whatnot, making them more challenging to move, at least for now. When blockchain technology comes into play, it can provide a layer of coordination for digital assets, granting users' ownership and permission to manage them and changing developers' relationships with their investments. All of this is possible thanks to 6 fundamental properties that set the rules for NFTs and represent the characteristics that make them unique.

Standardization

Standards serve to create a uniform set of rules that allow NFTs to integrate across platforms, be interoperable, and increase their utility value by extending their applicability.

As with all technologies, standards represent repeatable and shared ways of operating within a context. Standards arise from saving time and resources by eliminating unnecessary processes and are universally recognized within the community. A reference standard is always necessary to ensure that everyone operates compliantly.

When tokenization of a digital asset occurs within the blockchain, these tokens are enrolled through common, reusable, and inheritable standards. In other words, these are methods agreed upon and developed by developers that allow NFTs to operate in different ways. Each digital asset is represented differently—e.g., a game may represent its collection in an entirely different way than an event ticket. NFTs are based on a joint, public system whose standards include basic features such as ownership, transfer, and access control. That means that several purchased NFTs can interoperate within the same application if they are based on the same standard. Programmers can then create applications that use the same code to have all tokens within a decentralized platform, such as Ethereum's network. The three primary NFT tokenization standards on the Ethereum blockchain are:

- ERC721
- ERC998
- ERC1155

The acronym ERC stands for Ethereum Request for Comments. Anyone can create standards, but it is up to the author to explain them and promote support within the community. ERC was designed to provide information or introduce new features to the Ethereum network, so ERC is how programmers propose changes. Since Ethereum is based on blockchain technology, no one person can take over and make changes or adjustments to the protocols.

The numbers 721, 998, and 1155 represent the codes for those proposals. ERC721 in 2018 by Cryptokitties, where each cat to be adopted, nurtured, and raised was represented by an NFT. Before this standard, people could create fungible tokens such as Ether, but with ERC721, programmers can develop tokens with different properties, characteristics, and types, all from the same smart contract. ERC721 is the NFT standard that allows NFTs to be created and exchanged. While it is the most popular cross-platform, easy to integrate, and available NFT standard, it also has several inefficiencies depending on the use case.

ERC998 has a unique operation and was created to allow multiple ERC721 NFTs to be transferred within the network in a single bundle transaction instead of making several. With this standard, not only do you own an NFT but that NFT can also include your own NFTs, as in a sort of bundle. If an NFT is sold, all the tokens attached are sold. Thus, transferring the composition of the NFT means moving the entire hierarchy of associated elements. For example, a crypto kitty may own a scratching post and an eating dish that may contain fungible tokens, and in selling the crypto kitty, all of the items associated with it are also sold.

The ERC1155 token is a type of standard token that can store, within its authority, tokens that can act as if they were an ERC20 or ERC721 token, or both at the same time under the same address.

ERC1155 was created by Enjin, an Ethereum platform that allows non-fungible tokens and fungible tokens to be completed in the same contract. The standardization of NFT issuance makes possible a higher degree of interoperability, which benefits users. It means that unique assets can be transferred between different applications with relative ease.

The best example of ERC1155 can be found in blockchain games. Instead of requiring a new contract for each game item, multiple items can be created using the same agreement. Also, if, for example, both weapons and crypto coins are collectible in the game, you can write both with ERC1155, drastically reducing the resources needed to run blockchain-based games efficiently.

Interoperability

As we've already mentioned, all NFTs use the same standards to be on the same level and operate on the same Ethereum platform. That enables the transfer of NFTs across multiple ecosystems, immediately visible and tradable. Thus, based on the exact usage characteristics—

i.e., through standardization— interoperability allows NFTs to be freely tradable on open marketplaces.

Tradeability

That is the first time users worldwide can create NFTs that can be immediately available in marketplaces across the ecosystem. Here, people can buy, trade, sell, and auction NFTs. The extent of this property lies in the move from sales within closed marketplaces to the possibilities offered by a marketplace that has an open and accessible economy. The ease with which any user can create and trade NFTs worldwide through the blockchain is fantastic.

Liquidity

The speed and efficiency of blockchain-based marketplaces lead to a high level of liquidity, which describes how many people are making trades within the market and how often. This term is used to describe a group of activities within a market. High liquidity means that items are sold quickly and frequently. A marketplace based on blockchain technology allows for just such efficiency and speed in buying and exchanging, as is the case with bitcoins, which can, for example, be traded for real or fiat currency easily on Coinbase or Binance.

As with any other investment, anyone must sell and buy tokens quickly without lowering the price. To make this possible, the market you act in must be liquid. In other words, there must be a high level of trading activity, and the bid and ask prices must not be too far apart.

The NFT market must have high volume and good liquidity, especially for investors who buy NFTs, knowing that they have a large community of people to whom they can then sell them. For this cause, it is essential to keep an eye on the significant NFT projects to invest in. To understand if a market is liquid or illiquid, the best way is to look at three indicators: trading volume in a day, the depth of the order book, and the amount that separates the bid and ask price, which is known as the bid/ask spread.

With NFTs, it is also possible to develop real-world asset tokenization. These NFTs could represent fractions of physical assets stored and traded as tokens on a blockchain. That could introduce much-needed new liquidity into many markets that wouldn't otherwise have much, such as artwork, real estate, rare collectibles, and more.

Immutability and provable scarcity

Immutability, as the name implies, is the ability of a blockchain to remain unchanged so that it remains unaltered and indelible. To put it more simply, the data within the blockchain, as formerly mentioned, cannot be changed. In its technical nature, blockchain is configured as an immutable database, and it is not possible to manipulate the data already in the blockchain.

Each block consists of information, such as the transaction details, and uses a cryptographic principle called a hash value. That hash matter consists of an alphanumeric string developed by each block separately. Each block contains a hash referring to itself and incorporates the former one. That ensures that the blocks are paired retroactively. That is how this feature of blockchain technology ensures that no one can intrude into the system or alter the data stored in the league.

The most popular hash function is SHA256, or Secure Hash Algorithm 256. The hash value protects each block of code separately. The process of hashing generates a string of 64 characters. However, of the input size, the fixed length of the series, known as a digital signature, is always the same. That refers to the exact data entered, and the fundamental property of this hash value is that it cannot be decoded. The word immutable relates to something that can never be changed. Immutability is the key that imprints authenticity in digital assets and introduces scarcity. Immutability means that what belongs to a particular person in a game, for example, cannot be moved or changed.

Programmability

NFTs are fully programmable. They can, for example, be programmed to respond to triggers or actions taken by the owner. They can also react to external stimuli such as time or score. The programming possibilities of NFTs are endless.

TOOLS TO FIND UPCOMING PROJECTS FOR DIFFERENT BLOCKCHAINS

Platforms for NFT evaluation and Rarity can help you stay ahead of the game regarding NFT investing.

These are the shovels that will be used to locate the NFT gold nuggets. They will aid in the hunt for NFT rarities, the discovery of new NFT projects, the tracking of whale wallets, the making of wiser investment judgments and will undoubtedly be a part of your due diligence toolset.

Getting the appropriate information is crucial to the success of any crypto movement, as it is with any other. If you're a novice or a seasoned NFT collector, you'll need analytical tools to assist you in assessing the Rarity and availability of assets. Aren't you hoping to locate the next Bored Ape?

Fortunately, a few platforms have developed technologies that will undoubtedly assist you. While some are free to use, others require a subscription to access additional services. Here's a look at some of the best NFT analytical tools to help you along your way.

If you're a severe NFT investor, collector, or trader, you've probably used one, if not several, of the online NFT data analysis tools.

Rarity.tools

Rarity. When buying a non-fungible token, Rarity is one of the most important factors to consider. The best NFTs are extremely rare and highly sought after by collectors, which drives their price. Tools are an excellent NFT rarity tool for examining the NFT space.

Rarity. Tools is another website that collects real-time data on all NFT arts and collectibles—it's a popular choice among art collectors and artists (and one of mine), especially in the fertile art area.

Rarity collects and ranks NFT arts in order of Rarity, with a preference for new efforts. Unlike other tools structured primarily as charts and lists, the platform is developed with the aesthetics of an art-featured market in mind, and it has a charming appeal on the landing page.

Tools have a unique feature in that new projects can be listed in a few simple steps for 2ETH. The NFT collection list is also filtered on the free version by its unique traits, market volume, and sale prices. Users can click on any NFT to access additional information and pricing charts for Rarity's currency.

Rarity. Tools are also excellent for keeping track of upcoming NFT projects, allowing users to see them before going on public sale or mint.

On Rarity. tools, you may sort NFTs by their volume in ETH, average price, and market collections.

Each collection has its page, which lists all of the NFTs in that collection. Each item has its detailed card, on which you can view the asset's distinct characteristics. Rarity offers the added benefit of assigning a rarity score to each NFT.

The site charges a listing fee to creators. As a result, it's possible that it won't include all NFTs, as some may be unable or unable to pay the platform's cost.

Nft Calendar

NFTCalendar is the industry's first release and event calendar for Non-Fungible Tokens. It covers the most exciting events and NFT drops on various marketplaces and platforms.

NFT calendar is more than simply a calendar that copies information and data from the internet; it is a well-known platform that serves as an NFT calendar. It will be a complete marketplace containing information about NFT releases and reliable sites where traders may buy NFTs.

Whether you like to buy or sell NFTs, it will supply you with the necessary information. If you're looking to invest in new NFTs on any Blockchain, keep an eye on the NFT calendar for the most up-to-date information and details.

NFTCalendar is your companion in the world of Non-Fungible Tokens. It highlights crypto art and creators and reports on the latest news and events in Decentraland.

The purpose of the NFT calendar is to make the digital collectibles universe understandable and reachable to every NFT collector and movement follower. It lists all impending NFT (Non-Fungible Token) Drops and Auctions, ensuring that you do not miss out on anything significant.

Ethereum, Solana, Polygon, Cardano, Binance Smart Chain, WAX, FLOW, Cronos, Theta, Moonriver, Harmony, and EOSIO are among the blockchains on the NFT calendar.

Artists can include licenses when minting NFTs via secure channels provided by NFT marketplaces. The NFT calendar merely provides a medium for artists and collectors to communicate what they're selling and what they're going into.

Nft Scoring

All NFT initiatives are tracked and analyzed by NFT Scoring. It is a market research tool that aids in discovering exciting new projects.

NFT Scoring compiles all pertinent information regarding past and current NFT projects to assist you in identifying those with the most potential.

It keeps track of community size, growth, and engagement across all major platforms and provides a unique AI-driven rating system based on the most successful NFT initiatives. NFTScoring keeps track of social media and Discord activity to offer you a score for the best NFTs.

Twitter

The social media behemoth also changes the design of NFT profile photos, making illegitimate NFTs stand out if used as a profile image.

Tess Rinearson has been named as Twitter's new Crypto Engineering head, leading a new team focused on crypto, blockchains, and other decentralized technologies, including but not limited to cryptocurrency.

Twitter has unveiled a new crypto initiative that will allow NFT enthusiasts and creators to show off their ownership of the high-value virtual products as part of broader changes to the service that panders to the interests of its super-users. In keeping with its focus on crypto-communities, Twitter also announced that it would begin transacting in Bitcoin, allowing the service's top accounts to accept Bitcoin tips as part of a monetization initiative that started in 2021.

Icy.tools

Icy. Tools contain a plethora of knowledge that will put you ahead of the competition regarding NFT flipping. Icy allows you to spot trends early, such as the most popular NFTs in the last hour, the most famous NFT collections in the last hour, 6 hours, one day, and more. Based on the existing floor pricing, Icy also estimates the estimated value of all your NFTs in ETH.

Beginners love it because of its simple, transparent interface, ideal for a quick market survey. It offers a list of trending sales and projects, for example, ranked by volume and sale price.

The "Trending Collections" from the former day are the first thing you see on icy. Tools: If you have a wallet linked, you can narrow the ranking to the last three days or the last 15 or 30 minutes.

Each of the mentioned collections' floor price, average price, volume, and sales are displayed on the leaderboard.

The interface is simple, making NFT analysis simple even for inexperienced investors.

The top mints from the former day to the latest 15 minutes can be found on the "Discover" page. The wallet addresses of the top purchasers and sellers are also available.

The bonus version, on the other hand, has more features. Users can take advantage of transaction history on collections and balance searches on any wallet address. Users that want extensive research, available wallet tracking, in-depth market charts, and customized alerts should pay 0.03 ETH per month for the premium version.

Premium customers can also view the detailed pages for each NFT collection, including pricing charts and historical data for each NFT. Furthermore, premium accounts have access to each wallet address displayed under buyer and seller's trade history.

OpenSea

One of the most well-known platforms, OpenSea is home to coveted collections. This NFT platform can also function as an NFT tool for monitoring your future digital art investment, in addition to the remarkable digital art collection.

As a collector, you'll like OpenSea's comprehensive ecology, including the NFT shop and data. Having all the knowledge in one place makes deciding on the best NFT to purchase much more effortless.

OpenSea is the world's largest NFT marketplace, making it simple to track all activity and data for any NFT listed on the site.

Rankings and activity may be found under Stats on the main menu and provide real-time data about NFTs. The activity feed is convenient because it allows for a real-time feed of all activity on the OpenSea market.

OpenSea helps NFTs based on the Ethereum, Polygon, and Klaytn blockchains. Another benefit is that you can track NFTs on all three chains from a single platform. NFT can be filtered by nine different categories, including art, music, sports, and trading cards, in addition to blockchain.

Nansen

Many investors have long desired to identify opportunities in the NFT industry, and Nansen.ai was one of the first NFT platforms to do so.

This NFT analysis platform displays a leaderboard of NFT wallets ranked by total earnings. The analysis' findings can assist you in managing your assets and developing a strategy.

Nansen's analysis tool gives thorough information for each wallet on the leaderboard, including minting fees, secondary market fees, and all ERC-20 token details.

Nansen displays the leaderboard for each project, making it simple to identify and analyze owners. Furthermore, with this NFT application, you can track these wallets and their investments over time.

Nansen.ai is a must-have tool for anticipating trends and looking through the wallets of seasoned NFT collectors and traders with deep pockets, which are labeled. Nansen discusses the activities of over 90 million identified Ethereum wallets. So, you can tell the difference between the signal and the noise in blockchain data.

Nft Bank

NFTBank, a vital NFT instrument that can deliver rapid insights on investments, would delight NFT investors. The data presented include, among other things, ROI, activity, and spending. NFT Bank is one of the most excellent NFT portfolio management solutions available.

According to the company, investors that utilize NFTBank's platform uncover NFT investment opportunities ten times faster than others. Indeed, the user interface is simple and offers information that anyone can understand.

Users can track their portfolios and create a uniform profile that supports all NFT projects and blockchains using NFTBank.

Users can utilize the "Analytics and Signals" feature to locate new NFT investment opportunities because it gives indications to assist them in understanding the market and tracking other users' portfolios.

Nft Stats

NFT Stats is another simple-to-use and informative NFT utility. This NFT platform provides fundamental NFT collection insights. Trending collections, new collections, and the top collections in the last 30 days are all included in the NFT rankings.

The number of sales and total volume are used to rank the collections.

This NFT platform provides a quick snapshot of the most popular NFT collections sold in the former 24 hours, seven days, and 30 days. The NFT and the group it belongs to and when and how much it was sold for are all included in the data.

Each collection page includes information on recently sold NFTs as well as three-month pricing trends.

CryptoSlam

CryptoSlam is another excellent NFT tool for market analysis. Users can search for NFT collections based on a trading volume using this simple but powerful interface. Each NFT group has its complete website with live sales, marketplace, and minting information. You'll find a separate page for each NFT with all the information you'll need, including pricing, unique qualities, and rarity rankings.

Anyone may quickly locate and discover NFTs thanks to this all-time rating for all NFT collections.

NFT AS COLLECTIBLES AND DIGITAL ASSETS

What is an NFT, and why is it becoming such a big issue in the press these days? Cryptographic tokens, known as non-fungible tokens (also known as non-fungible tokens), enable someone to verify that an online asset is a genuine article. 2020 was a banner year for the cryptocurrency industry. The subject of decentralized finance has only gained prominence, with companies such as Tesla investing significant sums of money in cryptocurrencies and Bitcoin hitting all-time highs, among other things. Since the end of 2020, there has been a continuous increase in the popularity and usage of NFTs, which have sold for millions of dollars in some instances.

Cryptocurrencies such as Bitcoin are referred to be 'fungible' tokens since they are interchangeable and do not have a unique serial number. Therefore, if you were to trade one Bitcoin for another, you would be receiving the identical item. Each coin is similar to the others in terms of design. Non-fungible tokens, on the other hand, indicate something that is one-of-a-kind and cannot be replaced. An NFT may be stamped onto, for example, an original GIF or picture as evidence that the item being traded or sold is the genuine one. That is similar to trading or selling an original artwork that has been authenticated. Another way of putting it is that an NFT is a cryptographic token that enables someone to verify that an online asset is genuine. Because of this, resources are scarce, which in principle leads to the creation of value, even in the digital realm, where assets are not physically present.

You Are Maintaining The Security Of Your Nfts.

Given the potential worth of NFTs, it is only reasonable to consider the issue of protecting these digital assets from being compromised. Are they completely safe to use? In general, purchasing and holding non-fiat currencies (NFTs) is just as safe as buying and holding bitcoin. However, even though the technology that underpins NFTs is considered secure, there are certain precautions you should take to guarantee the safety of your investment. Here are some suggestions for keeping NFTs safe:

Select a safe and secure wallet. NFTs, like cryptocurrencies, is saved and utilized via a cryptocurrency wallet. The wallet you choose is critical since specific wallets are more trustworthy and safe than others. For example, a wallet that keeps your private key exclusively on your device needs strong passwords, supports two-factor authentication, encrypts your data, and requires you to set up a recovery passphrase are all desirable features. Hacken, a cybersecurity firm specializing in blockchain technology, conducted a case study examining nine non-custodial wallets. Based on different factors, including whether or not each wallet published its third-party audit results, whether or not each wallet requires strong passwords, and whether or not each wallet has a history of security breaches, they determined that Metamask and Enjin are the safest wallets available. For a more detailed description of the technique utilized and a list of wallets, please visit this page.

Make your password difficult to guess. You've probably noticed that you're using the same password for many different accounts. Please, don't do that! A long, one-of-a-kind, and complex password is required for your wallet. Pro tip: This recommendation should be followed for every account you have.

Enable two-factor authentication on your computer. Two-factor authentication, just like it does with your bitcoin wallet, is very beneficial. Due to the need for authentication before performing operations, the likelihood of an NFT being stolen or mistakenly given to someone decreases significantly.

Please make a note of your recovery phrase and keep it somewhere safe. If you forget your password, your passphrase will serve as a final option for regaining access to your account. If you are using a mnemonic phrase, be sure that your passphrase is not readily guessable and kept in a safe place. You will very certainly be unable to restore your account if you forget your recovery phrase.

Make frequent backups of your wallet. It is a good idea to keep many backups of your data. In the case of a system malfunction or the loss of a device, you can be sure that you will be capable of restoring your data.

Make sure to keep your software up to date. Security patches are included in software upgrades.

Make use of a protected internet connection. An attacker will have an easier time stealing your information if you use a public wifi network. If you must use public wifi, use a virtual private network (VPN) to protect your connection and turn off the Bluetooth connection on your device.

In addition to these measures, it is essential to be aware of your legal rights about your NFTs. Although NFTs demonstrate that a particular piece of data is one-of-a-kind, they do not prohibit someone from tokenizing anything that is not their own. Fortunately, there are legal safeguards in place that you may take advantage of. For example, NFTs may be subject to standard copyright legislation. Using the Digital Millennium Copyright Act (DCMA)*, you might, for example, submit a takedown request against the platform selling and the producers of these NFTs if you think your digital work is being stolen.

CoinDesk also advises that you specify what you offer to customers in your listing description. For example, what do you own if you hold the rights to a work you're selling? Do you own the underlying art (for example, an original GIF) or simply the digital representation of the work? Or, to put it another way, be precise on the front end by designing your smart contract to describe the rights that are being transferred when feasible or suitable.

WHAT GIVES THEM THEIR VALUE?

NFTs are created and issued using a variety of frameworks. ERC-721, a standard for printing and exchanging non-fungible assets on the Ethereum blockchain, is the most well-known of these frameworks. NFTs are built on Ethereum's permanent blockchain, suggesting they can't be changed. They're also "permissionless," which indicates that anyone can make, purchase, or sell an NFT without asking permission. Eventually, each NFT is one-of-a-kind and can be utilized by everyone. No one may take away the custody of an NFT or duplicate it.

Yes, it's like a one-of-a-kind collectible card shown in an always-open store window that everyone can value. Yet, only one individual (or cryptocurrency wallet, to be precise) may possess at any given time. A virtual artwork, such as a picture, will be used as a case in this book. In the NFTs platform, It's important to note, however, that it's not just about that picture (which can easily be replicated). The fact that it exists as a digital entity on the blockchain distinguishes it.

ERC-1155 is the latest and enhanced standard. It allows a specific contract to include both fungible and non-fungible tokens, which opens up a world of possibilities. The standardization of NFT issuance allows for greater interoperability that favors users in the long run. It essentially implies that specific assets can be easily shared among various applications. More will be explained on NFTs standardization later on in the book.

If you want to store and admire the elegance of your NFTs, Trust Wallet is the place to go. Your NFT will have an address, just like other blockchain tokens. It's worth remembering that NFTs can't be duplicated or exchanged without the owner's consent, including the NFT issuer. NFTs can be traded on open exchanges like OpenSea. These marketplaces bring buyers and sellers together, and each token has its meaning. NFTs, by their very nature, are subject to price fluctuations in response to market supply and demand.

But how can such items be considered valuable? Like any other useful item, the value of a functional object is assigned by people who think it is practical. Esteem is, at its heart, a common belief. You can do this in Trust Wallet with your NFTs. Your NFT will have an address, just like other blockchain tokens. It's worth remembering that NFTs can't be duplicated or exchanged without the owner's permission, including the NFT issuer.

NFTs can be exchanged on open exchanges like OpenSea. These marketplaces bring buyers and sellers together, and each token has its meaning. NFTs, by their very nature, are subject to price fluctuations concerning marketplace supply and demand. But how can such items be considered valuable? The value of a valuable commodity, similar to any other useful thing, is given by individuals who know it is functional. Value is, in essence, a common belief. It makes no difference if it's fiat currency, rare stones, or a car; they all have value, and people believe they do. Why not digital collectibles? This is how any valuable object becomes precious.

Characteristics Of Nfts:

Non-interoperable

CryptoPunks cannot be used as symbols in the CryptoKitties game, and vice versa. That also applies to collectibles like trading cards; a Blockchain Hero card will not work in the God's Unchained trading card game.

Indivisible

NFTs are inseparable, unlike bitcoin satoshis, and cannot be divided into smaller fractions. They only exist as a complete unit.

Indestructible

Each token cannot be lost, deleted, or reproduced since all NFT data is preserved on the blockchain through blockchain technology. The possession of these tokens is also unchangeable, implying that gamers and holders own their NFTs rather than the companies that make them. Regarding purchasing music from the iTunes store, consumers do not necessarily own the piece they are buying; instead, they are buying permission to listen to it.

Verifiable

Another advantage of storing past ownership data on the blockchain is that objects like digital art can be drafted back to the original maker, eliminating the need for third-party authentication.

Nfts Scarcity

The maker of an NFT is in charge of determining the asset's scarcity. Consider purchasing a ticket to a football match. The maker of an NFT may choose how many replicas there are, just like an event manager can decide the number of tickets to sell. 5000 General Admission tickets, for example, are often exact replicas. A ticket with an assigned seat, for example, can be issued in multiples that are very identical yet differs slightly. In another scenario, the creator may desire to make a one-of-a-kind NFT as a unique collectible.

Each NFT will also have a specific identifier (like a bar code on a standard "ticket") and only one holder in these scenarios. The NFTs' planned scarcity is essential, and it is up to the maker to decide. A maker may wish to make each NFT fully special to generate a lack or have good reason to make thousands of copies. Keep in mind that all of this material is available to the general public.

Nfts And Ethereum

Ethereum allows NFTs to work For a variety of purposes:

- It's easy to show ownership history because transaction records and token metadata are publicly verifiable.

- It's almost impossible to "steal" possession of a transaction after it's been verified.

- Trading NFTs can be done peer-to-peer without the need for sites that are willing to accept big commissions.

To put it another way, all Ethereum products can communicate with one another, making NFTs accessible through products. · The "backend" of all Ethereum items is the same. You can purchase an NFT on one asset and sell it on another. You can display your NFTs on several assets at once as a maker, and each asset will have the most recent ownership details.

- Since Ethereum is never down, your tokens will still be available to sell.

Fractional Ownership

Creators of NFTs may also create "shares" for their assets. That allows traders and fans to own a piece of an NFT without purchasing the entire investment. That expands the number of opportunities available to NFT minters and collectors. Fractionalized NFTs can be exchanged in NFT markets and even on DEXs such as Uniswap. That ensures there will be more buyers and sellers.

The price of an NFT's fractions may be used to determine its total cost. You have a more reasonable chance of owning and profiting from the things you care about. It's more challenging to be priced out of buying NFTs these days. You can learn more about Fractional NFT ownership om NIFTEX, NFTX.

It's possible that having a fraction of an NFT would entitle you to participate in a decentralized autonomous organization (DAO) for asset management in the not-too-distant future. In principle, this will allow people to do things like own a Picasso painting. You'd become a shareholder in a Picasso NFT, which means you'd be able to vote on issues like profit sharing.

Ethereum-based organizations enable strangers, such as global asset owners, to collaborate safely without trusting each other. That is because no money can be spent without the consent of the whole party. A developing market—NFTs, DAOs, and fractionalized tokens all progress at various rates. Nevertheless, since they all speak the same language: Ethereum, all their technology remains and can readily collaborate.

DIGITAL SCARCITY

The original creator determines the scarcity of an NFT.

An example below would give you more understanding regarding this topic. Suppose there is a sports event happening. It is only for the event organizer to determine how many tickets to sell for the event. Similarly, only the original asset creator has the right to decide how many copies he wants to create. Often the documents are a replica of the purchase. Other times a number of them are designed with a minute difference. In other cases, the creator may want to create an NFT where only one is minted, making it one unique and rare collectible.

Individually NFT would still have a unique identifier with a single one in the cases explained above. The creator decides to determine the scarcity of an NFT. It is something that matters. To maintain lack, the creator can create the NFTs entirely differently. If he wishes, he can also come up with many copies. All this is publically known.

Royalties

This concept is still under works, but it is one of the best. If your NFT has a royalty scheme programmed into it, you will receive your share automatically every time your art is sold. The ones who own EulerBeats Originals receive an 8% royalty whenever the NFT of their art is re-sold. Platforms such as Foundation and Zora back royalties for their artists.

The whole royalty process is automatic and stress-free. That is so that the artists who created the art don't have to go through a hassle and earn from their art every time it is sold again. Presently, there are a lot of issues in the whole royalties scheme as it is manual. Due to this explanation, a majority of the artists are not paid. If you pre-define that you will receive a percentage of money as royalties from the artwork in your NFT, you can keep earning from that art piece.

What Are Nfts Used For?

Below are a few more famous and widely known use-cases for the NFTs on the Ethereum blockchain network.

- Digital content
- Gaming items

- Domain names

- Physical items

- Investments and collateral

Maximizing Earnings For Creators

NFTs are widely used in the capacity of digital art. The reason for that is that the digital art industry has a lot of issues that need to be fixed. The platforms that they sold on would swallow their earning and profits generated, thus letting the artists suffer financially.

An artist puts up his work on a social network site and makes money for the platform that sells ads to the followers of the artists. That gives the artist publicity, but exposure and advertising don't make any money.

The NFTs power the new creator economy. In the creator economy, the original creators don't pass on the ownership of their content to the platforms.

Every time these artists make a sale, all the revenue generated goes to them directly. The one with whom he sells his art becomes the new owner. Whenever that owner would sell the art piece further, the artist would generate some revenue from the sale through the royalties' scheme.

The Copy/Paste Problem

Some people fail to understand the concept of NFTs and claim them to be of no use. The main statement that they pass over such a scenario is that if you can screengrab something and get it for free, why do you have to spend millions of dollars on it?

If you screenshot or google pictures of a painting by Picasso, it doesn't make you the owner of it.

If you own a real thing, that means that you won something valuable. The more an item becomes viral, the more in demand it is.

If you own verified something, it will have more value.

Boosting Gaming Potential

NFTs are commonly used in digital art, but they are also very applicable in the game development industry. The developers in the industry use the NFTs to claim ownership over the in-game items. It can help with the in-game economies and benefit the players in multiple ways.

You purchase items in almost every game that you play. If you buy an NFT, you can make money from it outside the game. It can also become a source of profit for you if the item is in demand.

The people who developed the game are the ones who issue the NFTs. That means that they have the right to generate revenue through royalty schemes every time an item is sold again. In such cases, there is a benefit for both the parties (i.e., the players and the developers.)

The items you have collected in the game are now yours, and that the developers no longer handle the game.

If there is no one to handle the game, the items would still be yours, and you will have complete control over them. Whatever you earn in the game can have a lot of worth and value outside of the game.

Decentraland is a VR game that allows you to purchase NFTs that symbolize the virtual parcels of land that you can use as per your liking.

Physical Items

If you compare the tokenization of digital assets and physical assets, you will realize that the tokenization of digital assets is more advanced. Several projects are working on tokenizing real estate, rare fashion items, etc.

Shortly, you will be able to purchase cars, houses, etc., all with the NFTs. That is because the NFTs are deeds, and you can buy a physical asset and then get an act as an NFT in return. With the advancements in technology, it will be real soon that your Ethereum wallet will become the key to your car or home. You will be able to unlock your door with cryptographic proof of ownership.

Nfts And Defi

The NFT space and the DeFi world are working together closely in several exciting ways.

Nft-Backed Loans

There are DeFi applications that allow you to borrow money using collateral. For instance, you collateralize 10 ETH so you can wring 5000 DAI. If the one who borrowed the money cannot pay back the DAI, the lender will be able to get his payment back. However, not everyone can afford to use crypto as collateral.

Presently, the projects have started exploring using the NFTs as collateral. Suppose you purchased a rare CryptoPunk NFT a while back with a present worth thousands of dollars. That means that if you put this up as collateral, you will access a loan with the same ruleset. If you cannot pay back the DAI, your CryptoPunk will be sent to the lender as collateral. Ultimately, you would see that it can work with anything you tokenize as an NFT.

It is not difficult on Ethereum. That is because both of these share the same underlying technology and infrastructure.

Fractional ownership

NFT creators can create "shares" for their NFT. Due to this, the investors and the fans have a chance to own a share of an NFT and not purchase it as a whole. That is an excellent way for the NFT creators and collectors to have more opportunities.

DEX's like Uniswap can help with the trade of fractionalized NFTs. The price of each fraction can define the total cost of the NFT.

Fractional NFTs are still a new concept, and people are still experimenting with them.

NIFTEX

NFTX

This means that you would be able to own a piece of a Picasso in theory. That is like you would become a shareholder in a Picasso NFT. You would be sharing revenue with every partner part of the NFT. Owning a fraction of an NFT will likely move you into a decentralized autonomous organization (DAO) for asset management.

The organizations powered and backed up by Ethereum permit strangers to become global shareholders of an asset. That would allow them to manage everything securely. They don't have to trust each other necessarily. In these systems, no one is allowed to spend a dime unless approved by every group member.

As we have been discussing, this is just the beginning.NFTs, DAOs, and fractionalized tokens are all developing at their own pace. However, their infrastructure has already been built, and all these technologies can work in close correspondence to each other as they are all backed up by Ethereum.

WHY YOU CAN MAKE MONEY WITH NFT

Nfts, Usability And Trends

The popularity of NFT has been increasing. From various trends to usability. The community has been innovative in providing a diverse range of NFTs and making them more approachable for newcomers to the Blockchain space. However, according to some statistics, only 47% of crypto users had learned of NFTs, and 57% had never used them. The most common NFTs were for collectibles (47 percent) and gaming (33 percent), according to a survey of nearly 30k people.

What do these stats tell us? Few people are comfortable engaging with NFTs, and that general knowledge about them is still restricted. The aim remains to bring more people into the space to understand Blockchain better and accelerate its development.

We must remain curious and pursue new projects to help space evolve and understand its functions to develop products for our users better.

A Little About Nfts

These are the most distinctive properties of NFTs, and it's important to remember them so we can understand what we can do with them and how they work:

Unique — Each NFT has its own set of properties, usually stored in the token's metadata.

Scarce is probably a small number of NFTs, with the most extreme example having just one copy, and the number of tokens can be verified on the Blockchain, hence its provability.

Indivisible — Most NFTs can't be divided into smaller denominations, so you won't be able to purchase or transfer a fraction of your NFT.

Like fungible tokens, NFTs ensure asset ownership, are easily transferable and are fraud-resistant.

The popularity of DeFi has recently aided the growth of the topic around NFTs.

How Can Nfts Be Used In Defi?

NFTs are considered the next big thing in the Decentralized finance universe. They can be used as collateral and represent other financial assets such as bonds, insurance, or options.

A DeFi borrowing and lending platform require collateral. That is where NFTs come into play to solve the problem. Yinsure uses NFTs in the insurance space; each contract is represented as an NFT, which can be traded on another platform (e.g., Rarible).

Another DeFi trend we have seen using NFTs is issuing governance tokens. Many sites and NFT marketplaces have begun to publish and distribute governance tokens.

How Brands Are Using Nfts

Technology has advanced in recent years.

Blockchain is one place that has seen some of the fastest advancements.

That does not mean cryptocurrencies like Ethereum, Bitcoin, and the slew of other cryptocurrencies own the crypto market solely.

Let's peek at non-fungible tokens (NFTs) and how labels can use them.

NFTs differ from cryptocurrencies because they have specific codes and metadata that indicate one NFT from another. Cryptocurrencies are fungible tokens because they stand all exact.

Because each NFT is unusual, it cannot be exchanged or traded for an equal NFT. As an outcome, each NFT is a digital collectible, an individual, non-replicable asset.

That's where the NFT craze originated. CryptoKitties, a combination of Tamagotchi and trading cards, burst onto the scene in 2017. Each kitten is unique and can be expanded, replicated, and sold for up to $140,000.

NFT mania was born, and interest in NFTs is increasing.

Why Are Non-Fungible Tokens (NFTs) Essential to Brands?

The ability to characterize digital files such as art, audio, and video is a critical reason NFTs are valuable to brands. They're so universal that they can be used to represent other forms of creative work like virtual worlds, virtual real estate, style, and much better.

What does this have to accomplish with your brand and marketing strategy?

NFTs have unlocked up new forms of brand storytelling and consumer interaction, which are the two critical pillars of a successful marketing campaign, thanks to the global interest they've created.

With NFTs, you can:

• Increase brand awareness

- Create unique brand experiences

- Encourage interaction

- Create interest in your product and brand

Finally, NFTs will assist you in increasing conversions and generating revenue.

Here are some examples of how companies use NFTs in their marketing activities.

Six Ways Brands Are Using NFTs

The concept of NFTs in marketing can be challenging to comprehend. The most effortless way to explain the most complex ideas is to look at examples.

Here are a few imaginative ways brands are utilizing NFTs. Hopefully, you will get some motivation from them.

Taco Bell GIFs

According to research, 83% of millennials choose to do business with companies that share their values. As a result, brands must publicly (and genuinely) endorse causes they believe in.

Taco Bell's basis has been doing this for years, but they obtained it to a whole new level by marketing taco-themed NFT GIFs to support the Live Más Scholarship.

All GIFs were reached within 30 minutes of setting their 25 NFTs (dubbed NFTacoBells) up for sale on Rarible. Each GIF had a starting proposal price of $1. However, they all marketed for thousands of dollars, with one going for $3,646.

Creating and selling NFTs was a wise move made by Taco Bell as it generated a lot of interest in mainstream and social media, which is always right for business.

Like Taco Bell, you can utilize NFTs to:

1. Drive brand awareness

2. Support a good cause

Both are potent factors that can aid in the growth of your business.

RTFKT Digital Sneakers

Looking for a way to make a reputation for yourself and disrupt the market?

NFTs can help you do that.

That's what happened when RTFKT, a relatively unrecognized Chinese virtual sneaker company, produced an NFT sneaker for the Chinese New Year and arranged it up for auction.

That's very special for a brand that's only been around for two years, especially given that they marketed a sneaker that can't even be handled, let alone worn. As impressive as this was, it was still way behind the $3 million they made from another NFT sneaker they designed with the 18-year-old artist, FEWOCiOUS.

While NFTs are still in their infancy, now is the most suitable time for marketers to get on board. It's a beautiful way to get people's attention and build a tribe of followers.

If you're a marketer examining new ways to use NFT technology, you can take a cue from RTFKT. Create restricted edition memorabilia to celebrate special occasions and holidays, and use them in your holiday marketing campaigns. You may give them away to the first X number of customers or sell them separately at an auction.

Grimes Videos

Six million dollars in twenty minutes.

Grimes made that much from a collection of ten NFTs auctioned on Nifty Gateway.

People are curious about NFTs, and brands can capitalize on that interest to sell their goods.

For example, you can:

- Partner with artists or auction sites to have your brand present at the auction.
- Conduct a contest (to generate leads) with NFTs as the prize.
- Make an NFT and auction it for charity.

Marketing is all about riding recent trends and using your imagination to capitalize on the buzz around them to attract attention to your brand.

The Launch of The Kings of Leon's Album "When You See Yourself."

The music industry has become highly competitive due to the many musicians and bands available building and maintaining a loyal fan base isn't as easy as it once was.

The Kings of Leon developed a strategy to get around that.

They unleashed their album "When You See Yourself" in the form of an NFT.

The Kings of Leon made history by becoming the first band to release an NFT version.

More importantly, it put them in the hearts of their fans by enabling them to own a digital collectible. That's a fantastic way to increase brand loyalty.

Kings of Leon have used three different types of tokens for this first-of-its-kind album launch. One type offered live show perks, the second featured exclusive audiovisual art, and the third featured a special album package.

The album is unrestricted on all music platforms, but the NFT edition was only available for $50 on YellowHeart.

The sale of the NFTs was only unlocked for two weeks, after which no more album tokens were produced. The tokens became a trade-able collectible as a result of this change.

Beeple Artwork

Mike Winkelmann, virtually unknown in mainstream art circles, has become a parable.

He marketed a JPG file for $69.3 million, making him the third most expensive living artist at the auction.

The file is a portion of art sold as a non-fungible token.

A flurry of bids came in as the auction was about to close, causing the two-week timed auction to be expanded by 90 seconds.

What lessons can brands learn from this?

Be swift to adopt new concepts and innovations. With the competition becoming more fierce by the day, you must be willing to take chances and be disruptive to outperform.

Nyan Cat GIF

A decade ago, the Nyan Cat GIF made a colorful impact on the digital scene. Developer Chris Torres created an NFT version of the GIF that sold over $500,000 on the crypto auction site foundation.

That's right! A vintage animated GIF sold for more than half a million dollars.

However, Chris didn't stop there. He organized an auction in which classic memes were marketed as NFTs. Bad Luck Brian, one of the memes, dealt for over $34,000 on the foundation.

What can brands learn from this?

The takeaway here is that consumers can pay for excellent service. Take benefit of this by converting some of your most successful ads into NFTs. Make an event where you auction them off and make sure it is well-publicized.

Not only would this increase brand recognition, but it will also help you reach out to new tech markets.

The Future Of Nfts

NFTs are still new, and their practical applications are still limited. However, people adore them and are willing to spend money on them. These are sure indicators that they are here to stay.

NFTs, including the blockchain technology that powers them, can play a significant part in the future digital world. Non-fungible tokens have opened up fresh ways to engage with your audience and create unforgettable adventures for them, which is particularly true for marketers.

Remember that most of the tools we use today (like social media) were once considered fads.

In today's world, we count on them for numerous things. NFTs can seem to be a fad right now, but they offer several benefits (such as clarity and security) that overcome the limitations of current technologies.

GROWTH OF NFTS

Nft Industry Growth And Cryptocurrency Markets

On-fungible tokens are gaining popularity in sports, events, and ID. Music, art, investors, and everyday use are examples of N management. New data has been discovered in many areas from a study that examined 20 million NFT trades. NFTs are still far behind other cryptocurrency cryptocurrencies and will need more attention from significant media outlets. While many mainstream media outlets monitor bitcoin rates, the large NFT transactions on OpenSea and WAX barely make the news.

NFT growth is hindered by public opinion. NFTs can only be traded privately, unlike crypto assets that are publicly traded. To put it another way: One market is open to all, while the other is hidden in the shadows. NonFungible is one example of an NFT aggregator platform that provides transparency in trading activity. Ironically, however, cryptocurrency and the blockchain technology underpinning them has paved the way to NFT growth. For various reasons, NFTs can raise funds much faster than cryptocurrencies. Let's look at three.

Affordability

The definition of meaning can be a bit fuzzy in theory. We believe something is essential because we think it is. Why is it that government-issued money has very little value? According to the system, that's why.

Money is an odd creature. Money is not just a promise wrapped in common metals, abundant (and renewable!) paper, and ink. Most people face financial challenges on both a macro and sometimes a fiscal level. The same applies to cryptocurrencies. Digitizing money can confuse people who have trouble understanding it.

What about tokens? Most people can grasp the idea of purchasing an item that has a specific and unique use. Anyone who has been to an arcade for video games will understand. That is the next step.

Gamification

Let's face facts; cash is boring. Indeed, some of the extravagant experiences and extravagances that money can buy can be pretty thrilling. But, looking at spreadsheets is not our idea of a good time. NFTs are, however, often associated with games and art. Their rarity and collectability are also boosting NFT awareness. NFTs are available to musicians, fans, players, and combinations thereof for many reasons.

OpenSea is the largest NFT marketplace in the world. NFTs allow gamers to take ownership of in-game items. As the public becomes more familiar with NFT, there are many new markets, including Nifty Gateway, owned by a billionaire. OpenSea, the most well-known group, is where we find the most data.

OpenSea users have increased from a few in mid-2018 to over 19,000 since then. Although this is a small number, it is a remarkable trend. Blockchain games and NFTs go hand-in-hand. NFTs are gaining popularity in tandem with videogames, which are experiencing a near never-ending rise in popularity.

Deeper Foundation

If you were alive before the Great Crypto Bullrun in 2017, you would be able to connect. Cryptocurrencies have been under the radar for almost a decade. The world began to notice bitcoin's rise in value, over $20k per coin. Coinbase accounts can be used for a variety of purposes. This massive increase in cryptocurrency wallets is a boon for the NFT industry. You are probably aware of the phrase "a rising tide lifts all boats."

As NFTs and crypto games often connect with crypto wallets, the number of users at 30 million is a good starting point. This number is only based on one transaction. NFTs have a home now, with hundreds of trades and wallet applications. NFTs don't have to start from scratch; they can build layers on a solid foundation. The creation of bitcoins and ethereum can be attributed to the growing popularity of non-fungible tokens.

Nft Use Case

It's more than a piece of art. Jehan Chu, the owner of the blockchain investment firm Kenetic, paid $84,000 for 680,000 HNS (HNS) NFTs. These NFTs give the bearer the ability to issue. The Handshake blockchain is used for NFT domain extension extensions. The Chu believes NFTs are the "real missing link" between offline and online items and that they can transform society, industry, and history. That is not a bold statement.

NFTs benefit from transparency because of their documentation on a publicly accessible ledger. That adds a layer of security for a collectible property that people tend to be attracted to. Rumors of NFTs playing a crucial role in decentralized finance (deFi) have led to proof of concept in Alpaca City's Ethereum based digital world. Alpaca's November tokens went on sale in less than 20 minutes and earned nearly 1,000 Ethereum. Alpaca NFTs won't be "bred" (remember CryptoKitties?). Their owners. NFT-collateralized loans and interest-bearing accounts could increase the tokens' value. NFT owners want to send and receive assets on different blockchains. This compatibility is crucial.

DeFi primitives can be found on many well-known blockchains like Ethereum and TRON. TRC-721 is the NFT standard of the latter, which allows users to track and transfer tokens on the high throughput platform. Individuals on both sides consider NFTs to be significant. Buyers want to play the game while firms offer safe and open NFT protocols. Many NFT projects are available on Ethereum, including CryptoPunks, Decentraland, Hashmasks, and CryptoPunks.

Why You Should Invest In Nfts

NFTs are a profitable venture for the following reasons:

Creates Value for the Tokenized Asset

NFTs allow tangible items like artworks to be tokenized. That prevents replication and gives exclusive ownership to the creator. That creates scarcity, which in turn generates demand for the painting.

It Increases Liquidity for Investors

Investors can leverage their assets more easily by tokenizing them. For example, a digital property owner might rent their digital property out to marketers or advertisers for a fee while still maintaining ownership. The owner still owns the digital property, but some have been rented out as rent.

Growth and development opportunities

NFTs can expand the land market. Virtual lands allow you to decide what you want to do with your property in real estate. Tying NFTs to the ground has allowed for tremendous growth and development. It can be rented out, used to advertise, or sold online.

NFT Projects with Increasing Growth

- Art Tokens

Boyart OpenSea has sold artworks worth over 400ETH and newer products fetching over 75ETH. Boyart is an artist with a lot of experience and has sold some of his art in tokenized form. The new mural paintings have been wrapped in NFTs and sold off.

Boyart has shown that crypto can create an art market in just a few months. That attracts investors who want to invest in assets of interest. The Digital Museum of Crypto Art also has Boyart's murals.

- Lil Moon Rockets

Lil Moon Rockets, a new NFT project, uses smart contracts to distribute unique works of art. The project uses vector art and computational genealogy to keep up with current trends. Every user will receive their own Moon Rocket picture right after the original artwork is sold. To prevent investors and first users from purchasing the best art, Lil Moon Rockets uses a "blind sale." All paintings will become public after the smart contract has ended. Unlike other NFT projects based on Ethereum blockchain, Lil Moon Rockets uses the Binance Chain for its NFTs and subsequent tokens.

While NFTs are a valuable source of revenue for Ethereum, Binance Chain allows easier transactions at lower fees.

- Cryptopunks

Crypto punks are one of the most standardized art forms for NFTs. They are a great example of the attraction to NFTs. Despite being standardized art, crypto punks rose in popularity and became one of the most loved collections.

After a specific social media campaign from prominent crypto personalities, Cryptopunks became the go-to place for risky investments and collections. Due to a combination of scarcity and growing popularity, the 10,000 characters of Punks are also enjoying a stable market for resale. The NFTs were modestly launched with an airdrop for anyone who has an Ethereum wallet. Prices climbed to $57,000. The market is highly active because of network effects of popularity, and the price does not matter how early tokens were distributed.

- Beeple's artwork

An artist known as Beeple is a member of the NFT global marketplace. He had been active on Instagram for many years and only recently gained recognition. Beeple's work has been compared to Pascal Boyart's. The market also values the more computational approach that combines art with technology.

- Hashmasks

Hashmasks is one of the most prominent projects in the NFT space. These collectibles feature alien or robotic backgrounds and are made postmodern. Over 16,000 images were assembled using computational combinations and artists' work. It is impossible to predict where these works of art will end. Hashmasks have become an identity mark in crypto-related social media.

They have been used in visual identities and social media games until now. The most expensive hashmask, which costs 420 ETH, has been until now. The most costly hashmask, which costs 420 ETH, has been 4 ETH.

ADVANTAGES AND DISADVANTAGES OF NON-FUNGIBLE TOKENS

Presently, NFTs have their advantages and disadvantages like any innovation, and in this segment, the accompanying can be featured.

Nfts Advantages

They permit us to address computerized and genuine items inside the blockchain in an exciting and unrepeatable manner. So we can utilize this innovation to deal with these articles securely and consistently. Would you like to tokenize your home or your vehicle using NFT? You can do it. Your creative mind is the cutoff.

The advancement prospects of NFTs are perpetual; anything that you can address carefully can turn into an NFT. For instance, space names (those used to distinguish website pages) can be addressed as an NFT inside a DNS on the BlockchainBlockchain. That is what occurs with the Namecoin project and the Ethereum Name Service.

The production of NFT can be adjusted to any blockchain, and it tends to be executed in a highly secure manner. A model is Bitcoin, which with its restricted programming limit, can address NFTs, keeping the security hazards for such resources for a base; it concludes out how to handle NFTs.

The presence of norms makes their creation, execution, and advancement simpler.

Opportunities for cross-chain interoperability with tasks like Polkadot or Cosmos.

Nfts Disadvantages

While there are norms for creating NFT, they are neither dependable nor complete as far as usefulness is concerned. The formerly mentioned is the primary motivation behind why, for instance, the ERC-721 badge of Ethereum (the most utilized for NFT in Ethereum) tries to be supplanted by the ERC-1155 token significantly more secure and has new capacities.

NFTs are overseen by complex shrewd agreements, making their tasks mind-blogging and weighty (as far as data). These two things raise the estimation of the commissions paid to complete exchanges. So, running NFT can be costly, mainly if the organization is blocked and commissions soar.

Like Defi, NFT stages are more defenseless to hacks since everything is taken care of by brilliant agreements and different interfaces to control them. This whole programming layer adds assault vectors that programmers can misuse for malignant increase.

Non-Fungible Tokens Value

NFTs derive their value from the same deflationary principles as bitcoin—the number of tokens is limited, and the articles cannot be replicated. Thus, owners of NFT tokens can fully own these individual digital assets knowing that they hold only such tokens. Authenticity also plays a role in verifying and can always be traced back to the original creator.

The value of NFTs is also based on the immutability of the product. NFTs cannot be destroyed, deleted, or duplicated. The token only exists on its native platform. It is stored on the blockchain items from one platform and cannot be moved to another.

The Nonfungible website found that NFT buyers increased by 66% in 2020, while the value of transactions rose from around $63 million to $250 million (52 to 207 million euros).

Non-fungible tokens are unified and extraordinary crypto resources that help make computerized shortages. NFTs have been made on the Ethereum (ETH) blockchain, as per the ERC-721 norm. Today, in any case, they are accessible on numerous other blockchains, similar to EOS, TRON, and NEO, and have many use cases. For example, NFTs can address advanced collectibles, craftsmanship, or in-game resources.

NFTs and their intelligent contracts contain distinguishing data, making each NFT special. Thus, no two NFTs are similar. For instance, you can trade one ticket for one more of a similar segment on account of banknotes. They have equal worth, so it doesn't make any difference which one you own.

Bitcoin (BTC) is a convertible token. However, its worth is as yet equivalent to one bitcoin. You can send 1 BTC to somebody; at that point, they can move it elsewhere. Since convertible digital currencies are separable, you can likewise send or get a more modest part of bitcoin-satoshi.

One of the primary NFT collectibles was Cryptokitties, an Ethereum blockchain-based game that permits clients to gather and raise virtual felines. Each blockchain-based talk is fascinating.

Most Expensive Non-Fungible Tokens Ever Sold

- Beeple, every day (The First 5000 Days, $69 million)

Beeple takes the top spot in our ranking, thanks to this period's most remarkable and surprising sale. Christie's closes his first online auction on March 11th, in which he has a work NFT that soars from an initial evaluation of $100 to a record of $69 million in a brief period. Beeple, therefore, found himself the third living artist most expensive in the world behind himself in Jeff Koons and David Hockney.

- Virtual Images of Rick and Morty ($2.3 million)

Another craftsman who has to conclude how to sell show-stoppers as NFT at an over-the-top cost is Justin Roiland, the maker of the famous energized arrangement "Rick and Morty." His assortment of 16 masterpieces was sold for 1,300 ETH, near $2.3 million.

A part of the closeout returns was dispensed to assisting the needy with peopling in Los Angeles, with Roiland saying it was an approach to test the restrictions of crypto artistry.

Strangely, a portion of Roiland's work of art has been delivered in numerous duplicates. Works named "It's Tree Guy" and "Qualified Bachelors" cost $10 and $100 for each piece, separately.

Show-stoppers made in a solitary duplicate were sold at higher costs because of their uniqueness and extraordinariness. The play called "The Simpsons" sold for $290,100. The closeout's beginning cost was $14,999, with its actual being sold for a similar sum.

- Land on Axie Infinity ($1.5 million)

In the first and second positions, we put computerized craftsmanship assortments sold through different exchanges. This time, nine land plots on the well-known blockchain game Axie Infinity were sold in a solitary NFT exchange. The client who made the buy paid 888.5 ETH, or $1.5 million, at that point.

Axie Infinity permits clients to construct a realm in which fabulous characteristics live. The existence where you can purchase virtual land is called Lunacia and has many spots. The entire plot is separated into 90,601 more modest plots, 19,601 more modest plots, 19% of which players possess.

Hawk called attention that the land he purchased is in a great area. Moreover, the pattern on Axie Infinity is consistently expanding, as confirmed by the developing number of dynamic clients. Later on, it will likewise be feasible to arrange occasions, like celebrations or shows, on "your territory" and accordingly bring in cash.

- Collectible character on CryptoPunks ($762,000)

Toward the finish of January, an NFT portraying a character from the CryptoPunks game was sold for 605 ETH, or $762,000, at that point. The universe of CryptoPunks is enlivened by crypto artistry development and comprises more than 10,000 extraordinary advanced characters.

Today, they can be purchased and sold in the committed CyberPunks market. It ought to be referenced that already the characters in the game were free, and you expected to have an ETH wallet to get them.

The NFT, initially founded in 2017 and sold at an exorbitant cost, is $2,890. It is a very uncommon 'punk.'

- A visit to the blockchain game CryptoKitties (600 ETH)

The most costly NFT in history is Dragon from the blockchain game CryptoKitties. This adorable advanced feline was sold for 600 ETH, or $200,000, at that point. Today, a similar measure of tokens costs around $1,000,000 million.

CryptoKitties is one of the primary endeavors to utilize blockchain innovation for diversion. The Axiom Zen studio created it. Like real felines, each virtual feline has a unique DNA and qualities called "credits," which can be given to posterity. Furthermore, each virtual feline is one of a kind and can't be repeated or moved without the proprietor's permission.

As a rule, past ages of virtual felines are viewed as more critical. Dragon uncommon—this is the 10th era of CrytoKitty.

- A Delta Time F1 vehicle ($110,000)

Another NFT is a Formula 1 vehicle on the F1 Delta Time game, explicitly the 1-1-1 model. An unknown gamer purchased this dashing virtual vehicle for a fantastic measure of 415.5 ETH. At the hour of procurement, it was more than $110,000. Until now, such a measure of ETH is worth around $665,000. This buy got the title of the most excellent NFT exchange in 2019.

- One F1 Delta Time track ($200,000)

This time, nonetheless, not a vehicle but rather part of a track. Toward the beginning of December 2020, a piece of the way on F1 Delta Time was sold for more than 9,000,000 REVV tokens, or $200,000, at that point. From that point forward, EVV has developed by 500%, and at the hour of composing this book, it would cost $1.2 million for a similar measure of REVV.

For F1 Delta Time, all significant game resources are addressed by NFTs. For example, the Circuit de Monaco's virtual track comprises 330 badges of this kind partitioned into four levels—from "Uncommon" to Summit." Each token addresses a virtual track share, giving its proprietor many advantages.

For this specific NFT, it was at the "Zenith" level. As a result, its purchaser will get 5% of all in-game income and 4.2% of first-class marking benefits from player stores. Both will be paid in REVV utility tokens.

- NFT Guarantee Money Insurance (350 ETH)

"5000.0 ETH-Cover-NFT" is a protection strategy dependent on insure. Money, an undertaking upheld by Yearn. Financial Because of an enthusiastic advanced approach, its proprietor profits by protection against mistakes in keen agreements on Curve.fi up to 5,000 ETH. NFT costs 350 ETH, which compares to more than $560,000 today.

Yinsure is otherwise called Cover, So, it is a consolidated protection inclusion ensured by Nexus Mutual and another sort of tokenized protection. Protection approaches are represented as NFT. Every one of them is a special NFT. Otherwise called NFT, and can be moved, purchased, or sold.

- 12,600 square meters of virtual land in Decentraland (514 ETH)

Somebody purchased 12,600 m2 for 514 ETH on the Decentraland blockchain game. The game is an Ethereum-based decentralized augmented experience stage. Its clients can make, analyze, and adapt their substance and applications.

Decentraland has a restricted 3D virtual space called LAND. It is a non-fungible computerized resource kept up by Ethereum shrewd agreements. The landowner has complete control of their virtual land.

- Land at 22.2 in Decentraland (345 ETH)

Here is Decentraland once more. This time, it's a land parcel in a "great area" at 22.2. In the realm of Decentraland, the size of the land is fixed. About 80% of its space is private, and the vast majority of the rest is sold and rented by Decentraland. Like streets and squares, the excess land doesn't have a place with anybody. Players can walk their characters on their territory and public land, so the situation is significant. Parts nearer to well-known regions will be more costly than those situated in more distant zones.

Taking a gander at how quickly the NFT markets are developing and what costs non-fungible tokens are sold, we can accept that this will be another gigantic pattern just after Defi. A significant quality of NFTs is that each has its own remarkable and exciting attributes.

PROBLEMS WITH NFTS

Risks Associated With Purchase And Sale On Nft

Like any new resource in the beginning phases of advancement and appropriation, NFTs convey some danger similar to far from mass acknowledgment. If a financial backer picks to purchase an NFT and interest in exchanging them slows down or even disappears, costs will fall, and the purchaser could be left with huge misfortunes.

NFTs are not absolved from misrepresentation. NFTs professing to be crafted by notable specialists have been sold for many dollars; however, they have been uncovered to be phony. Furthermore, similarly that digital forms of money can be taken, NFTs can depend on burglary, relying on how they are put away. Another danger to consider is that computerized content isn't altogether liberated from weakening in quality, record designs getting out of date, sites going disconnected briefly or even forever, or the deficiency of wallet passwords. For makers, printing NFTs to sell content doesn't ensure legitimate rights to responsibility for work, giving less assurance from burglary than they may anticipate. While NFTs and the commercial centers that sell them are decentralized, there can, in any case, be obstacles to acquiring segment and openness for their work.

Similarly, many stages are greeted as craftsmanship exhibitions, and other actual scenes select specialists address. Since NFTs can be created dependent on essentially anything computerized and advanced things can be effectively duplicated, there's the potential for misuse. In particular, there's nothing preventing anybody from making their own NFT dependent on computerized things created by others. In one model announced by Decrypt on March 13, craftsman "Odd Undead" has discovered individuals taking advanced works of art from their tweets. The pictures were utilized to create NFTs and were sold on an NFT commercial center, which the craftsman attempted to end. Bizarre Undead alludes to the training as "crazy and trivial copyright encroachment," which advantages the retail centers and individuals taking the pictures, not simply the craftsmen. The movement isn't restricted merely to fine arts. Likewise, there have been issues with individuals tokenizing tweets by others as NFTs and selling them. Once more, the training doesn't include the individual who composed the first tweet, who might eventually possess the copyright for the content. While it is conceivable for an artisan or the maker of media to sue under the existing brand name and intellectual property laws, the idea of how blockchain works can make it hard to discover who initially encroached to make the NFT. There's additionally the issue of which commercial center to trust in any case. Different blockchain administrations could each guarantee they have records that a particular NFT is interesting and the expert for the work. That is what might be compared to two closeout houses asserting they are the scene of an offer for an extraordinary piece of craftsmanship.

It seems to me that there is a level of participation between significant commercial centers regarding the matter. However, there has been no assurance that things will remain later on. Include that it is therefore workable for individuals to set up their commercial centers on blockchains. It gets more diligent to police the non-fungible tokens as being set available for purchase. These are issues that should be tended to eventually, both to make sure of specialists' occupation and to keep the deals of NFTs legitimate. For the occasion, these issues haven't blunted the craving for all-around obeyed purchasers. For Nadya Ivanova, COO of L'Atelier BNP Paribas, a developing statistical surveying firm that teamed up with Nonfungible on a report on non-fungible tokens in February, the innovation's most unique strength is additionally one of its significant shortcomings. Anybody on the web can make an NFT out of, in actual circumstances, anything, which implies there are a lot of "truly downright awful" out there, Ivanova reiterated in the meeting. It takes a prepared eye to remove what merits gathering or putting resources into. "That applies to the actual artistry market too — it's normally space for the educated. The same thing with NFT craftsmanship," Ivanova said. Also, despite the fact Ivanova views the NFT market as at last developing and proceeding with its course into the standard, she perceives a modest bunch of extra dangers and vulnerabilities new gatherers ought to consider about the maturing space.

The non-fungible token market experiences tremendous unpredictability, Ivanova said, to some degree because there aren't any instruments set up yet to help individuals value resources. Throughout 2020, the estimation of probably the most famous kinds of NFTs spiked by around 2,000%, L'Atelier's report found. On the Top Shot, a few features first traded for a couple of dollars are currently worth many thousands. Regarding liquidity — how promptly a resource can be sold for money —, NFTs are much more like baseball cards or art pieces than bitcoin or stocks; in cognizance of the circumstances, each merchant needs to discover a purchaser who will address a specific cost for a particular, unique thing. That can place authorities in a troublesome spot on the off chance that they, say, burned through $100,000 on a top-notch second the marketplaces start to tank, Ivanova said. Yet, illiquidity can likewise be something to be grateful for since it keeps individuals from settling on careless choices, Andrew Steinwold, a crypto-financial backer who began an NFT venture store in September 2019, told Insider. If individuals don't have the alternative to freeze and offload their NFTs, the market could keep off from the sort of falling qualities that would start such a selloff in any case, he said.

Most Popular Projects

It seems that hundreds of new projects are being created daily, even though millions of NFTs are available for purchase. How do you sort via all of the noise to determine which NFT efforts are the most promising and worthy of your time and attention, as well as your potential investment?

In the first instance, and depending on the amount of money you have available to spend, you may not want to consider NFTs as a potential investment choice at all. Existing assets on OpenSea (the most popular NFT marketplace) total 4 million, with potentially millions more on other exchanges, such as Bittrex and Coinbase (Rarible, Foundation, SuperRare, NBA Top Shot, and more). Because of the breadth and ongoing development of the NFT universe, it is reasonable to expect that not all of these assets will increase in value in the future.

If you're looking for traits in a project, you may be wondering what to look for. According to us, NFTs with practical applications (as mentioned below) is an ideal starting point for learning about NFTs and their potential future uses.

A utility NFT provides a practical use for a digital asset rather than just owning a piece of artwork. You can get a utility NFT if you purchase an NFT to utilize it later. A utility NFT might be anything from a genuine work of art that matches the NFT you purchased to exclusive access to an event, exclusive in-person memberships, or future use in the digital world (think to the game).

Remember that there is always the potential to come across a project that has a goal you can relate with and that will also benefit you. Because of this, you acquire more from your NFT purchase than only digital ownership of a tangible asset, which is a significant advantage (art, photo, video, audio, etc.).

Here are the most promising NFT projects for the year 2021.

Veefriends

One of the most successful serial entrepreneurs globally, Gary Vaynerchuk, founded VeeFriends in 2011. Gary operates in various capacities, including as Chairman of VaynerX, CEO of VaynerMedia, and owner/creator of VeeFriends, among other positions and duties.

Simply put, VeeFriends tokens are a ticket to Gary V's multi-day mega-conference, which is solely open to holders of VeeFriends tokens and is not available to the general public.

That is the world's first ticketed NFT conference, and it is also the first of its type in the globe. An event where token holders of VeeFriends tokens come together as a community to create long-lasting friendships, share ideas, and learn from one another is called a VenCon.

Crypto Baristas

The world's first NFT-funded café, among other things.

Season 1 of Crypto Barista will premiere with 60 caffeine-loving individuals whose ownership will aid in the conceptualization and opening of the World's First NFT-funded Café.

Caffeinated bonuses are available to Crypto Barista owners at all future cafe locations and websites for the rest of their lives. The "Barista Bank," a 15 percent fund put aside from the project's earnings for future use in the coffee industry, is likewise under the owners' authority. Some possible applications for the Barista Bank include supporting charitable organizations in the coffee industry, advancing the Crypto Barista initiative, and launching a new venture.

"The mission of Crypto Barista's is to create a community of like-minded people who share an appreciation for art, coffee, entrepreneurship, and innovation," says the company. The project aims to establish a physical venue in New York City where art and innovation will be at the heart of its processes. The destiny of Crypto Baristas will be determined by the holders and followers of our campaign beyond this point," says the founder.

Dan Hunnewell is the author of this piece (Owner, Coffee Bros.)

Aiming to address three issues in many NFT projects: governance, community, and ownership, the Coffee Bros. Crypto Barista project seeks to address these issues. Seasonal launches will be used to guide the project's development, with each season focusing on a different venture within the coffee area while also delivering benefits and governance to all holders.

Moon Boyz

Known as the Moon Boyz, they are a collective of 11,111 distinct individuals that live on the Ethereum Blockchain. Each NFT is one-of-a-kind and 3D created, and it includes unlimited membership to an ever-growing community and great utilities.

- Moon Boyz Party (the holders of the most irregular characters)
- Exclusive merch for holders
- Private club access
- And more

Mekaverse

In the MekaVerse, which has 8,888 generating Mekas that incorporate hundreds of components inspired by the Japan Mecha worlds, Mekas is created by the MekaVerse.

In the case of the MekaVerse project, Mattey and Matt B, two friends who are also 3D artists, came up with the concept and decided to go headlong into the NFT arena.

It is planned that high-quality 3D-printed toys will be accessible shortly to bring the Mekas to life as part of the MekaVerse project's implementation roadmap. The MekaVerse project is currently in its early phases, with the roadmap for the project being developed by the project's designers and the proprietors of the characters included in the project. Streetwear development, collaborations with well-known artists, and short films based on the characters are all planned for the project's future.

Creature Wor

Danny Cole, a 21-year-old graphic artist from New York City, is performing on a project called Creature World, in which he is aiming to bring the dream to reality.

In terms of the project itself, there has been a tremendous degree of curiosity among those in the NFT community, albeit it remains somewhat mysterious. An interactive segment where the animals join you on your virtual voyage may be found at the website www.creature.world. It is yet ambiguous whether or not your purchased characters will eventually emerge in the virtual world, as well as what the project's overall objective is. In any case, we're looking forward to seeing where this one goes, regardless of which direction it takes, since the mystery around the project is fascinating.

Adam Bomb Squad

If you are a lover of streetwear fashion, the Adam Bomb Squad project will be just up your streetwear fashion alley. This project, known as the Adam Bomb Squad, was devised by The Hundreds and financed by the National Science Foundation (a famous streetwear brand launched in 2003).

The project's three-fold premise is to instill a feeling of identity, community, and ownership in those who participate in non-formal education programs and activities. The "Adam Bomb" is the most well-known logo/character associated with The Hundreds, and the Adam Bomb Squad effort tries to record the character's 18-year history and widespread use.

As has been the subject in the past, we will continue to reward NFT members with incentives such as exclusive items and early access to drop dates. No matter how far ahead of the infrastructure our concepts are, a breakthrough with these NFTs will finally resolve the outstanding Ownership aspect in developing a brand. We are working on technology that will allow Adam Bomb Squad NFT holders to 1) buy The Hundreds gear that depicts their bomb and 2) get reimbursed for the clothing sales to others in return for their token (which is currently under development). There's no reason why our community shouldn't benefit from The Hundreds' win, and there's no reason why they shouldn't profit from The Hundreds' success."

The Hundreds are a group of individuals who reside in the Hundreds and are related.

Claylings

It is yet another highly sought-after project, and it is now ranked 5th in terms of total trending volume ($6.42 million as of the time of publishing of this article) in the world.

Known as Claylings, this project attempts to introduce clay animation to the blockchain to introduce 4,040 characters in the project's initial phase. To achieve one of the project's aims, a short 1laymation film starring at least one of the formerly developed characters will be produced (it would be cool to see your character in the movie).

Autograph.Io

Rather than a single effort, Autograph.io is more of a marketplace, with an intense concentration on sports, entertainment, culture, and one-of-a-kind digital experiences as its key focal areas.

In addition to Tom Brady's co-founding of the program, it received tremendous support from various advisors, including Naomi Osaka, Wayne Gretzky, Tiger Woods, and other noteworthy personalities.

Athletes are now driving the development of NFTs centered on Autograph.io, such as the actual signature of a professional athlete, access to future drops, and entry into a private Discord channel.

Because of the excitement and support displayed by everyone involved, it will be intriguing to observe how this effort develops in the coming months. Watch out for rapid development into entertainment and one-of-a-kind digital and in-person events, even though it is now primarily focused on sports.

Decentraland

Decentraland is a virtual environment with its own DAO (Decentralized Autonomous Organization), which decentralizes control of the virtual space and distributes it to the virtual space users.

The virtual in-game assets in Decentraland's environment, such as land, wearables (for your characters), and other objects, are driven by the marketplace for virtual in-game purchases on the Decentraland blockchain.

To be successful, all you need is a web browser and a cryptocurrency/digital asset wallet, such as MetaMask, to play the game. Even though it is not required, the wallet improves the entire game experience by protecting all of your digital assets, such as your names, valuables, and LANDS, from being stolen or otherwise lost.

ETHEREUM AND NFTS

How Is Ethereum Helping In Leading The Way For The Nfts In The Future?

Do you know what cryptocurrency is and what Bitcoin is? Here, in this case, we will be discussing and talking about Ethereum to divert the readers' focus towards this technology. Ethereum is important to understand if you are looking to invest n the NFTs. Ethereum blockchain is one of the essential parts affecting today's cryptocurrency markets. If you need to venture into this market, you know all the basics. It is something that you need to know at all costs because it is the future.

What Is Ethereum?

Ethereum originated in July 2015 as open-source blockchain technology. This technology came as a support to the decentralized applications and the functionality of the smart contracts. Ethereum came into existence to inflate and develop the abilities of Bitcoin by introducing the practice of intelligent contracts. It is a system of decentralized apps that are independent of each other. NFTs are influenced and controlled by the blockchain that uses the ERC-271 non-fungible Ethereum token standard.

What Is An Nft?

NFTs are non-fungible tokens that are in everyday use nowadays. They are used to display the copyrights of digital assets by any digital artist. That is an excellent practice for these artists to trade their work digitally worldwide without fearing their work being plagiarized. NFT is a token that is based on the Ethereum blockchain technology. All the transactions among the artists and the collectors are stored on a digital ledger over the blockchain network.

How Does Ethereum Play A Role?

Ethereum blockchain is used to distribute the ownership of these tokens. Using the Ethereum smart contracts, the man in the middle of all the transactions has been eliminated, and all the transactions are exclusive between the creator and the collector. The Ethereum blockchain technology used in these NFTs also enables people to see and track down the owners who formerly owned these NFTs. Ethereum blockchain networks make it easy to securely store this information on the digital ledger and record all the data using smart contracts.

Why Is This Intriguing?

What makes these NFTs special is their uniqueness. This uniqueness helps them provide solutions to all the problems that may come up due to the selling of fake and counterfeit products and goods. These tokens are legit and legal. They ensure the authenticity of the product. You cannot trade one ticket for another because they are non-fungible. Every key is unique from one other. Gaming and art industries have extensively utilized the NFTs.

Many gaming companies have tokenized avatars and add-ons that come built-in with the game for generating profit. For instance, a $270,000 digital cat was sold as an NFT by CryptoKitties' Dragon. The worth of certain digital assets such as Twitter handles domain names, merchandise, art, music, and more impel huge fiscal assistances that people often oversee. That is accredited to the scarcity of these assets and their failure to be copied. That is lacking in such industries. That is because people have access to all the information. The information that they have access to is not owners. Presently, they choose some people who agree to pay and can do so.

What Does This Mean For The Future?

The market has been growing consistently since the first NFT was launched in 2017. Currently, $207 million has been spent in the market, and this number is enough for people to see the future of this technology.

With the suggestion that Ethereum' layer 2' scaling will make its first appearance shortly, these transactions will be quicker and inexpensive. The majority of the creators have started to tip the iceberg into discovering the opportunities of NFTs worth in the music industry. Artists currently can monetize their work in the digital environment. As well as their merchandise, tickets, and much more drive up equitable worth and mention to a new individuality factor and standing from digital ownership. It is highly likely to see music festivals, where the ticket would look like an NFT that is unique and based on the QR code. That would prove the ticket's ownership and the validity of their acquisition during entry. As other creators realize the abilities these NFTs can provide their work and help them gain profits from the work they produce, they would likely choose NFTs over anything else.

OPENSEA

Opensea Market Place

OpenSea is a democratic and flexible marketplace for purchasing and sales of NFTs that is changing the game in the NFT industry. NFTs stand for Non-Fungible Tokens, which are distinct, collectible digital assets such as in-game assets, avatars, trading cards, and art.

There was a high level of NFT transactions on OpenSea in August 2021 only was well over $3.5 billion. Given that it only had $21 million in amount for the entire year of 2020, it's logical to conclude that the 12,000 percent increase in trading volumes is a clear positive indicator that OpenSea is experiencing growth in leaps and bounds.

The Bigest Nft Market

OpenSea prides itself as the first and biggest NFT marketplace in the globe. To put it another way, OpenSea can be likened to eBay for digital artifacts and collectibles. Going by its staggering quantity and achievement, that does not seem far from the truth.

Initially, the OpenSea group had a lot to prove to everyone. Besides initial sensations like Crypto Kitties, NFTs had failed to pick up on before 2021, which was quite disappointing. However, the team's prediction that people will cherish digital goods as highly as — if not more than — natural objects began to come true. Here are some background attributes to help you know what OpenSea is all about.

Cryptocurrency token buying and selling laid the groundwork for the present NFT craze. People are trading virtual money and utility tokens worldwide at all hours of the day and night. They're okay with owning things they can't see or touch virtually, signaling that the digitally savvy era has arrived.

As more and more people live their own lives digitally, interacting with digital items has become more common. Rather than bringing the physical into the digital in the early days of the internet, the present state is mostly about virtual inventions, such as good memes, games, and immersive experiences. All of these point out that humans have attained a digital era where digital items are now held in high esteem.

This is why users are ditching selfies in favor of personal pic caricatures on social networking platforms like Instagram, Twitter, and TikTok. Penguin avatars, pixelated punks, and jaded apes with laser eyes are taking over instead. And it is not just a fad anymore; it has come to stay.

In a larger perspective, every one of these signs speaks to the start of the Metaverse, a shared virtual realm that we all create and own collectively, or in which NFTs play a tremendous role. When considering or thinking of OpenSea, it's simple to conceive of it as the eBay of virtual things, but it's so much more.

When you purchase an NFT, it is akin to what foodstuffs do after purchase. But what if you want to switch it, sell it, or look for others similar to it? What if you're planning to purchase an NFT but want to check its possession background quickly?

Before now, there was no straightforward method to do any of these things before OpenSea.

Yes, OpenSea is a peer-to-peer NFT platform. Still, it's also the user experience layer that connects the network to ordinary people, making it easy to buy and utilize NFTs.

On OpenSea, you can do a lot of cool stuff. Trading, selling, and buying various types of NFTs are, obviously, the most popular actions. Furthermore, you can utilize the site to learn about the NFT business and novel initiatives. Again, with no former knowledge, OpenSea makes it possible to create your own NFTs. To begin, you must first create an NFT portfolio. After that, you can start submitting NFTs in the appropriate formats.

NFTs can symbolize any item on the chain, whether real or virtual. Isn't that a sweeping generalization? Thankfully, OpenSea has restricted the reach to a few valuable categories that capture the most prevalent NFTs today. Artwork, songs, web addresses, virtual communities, trading cards, collectibles, sports assets, and utility NFTs like membership passes are all available.

OpenSea has accumulated the most extensive stock of NFTs for sale on the planet. As a result, it has become the de facto marketplace for retail customers purchasing NFTs and an essential arena for innovators. On OpenSea, developers may quickly build specialized NFT marketplaces for selling in-game products, fundraising campaigns, and producing user airdrops, among other things.

For NFTs, Ethereum is the most essential and efficient blockchain on the planet. NFT artists, engineers, and enthusiasts have already given Ethereum the crown, much like decentralized financial projects.

Because of its weak scaling, the Ethereum service is not without its drawbacks, as so many people know. Due to high gas expenses, deals involving NFT sales and transfers are pretty pricey.

OpenSea's Polygon inclusion is particularly significant given Ethereum's existing flaws. Polygon is a chain that allows Ethereum tokens, such as NFTs, to be transferred quickly and cheaply. Indeed, Vitalik Buterin, the inventor of Ethereum, actually pushed NFT projects to move their tokens to Polygon.

On OpenSea, shifting between the Polygon and Ethereum networks is as easy as clicking – a good user-friendly feature that's simple for newbies.

Compared to distributed finance and other crypto industries, the NFT market is very young. Finding data and insights about single NFTs and many NFT indicators might be difficult if you don't know where to go. By basically gathering its market info for anybody to sort based on the most recent ranks (by overall sales) and activities, OpenSea has made this procedure a lot easier.

The idea is that OpenSea offers the NFT marketplace infrastructures for free, while customers pay a 2.5 percent fee on every NFT sale to finance the platform's maintenance. When you consider that eBay costs are about 10% for a start and go up from there, OpenSea's flat-rate sales fee is quite fair and decent. The charge given to OpenSea remains the same whether your NFT sells for $10 or $10,000,000.

When considering the number of various digital currencies available, purchasing NFTs can be difficult. The same NFT is likely to be valued in multiple currencies, including ETH, DAI, and USD, to make matters even more complicated. Ethereum is the most often utilized base currency for buying and trading NFTs. Is it also the most frequently used money on OpenSea? Although there's one thing, you must know: OpenSea adopts WETH, which is a rebranded version of ETH (wrapped ETH). Ensure you've switched some ETH to WETH before participating in an NFT auction. The most straightforward approach to convert is to use your OpenSea wallet. You can then choose a wrap for the fixed amount from the dropdown menu. You will also need some ETH to finish the work and pay for gas, but once that's done, you're ready to start bidding on OpenSea.

WALLET

Hold it right there. I can notice the twinkle in your eye. You want to dive headfirst into the NFT pool right now! Good for you. But before you start going fishing with hooks baited with diamonds, you're going to have to have a wallet for your NFTs and your profits to live in.

Not all crypto wallets are created equally. Just as there are a variety of blockchains, there are various wallets, and they aren't all compatible with each other or the marketplaces. Imagine the tragedy of minting an NFT that nets you several million dollars. Still, you don't have a digital wallet to receive the funds, or worse, you don't have a digital wallet that's compatible with the payment! Keep such nightmares from ever happening by doing your homework on wallets and matching your needs.

All About Crypto Wallets

So what exactly is a cryptocurrency wallet? Is it electronic? Is it a piece of hardware? The truth is it can be both. You cannot purchase and own Bitcoin or any other cryptocurrency, including NFTs, without a cryptocurrency wallet. And you better make sure that your wallet is compatible with your NFT and the cryptocurrency you want to deal in, or you'll have a payment that isn't collectible and essentially has given your NFT away. Whichever route you go, one thing is sure.

It's interesting how much a crypto wallet has in common with a physical wallet. Any paper money it contains in your physical wallet represents the value in storage at the United States Treasury. So a crypto wallet also holds proof of your digital cash. It has the public and private keys needed to buy any cryptocurrency, including Bitcoin. It also provides digital signatures that authorize each transaction like a blockchain. As mentioned before, these wallets can take the form of an online app, a website, or a physical device that you can carry around with you. You would want to protect your keys the same way you want to save a password since those keys allow you to trade or spend your cryptocurrency.

Before moving forward, we should mention that an Ethereum wallet doesn't work exactly like a conventional physical wallet. Your crypto wallet does not store ether. It's not stored anywhere. Ether doesn't exist in any definite shape or form. The only thing that exists are records on the blockchain, and your wallet contains the keys necessary to interact with the blockchain to enable transactions.

Let's suppose you decided to focus your NFT endeavors on where NFTs were born: the Ethereum blockchain. There are two primary flavors of wallets—hot storage and cold storage.

Hot Storage

A hot storage wallet maintains a constant connection to the internet. The excellent information about this arrangement is that you can easily access your funds from virtually anywhere in the world. But as history has demonstrated repeatedly, anything connected to the internet is vulnerable to theft. A determined hacker with no time limit can eventually find a way to steal your funds. Is it likely that this will happen? Who can say? But it is possible.

Cold Wallet

Therefore, cold storage wallets store your keys offline and only connect to the internet when you want to. That is a greater degree of security for your precious cryptocurrency.

Desktop Wallet

As the name implies, a desktop wallet is stored and runs on your desktop computer or a laptop. Depending on how much storage space you have on your machine, you have options. You can download a full client with the entire blockchain or use a light client. Light clients are easier to use and store, but a full client also has extra security since it doesn't rely on miners or nodes to pull accurate information. All the transactions are validated at the home base.

Desktop wallets aren't bad. They are convenient and relatively secure. You can only use them from the one computer where they were downloaded. But laptops and desktops are also connected to the internet, so it would be a good idea to spruce up on your cybersecurity measures. Ensure that the machine in question has not been hacked and is not infected by malware. And even more so, make sure that the computer in question is not at risk of being stolen.

Web Wallets

Web-based wallets have several things going for them. They're based on cloud storage technology which means that you can access them from pretty much anywhere in the world. They also clock a bit more speed than other kinds of crypto wallets. But in the eyes of many, a web wallet completely undermines the purpose of cryptocurrency. Since the wallet is stored online, your keys are also stored online.

Don't forget that the cloud is a third-party server, which means the security of that server is entirely out of your hands. The security of your funds and your keys rest squarely in the hands of whoever owns that server. That means that you are defenseless to take measures against hackers, cyber-attacks, malicious malware, phishing scams, etc.

Hardware Wallets

If you can't do without the familiarity of feeling a physical object in your pocket associated with your money, then there are hardware wallets. That is the ultimate cold storage method of cryptocurrency. They aren't unlike portable hard disks, except they are specifically made to work with cryptocurrency and blockchain technology. You can fill them into just about any computer when it's time to complete a transaction. Better yet, key generation takes place offline. No hacker alive is going to be able to get past that.

Aside from that simple feature of being completely isolated from the reach of cyber-attacks, many hardware wallets come with backup security options to ensure that you won't lose your cryptocurrency. Many also provide the opportunity of two-factor authentication and a password for an added level of security for your currency. There are now wallets on the market that also have a screen that allows you to sign for transactions on the device itself.

The extra security and peace of mind with the hardware wallet also comes at a price. You will lay down more money on a hardware wallet than you would on a software wallet. But if you're storing a large amount of cryptocurrency, then the investment will be more than worth it.

And like any device that was made for one singular function rather than a wide range of applications, hardware wallets weren't manufactured in massive quantities. So finding one for purchase might take a minute.

Custodial Wallets

Every so often, someone makes the news for losing their password or their security key to well over a billion dollars in cryptocurrency. The irony is almost too bitter about fathoming since the wealth exists in storage. Still, the means of accessing it has evaporated from existence, effectively separating its owner from the wealth.

A safeguard against this is utilizing a custodial wallet.

Again, some people see this as something that completely defeats the purpose of cryptocurrency. Since one of the whole points of crypto is to have complete control over your funds. A custodial wallet is third-party assistance that offers storage and protection of your digital assets. So, if, for some reason, you lost access to your funds because of some unforeseen loss with your keys or otherwise, you would be able to restore your ether from any other device.

Your security keys and your funds are both backed up by the provider's servers.

Minting Your Nfts

So it's time to bring a new NFT into the world. All of the marketplaces we just cited offer a page for minting a new NFT that is just as straightforward as uploading a picture to the internet and captioning it. The difference is that you're going to spend some crypto in the genesis of your new baby. But the actual creation of a new NFT is never rocket science. Whichever marketplace you do it in, you'll be walked through it step by step.

STRATEGIES TO MAKE MONEY

Tips And Secrets To Reach Huge Profit From Nft Investing

Many NFT creators, artists, and collectors are now clamoring to participate in this burgeoning trend. However, is there a lot of profit to be made from NFTs? In fact, how do you earn a profit on non-fungible token purchases? So, after accomplishing a lot of research on this topic, here's what I discovered.

You can profit from your NFT purchase in several ways:

- Flip Your NFT (Buy NFTs, then swiftly resell them for a profit.)
- Your NFT can be sold (When there is a sudden spike or steady climb in recent sales.)
- Hold Onto Your NFT (If your NFT has underlying value, it'll likely rise in value over time.)
- Unlockables (This is exclusives available to the NFT owner.)
- Purchase what you believe in (Buying an NFT you believe in can result in better-educated purchases.)

Now, let's take a tighter look at the many ways to profit from your NFT purchases.

Flip Your Nft

Flipping an NFT is one of the most typical ways to profit from purchasing. To convert your NFT, buy one and immediately put it back on the market for a higher price. The best part of restoring a non-fungible token vs. a traditional item like a house is that it doesn't require remodeling or updating. It's as simple as buying it and then selling it.

If you want to have the highest chance of flipping your NFT, look for one that has a constant upward sales trend. Furthermore, suppose you have the opportunity to purchase a low-cost NFT from a well-known developer. In that case, you may be able to immediately sell it for a significant return on investment (ROI).

Resell Your Nft

Rather than purchasing and immediately flipping your non-fungible token, you can buy one and hold onto it for a while until you witness a drastic increase in sales/sale prices or a constant and consistent growth over time. The secret to successfully reselling your NFT is to not keep it for too long.

It may be an excellent concept to sell your NFT shortly following a steady increase in sale prices or a sudden rise. If you wait too prolonged, you might not make any money or possibly lose money. Remember that you must ride the wave, but every wave will eventually end.

Hold Onto Your Nft

If you are in the NFT space for a long time and not simply looking to make a quick profit, investing in a long-term NFT could be a good idea. If you can find an NFT with underlying value for a low price now, it could be worth a fortune in the future. The most important aspect of this strategy is to ensure that the non-fungible token you buy has real value and is not just a quick fad.

Anything valuable, exclusive, or unique could be a wise long-term investment.

Unlockables

NFT Assets held on a decentralized storage network are known as unlockables. When someone buys a non-fungible token with these unlockables, they gain access to a variety of benefits, including:

- Merch Deals
- VIP access to live shows
- Monthly Meetings
- Exclusive Calls
- Physical Product
- Follows on social media

When it comes to NFT unlockables, the options are unlimited. I recommend purchasing NFTs with valuable unlockables if you can. You can take benefit of all the perks even if you don't resell it!

Buy What You Believe In

It's essential to purchase an NFT that you're passionate about. In general, if you are interested in a subject, you will better understand that subject. That means you have a better chance of buying something profitable because you know better.

It's just the right thing to do. You may either jump on the bandwagon and start buying trendy items you know nothing about, or you can make a more informed decision and support someone who makes something you genuinely enjoy. It's entirely up to you, but I only purchase items I like.

Overall, if your primary goal is to profit from NFTs, you must research to guarantee that you purchase an NFT that will deliver a return on investment.

Nft Categories With High Potential Profit

There are many different kinds of non-fungible tokens to choose from, and the list will only get longer. Here are some of the multiple famous NFT categories available to purchase and profit from:

- Art
- Gaming
- Photography

Art

Thousands of digital art NFTs are available for purchase. Look for one that has the potential to be valuable in the future. Also, anything you think would make beautiful memorabilia.

Digital art is fantastic because you can create it and transfer it to someone else right away. It is now possible to purchase a portion of digital artwork. That's exactly what the $69 million buyers of Beelple's piece did. He sold shares of the article to multiple people.

The good news is that if you are a creator, you can not only sell your work, but you can also set up NFTs so that you automatically receive a percentage of all secondary sales, which is known as a royalty. Formerly, as an artist, you could not receive any proceeds from secondary sales in the art world, but that is no longer the point.

NFTs can be utilized to make programmable art as well. Programmable art refers to artwork programmed to exhibit dynamic qualities based on how the code is implemented on the blockchain. A digital marketplace called ASYNC art is where you can make programmable art. You can not only make your master

copy there, but you can also add individual layers and change their attributes.

Individuals can contribute to the art, and different group members can control their activities. As a result, NFTs allow for collective art. Your art can be displayed on online marketplaces such as SuperRare and OpenSea, where it can be bought and sold once it has been created.

Music

NFTs have massive potential in the music industry! You can get lifetime VIP access to events, meetings, phone conversations, and more, but that's just the beginning. Consider this: music artists can suddenly use non-fungible tokens to fund their careers. That means that record label deals may no longer be necessary for musicians, and the artist may keep a more significant portion of the profit for themselves.

Furthermore, NFTs allow the artist and the audience to connect on a much deeper level than before. Musicians have so many customizable possibilities to include anything they want when it comes to minting tokens.

Gaming

With the purchase and sale of in-game items, money is made on popular video game platforms. Games like Dota 2 and Team

For example, fortress two on the Steam marketplace is extremely popular and sells quickly.

Crypto Kitties is another NFT phenomenon. Crypto Kitties are being purchased and bred to sell them. Another attractive niche to profit from is in-game items.

Furthermore, because it is decentralized, there is no limit to the types of game items that can be sold or the amounts that can be sold. Axie Infinity, one of the most popular games, has seen some high-ticket purchases. Other games, such as Skyview, Gods of Change, and others, can be swapped or sold for different cards.

Photography

Kate Woodman recently received $20,000 for a single NFT photograph. Photographs are ideal for NFTs because they are now digital.

Photographs capture moments, and some of these moments are significant to people. You can buy images or make your own NFTs and sell them on the various marketplaces.

The most promising part is that you don't have to give up your copyright or reproduction rights as a photographer. You are just selling the buyer the ownership of the NFT piece. You can keep showing that image or photograph, sell prints, or license it to companies.

Once you've determined whether you'll buy or create NFTs, you'll need to decide which type of NFTs you'll use. The next stage is to put them on the marketplaces for sale.

Best Tip To Sell Your Nfts For Profit.

Determine Which Marketplace you want to sell on

If you have NFTs that you purchased and want to sell, you can do so directly on the marketplaces. You can go to prominent market spaces like OpenSea, SuperRare, and Nifty Gateway once you have the digital asset you wish to sell. However, it would help if you inquired about the fees charged.

You have complete control over the number of editions you wish to sell. It does not have to be only one edition. You can have multiple editions of the same digital asset, and each will be distinct and have its token id. Please keep in mind, though, that having more can potentially lower the value of your asset.

Once you've done this, your digital item can't be duplicated or replaced in any way. As a result, no unique abilities or talents are required. You can benefit from locating or constructing an NFT that appeals to people in a specific niche.

Set a reserve bid, which is the lowest price you're willing to sell it for. That is similar to auction websites such as eBay. Don't overprice it or underprice it. Look for a reasonable profit margin, and it will sell.

Finding solid digital assets that have underlying value or that you believe will have value in the future is one method to profit from NFT. Invest in NFTs that you are confident will yield a profit when sold. Once you've purchased these, you can resell them for a considerably higher price on a marketplace. You can also utilize a variety of advertising methods to increase bids.

The value of NFTs is determined by two factors: novelty and scarcity. Focusing on these two aspects can result in high weight for your digital content. One of the secrets to profiting is acquiring appealing and unique creative art, music, and collectibles. Knowing the fees and transactions is vital to avoid losing money on your trades.

GAMING & NFTS

What Is Play To Earn Games?

The business standard known as Play-to-Earn is the most current innovation in the gaming industry. It is a business strategy that embraces the notion of an open economy and bonuses all players who supply value to the game environment via their contributions. It's likely to add new game concepts and retention models to current gaming that haven't been seen before.

As technology became more available to the general public, business models for video games developed. In the late 1970s and earlier 1980s, we recreated our games on arcade machines in neighborhood gaming centers. With only a quarter in their pocket, gamers would vie for the most elevated score.

Nowadays, we play matches on our smartphones when on public transportation or taking a break. We launch a game on our computer or home console when we desire a more immersive experience. However, each participant may find a business plan that works for the platform.

The foundation is free-to-play.

Consumers must acquire a license to access a premium game. They accomplish this by purchasing a request from a digital retailer or a physical copy from an online or brick-and-mortar retailer. Financial commitment is rather significant since paying $60 for a freshly launched game is not uncommon. While this is still a massive market, the free-to-play model has experienced the most growth in recent years.

The free-to-play business model enables gamers to obtain a game free of charge. Free-to-play or freemium games are constantly available for download and provide users with a confined/limited experience. Gamers will be required to pay to accelerate their progress or gain unique equipment. Users may be instructed to pay for in-game currency, more material, or specific cosmetics for their game symbols.

Several of the most famous games on the market are complimentary. Fortnite alone caused 1.8 billion dollars in deals last year, even though the battle royale game is free. Selling cosmetics to enable more personalization is a lucrative industry. Among the most famous games on the market are League of Legends and Hearthstone, which are almost entirely free. Each developer has its strategy for charging customers for more material or aesthetics.

These complimentary games have generated billions of dollars in revenue, and there is no reason to believe they will stop. That demonstrates that the free-to-play business model has developed and that developers have mastered the technique of monetizing free-to-play games.

The play-to-earn business model shares several characteristics with the free-to-play business model. Often, a play-to-earn game will incorporate mechanics from free-to-play games. However, play-to-earn games provide an opportunity for gamers to earn money or valuable digital goods.

Explanation of earn-while-you-play

Giving gamers the right of in-game assets and the ability to grow their worth via dynamic gameplay are essential components of the play-to-earn business model. By hiring in the in-game economy, players contribute to the game's development and benefit other players and the creators. They are rewarded in-game assets as a result. These digital assets might range from cryptocurrency to gaming assets tokenized on the blockchain. That is why the play-to-earn business model complements blockchain plays exceptionally well.

The play-to-earn business model rewards gamers for their time and effort invested in the game. For instance, participants in Axie Infinity win Small Love Potions (SLP). Players require these tokens to breed more Axies, but they may also sell them on the open marketplace to other players. Additional examples are the resources available in League of Kingdoms and the rewards available in the fantasy football game So rare.

Acquire worth to participate

In essence, a pay-to-win game should also be free to play. That is not always the case, though. At present, gamers must purchase three Axies before they may battle within Lunacia, Axie Infinity's universe. Additionally, So rare to ask users to spend money on player cards before earning cards through weekly tournaments. While games like Chainz Arena and League of Kingdoms are free to play, their idle gameplay mechanics and restrictions compel gamers to invest some money in the game. Thus, even if gamers gain anything, they must also pay.

It requires money to develop a video game, which firms generate. The virtue of the play-to-earn business model, on the other hand, is that a gamer will always generate something of value that can be sold. Even if a player must pay to begin, these obtained things may always be resold. Each card in So rare, as well as each Axie in your wallet, may be sold. Simultaneously, games like Fortnite and League of Legends generate billions of dollars. Players spend money and deposit their worth in an infinite pit. Their finances will be depleted when they quit playing these games.

That is altered by play-to-earn. Each thing collected has a monetary worth. That means players will always earn money even when not actively playing a game.

How Do Play-To-Earn Games Change The Economy?

When we hear the word "globalization," we instantly associate it with governmental policy, trade agreements, immigration, and large corporations. However, much of the globe's networking occurs outside of boardrooms, in virtual settings accessible from anywhere in the world. MMO (Massively Multiplayer Online) games have altered how we communicate, build friendships, and form communities by enabling individuals to connect and socialize without regard for geographical boundaries in virtual, fun spaces. One of the fascinating features of this fast globalization of communities is the economics that has developed duhow, how participants value and position digital products and services. Online games, mainly MMOs, have been at the forefront of creative economic techniques that allow for global involvement. That has included players seeking to sell their digital items in exchange for real-world cash, as well as giant corporations developing new business models.

Virtual Economies' Real-World Applications

While the practice of purchasing and selling digital items for real money is not new, it has become increasingly widespread as online communities have grown in size and become huge businesses. Venezuela gained international headlines when many residents switched to gold farming as their principal source of income, discovering that it offered greater financial security than traditional jobs. The practice has grown in popularity to the point where it now has its own Wikipedia and Encyclopedia Britannica entry.

Most game businesses have stringent Terms of Service (ToS) agreements that prohibit Gold Farming monetary exchange of in-game goods or account transfers. While these methods are intended to safeguard the community, they are more likely to establish control over the in-game economy, minimize exposure to KYC/AML regulations, and maximize revenues. These prohibitions preclude an individual player from realizing value from assets acquired or gained via games. By limiting trade, users cannot resell goods they have formerly received, highlighting that they do not purchase their purchased items. These methods have pushed some participants into the grey markets, where they face counterparty risks and account closures if caught.

Without a valid, transparent exchange of products, it becomes practically tricky for gamers to recoup some of the expenses associated with former purchases, much alone profit from their accounts and virtual goods gained while gaming. These closed systems may be restricting the economic possibilities of these gaming communities, as game companies own their growth.

Worldwide, new game economic models are as blockchain technology spreads worldwide emerging. In 2020, the Philippines witnessed a massive migration of non-traditional gamers to cryptocurrency-based video games to make money during the COVID-19 lockdowns. Grandparents, single moms, and taxi drivers turned to video games to supplement their incomes, creating, constructing, and exchanging digital commodities they could later sell on public blockchain markets for cash. What distinguishes these games from MMOs Gold Farming games are based on open economies, the elimination of restrictive Terms of Service, and innovative technology leveraging Non-Fungible Tokens (NFTs) that operate on the blockchain. These new models restore individuals' power by facilitating the ownership of their acquired and earned assets.

The System is Being Gamed

As early video games transitioned from boxed items to continuous-play online services, several facets of game design shifted accordingly. Online games built long-term relationships with their customers, necessitating the evolution of economic structures. Subscriptions and, eventually, microtransactions enabled incremental on-demand purchases. Regrettably, several areas of the game design remained incompatible with these new models. Randomized "Loot Boxes" offered motivation and reward in early video games but were not associated with commercialization in single-purchase, packaged goods game cartridges.

When marketed as microtransactions, certain publishers may monetize these randomized game components. When taken to its logical conclusion, this activity can be classified as gambling. More often than not, practical "Free to Play" games rely on retaining their most devoted players by granting them the ability to speed their game progress. Unfortunately, this might irritate some players, resulting in a lack of incentive to pay and placing the weight of income generation on a small percentage of the player population. A design that favors high rollers can irritate and stratify the playing base.

Thus, what do gamers enjoy? As it turns out, the virtual world closely resembles reality. Players enjoy amassing limited-edition digital items and expressing their social standing via the customization of their identity and virtual environment. The cosmetics sector alone is estimated to be worth $40 billion a year and continues to rise. The addition of blockchain to paid cosmetics and virtual goods has the potential to create new economic models for the gaming industry - models that are likely to be dominated by non-fungible tokens, which give players ownership over their purchases while sharing resale revenue with developers and adding economic value to the game community.

What Does This Mean for Investing Professionals?

While many investors look to major, publicly listed corporations for market direction, astute industry participants will monitor and wait to see how newer, more nimble companies perform before committing to these new ways to market. These investors are more inclined to adopt a wait-and-see attitude, allowing independents to take risks and evaluate proofs of ideas. Their tactic is frequently to enter after new models have been established and lucrative.

That is a unique chance for entrepreneurs, independent developers, and investors to get in on the first floor. While creator-based economies are not new, blockchain technology can expand existing economic models and propel growth to new heights. Cryptoeconomics offers gamer communities the opportunity to contribute to the success of the games they like.

The world closely monitors the present crypto and NFT excitement and anticipates what will transpire over the next 12 months. In truth, astute investors and developers will be looking at the next 3-5 years as the make or break moment for this technology and the associated new business models. If high-quality games are developed, blockchain-enabled open economies can become the fastest market segment of a market, reaching $200 billion.

TOP VIDEO GAMES THAT ARE AN OPPORTUNITY

The phenomena of video games that have incorporated NFT translate into a clear opportunity; the beginning has been Axie Infinity, and then more options have been developed within this industry, which has allowed the lovers of the gamer environment to receive a handsome percentage of profit.

The best NFT video games that yield substantial profits follow the dynamics and relevance of blockchain technology, all this has transformed into a path full of profitability, and you should know one by one to decide to invest in the one that best suits your aspirations within this field,

The Main Options Are As Follows:

- Axie Infinity.
- PVU.
- Wakana Farm.
- Crypto Cars World.
- Block Farm Club.
- Overlord.
- Binamon.
- MIR 4.
- CryptoZoo.
- Sorare.
- Alien Worlds.
- Dragonary.
- CryptoBlades.
- CryptoZoon.
- Splinterlands.
- Upland.

On the other hand within the NFT games sector, there are going to be essential releases such as the following:

- Battle Hero.
- Tethan Arena.
- Mist NFT.
- Block Monsters.

- Ember Sword.
- Illuvium.

The impact caused by each of these games ratifies the power that is being manifested on these investment options; they are also games that endorse the concept of "play-to-earn," that dynamic is the dream and goal of any lover of games, where the entry of some is free because the NFT is acquired according to your progress, or subsequent investment.

The blockchain ecosystem has included video games as one of the forms of investment, and even fluctuation; the success of Axie is the direct support, but so is the AXS that is presented as a governance token that is part of the game, i.e., it is a universe composed of cryptocurrencies, video games and NFT.

If you want to decide on one of the main games that you are betting on today, you should study the volume of each one, and especially from when it was launched to the acceptance of the same.

This game, frequently mentioned in most social platforms, is governed by the recognized token AXS, its capitalization has statistics of; $2,67,003,328 to this is added the participation of partners of the size of Ubisoft or Samsung, which follow the inspiration of Pokemon to carry out the creation of the game.

To start being part of this investment option, you must purchase three creatures with which you will battle and generate profits; that purchase is produced from its Marketplace, although there is the option to enter as a scholarship and play someone else's account, in general, the profits arise from battles, Axies broods, or investing for Lunacia resources.

Wakana Farm

In the middle of the video game, there is the opportunity to be a day laborer, that is the central role and within the game, where in addition to everything you can make purchases of items from the WanaShop, this fulfills the purpose of carrying out purchases and sales of items of collectible qualities.

The trading marketplace of this farm-style NFT trade is conducted using the WANA token, which makes it easy for users to buy items to keep their virtual lands in order.

Block Farm Club

Block Farm Club is presented as a game with a decentralized operation; that way, any user has the opportunity to earn tokens and NFT from the game farm; the profitability of the game has been positive during its first days, its operation has caused it to be compared to PVU.

The main distinction of this game lies in the other browser entertainment alternatives; it has innovative mechanics, it does not have a PAY TO WIN response, but you must buy tokens to start from the platform itself; that way, you can play and get tickets, energy, characters or others to exchange them.

Battle Hero

That is an NFT gambling project launching in 2021, during its operation, it has accrued striking fees that equal CryptoMines for example, it meets the earn to play mode, it has been strongly preferred in Spain and has not yet finished its development, but it is possible to make money from speculation.

The token cryptocurrency associated with this video game is BATH; it is generally a Battle Royale shooter genre. Also, the dominant mode is the free-to-earn, where you can earn money without investing, but rather that money you can spend on the purchase of unique items.

CryptoBlades

It is one of the free games that have the most significant number of users, under the token SKILL is managed by the company Riveted Technology, to offer a choice of entertainment and investment combat, operates under the Smart Chain network Binance, so it has become one of the most popular video games.

The attributes of the game are on the weapons and equipment; thus, the characters face each other; the outcome of such battles depends on a mathematical calculation that merits a considerable investment, thanks to the fact that a large diversity of SKILLs is generated from the exchange of weapons, with a high capacity of token generation.

Overlord

Overlord represents a copy of Mist, a play-to-earn mode is implemented, it has gameplay facilities to be available from a mobile version, the ecosystem is not promising but for the low entry fee is interesting, its launch has been rushed and therefore generates some doubts. Still, it is an alternative to follow closely.

Binamon

The inspiration of this project is to simulate and match what was generated by Axie; it presents a fusion between earn to play for profit without losing the quality of the game, surpassing the development of Alien Worlds or the intention that exists on CryptoBlades, thanks to bet on the theme of adventure, skill and an interface that fights monsters.

This approach is not new but seeks to compete from the similarity with Illuvium, Splinterlands, or Block Monsters; the fight against this type of creatures is one of the most fundamental concepts.

MIR4

MIR4 is not like other NFT games, as it has a high-level graphic design for an accessible mode, that's why the amount of interested users increases every day, it's a great option before the release of My Neighbor Alice and also Ember Sword; this happens through the user base, over the criticism it's a strong alternative.

Splinterlands

It is known as one of the most played NFT in the world, formerly known as Steem Monsters, where a dynamic of collectible cards is developed on Hive blockchains, a different type of battle is managed, and deck building is required to be carried out.

This game's preparation is strategic battles; unlike other NFT games such as Dragonary, this game takes strength thanks to its growing community.

Diversifying The Portfolio Of Video Game Nfts

Investment diversification is a guarantee to offset any risk; it is one of the principles that has ruled within cryptocurrencies and carries over to the NFT sector, especially when it is a market that frequents many video game projects from which it is possible to profit.

Putting together NFT investment diversification is possible, as long as you have different business models included to ensure that you follow the course of any winning dynamics or can amortize the lack of confidence that other paths may cause; for this, you should consult the following games that between them complement a good investment wallet.

The income value that is obtained utilizing this video game is striking, thanks to the point that the in-game currency can be obtained from internal battles that force you to have and use a good, competitive team that along with the gameplay is what creates an income that you can take advantage of.

Alien Worlds

As an investment, it is interesting because it follows a fantasy of creatures that have different races and qualities; as a result of these distinctions, you can use the cards to win most of the games within this game, on the side of the quotation of the virtual properties of the game, they depend directly on Trillium as its official cryptocurrency.

The community that defends the development of this game ratify the excellent decision to bet on cryptocurrencies, although it is best to evaluation its platform to consider the blockchain operations and base yourself on those numbers that are being generated as a result of the game, that is the ratification of how it works.

0x Universe

This NFT game maintains a wide availability from the Play Store for any Android user. Still, beforehand you should know that it is a game that pays off slowly, so it deserves patience and considers that you do not need to invest as a positive side of this option.

The game's main idea is to build ships, collect enough tokens to acquire planets, each of the properties you get to buy NFT; finally, the profits can be easily exchanged for Ethereum, the progress within the game is accelerated by investing in continuing accumulating more properties.

Sorare

If you are passionate about sports games, this option is to your liking because the primary motivation is fantasy football, which is fashionable in the gamer sphere, with the contribution of earning money for free, as long as it is possible to build teams, management, and other competitive football activities.

Like other NFT games, the start is framed by non-tokenized tokens; then there are internal gains in the game that make it possible to continue to invest; as you engage with the game, substantial gains will begin to occur, from the tokens or cards in the game a differential value emerges that you can trade with.

One of the NFT games that get a lot of attention is CryptoBlades, because it brings medieval role-playing to life, with the option to do battles against monsters and use weapons, all of which are easily converted into money.

The NFT within the game is on the weapons, that way is distributed up to 800 thousand tokens open to users, for that you must invest in weapons to raise the level of each of them, but the advantage lies on a free registration until you get the official currency of the game called as SKILL.

Gods Unchained

The popularity of God's Unchained causes must be about diversifying your NFTs through a card mechanic to earn rewards from digital tokens anchored in Ethereum; monetization is on the side of the coin that receives the designation as Flux.

The initial registration does not earn any token, but it is necessary to be part of an advance within the game until reaping the rewards, likewise, the funds are received in the same measure in which you play, it is essential to allocate time to play until you find the long-awaited gains you expect.

Snook

It is striking as a game as it is very similar to the typical Nokia entertainment, where users spend hours having fun controlling a snake that evolves as it feeds on the elements presented in the game. Still, this opportunity facilitates the generation of income.

When the snake goes eating everything you get in its path, it receives masks that increases the price quotation of the NFT thanks to that is evolving, in this case, the official currency is SNK that has presented good moves to motivate users to be part of this ecosystem, everything is measured according to the player's skills.

SMART CONTRACTS

We will take a more close look at some essential concepts to understand better NFTs and how to use them:

- Smart contracts are protocols that facilitate and verify the negotiation and subsequent execution of the contract. These are contracts in the form of programming language.

- Ethereum is the decentralized platform where smart contracts are created and executed.

- An API (application programming interface) refers to procedures aimed at solving a given task—in this case, the goal prescribed in the smart contract.

- The gas fee refers to a price or value required to successfully conduct a transaction or execute a contract on a blockchain. Gas in Ethereum is a division of measure for the work done by Ethereum to perform transactions or any interaction within the network. In Ethereum, the developers decided to attract constant values to the different operations performed in Ethereum. In this way, every activity in Ethereum has a defined gas value, which does not vary and is not altered by the increase or decrease in the value of Ether, Ethereum's native currency. The fact that this gas value is a constant response to the fact that although the price of Ether is volatile, the computational cost of operations always remains constant.

Now that you know these terms, we can delve into smart contracts.

Smart contracts are computer protocols that facilitate, verify, and enforce contract negotiation. They are programs executed on blockchain nodes and simulate the logic of contract clauses. The clauses and validating nodes represent a change of state of the blockchain itself; therefore, the transaction is created must find consensus through a community system. That is called "proof of work."

Any data can be recorded and inserted within the blockchain in a distributed, decentralized, and transparent chain. Data validation is done through peer-to-peer verification called "proof of work" or "PoW." None of the recorded information can be deleted or modified once encrypted. The nodes within the blockchain, as we have seen, exchange value in an entirely new trustless situation, which involves the absence of a third intermediary. Due to this nature, blockchain can hold and store all sorts of digital values and virtual assets.

The use of blockchain technology is limited to digital assets; dematerialized tangible assets can also be recorded within it. Smart contracts come into play when the data transferred on the blockchain platform must respond to predetermined conditions. Then, the platform is used to certify the transactions. Nick Szabo defined the concept of smart contracts in 1997, before blockchain. However, blockchain has played a vital role in ensuring the implementation of smart contracts by allowing information and transactions to be managed securely.

A smart contract is a computer protocol that facilitates and verifies the execution of a contract between two or more users. It automatically verifies the terms based on the clauses that have been agreed upon. It is called an intelligent contract precisely because of its ability to be brilliant in the sense of executing an agreement. It typically uses the "if/then" functions built into computer software and can only manage what has been predetermined in the programming phase.

The different stages of implementing a smart contract are as follows:

- Definition of the agreement between the parties involves the translation and registration of the details in a smart contract.

- Related verification and inscription of the smart contract in the blockchain is registered and made exclusive. The blockchain guarantees the automation of contractual obligations and their transparency in case of execution and the immutability of the collected data.

The smart contract then becomes an identified block simply by transforming into a hash value that allows for the maintenance, accessibility, and correct updating of a shared ledger or distributed ledger.

The proof of work (PoW) mining inside Ethereum occurs when the miner solves the cryptographic puzzle and sends it to the whole network. At this point, the contract applicant pays a fee, and the contract is registered.

The block is added to the immutable and certified chain. The whole operation has a public value and is entirely accessible. The hashes in the sequence are safe and cannot be counterfeited.

At this point, the smart contract can access third-party (external) applications to know the conditions of certain situations and occurrences for which it was programmed—for example, to know flight times to communicate delays. In practice, it queries the APIs to get the necessary information. This way saves a considerable number of resources in negotiation and execution, speeds up performance, and considerably decreases the chances of disputes between the parties.

Unlike a traditional contract, an innovative agreement is binding by its very nature—i.e., its particular technology. The blockchain node prevents pre-established conditions from being violated, and conditions related to the individual's conduct take a back seat. This irrevocability, which is triggered when the data is entered into the blockchain technology, leaves no room for exceptions.

Ethereum's virtual currency is Ether, which serves as the unit of measure and cryptocurrency. However, Ethereum, unlike Bitcoin, is not just a network for transferring value; it is a trustworthy platform for running smart contracts. Intelligent contracts can define rules as standard contracts and enforce them automatically through code. However, they are not controlled by a user. Instead, they are deployed on the network and executed as initially programmed. A smart contract on Ethereum uses the same operation as a vending machine: you receive the snack if you insert the coin and select the snack. The vending machine follows programmed logic in the same way as a smart contract. Any programmer can write a smart contract and deploy it on Ethereum's blockchain network. Deploying an intelligent agreement is technically a transaction, so you have Ether pay the gas fee just like a typical transaction. However, the costs of implementing the contract are much higher.

Since each Ethereum transaction requires computing resources to be executed, each trade requires a fee. Gas is the fee needed to successfully conduct a transaction on Ethereum. The ether and gas gee on Ethereum is essential to keep the network security to prevent any spam.

Ethereum has developer-friendly languages for writing smart contracts, such as Solidity and Vyper. Intelligent contracts are public on Ethereum and can be considered open APIs. That allows intelligent contracts to be composable. Moreover, you can start a smart contract on an existing one. It is also possible to enable a self-destruct option, which removes programs that are no longer used to improve effectiveness and performance.

With the help of smart contracts, digital assets can be programmed in such a way as to have additional functions compared to traditional modes. Digital assets based on a smart contract can execute clauses entirely autonomously, without the intermediation of third parties, thus increasing transparency and legal security.

For this reason, they have many possibilities within different areas and applications, such as the following:

- Cybersecurity: Although it is a system visible to everyone, everything in the blockchain is inscribed through encrypted keys that verify the data within it. The transmission of data is protected from interception and manipulation.

- Election systems: Blockchain enables voter identity authentication, secure record-keeping, and accurate and transparent counting.

- Internet of Things (IoT): When objects become intelligent and talk to each other, they can facilitate and verify the execution of operations within an enterprise. Smart contracts provide the backbone for the Internet of Things and allow for a ledger that can manage many devices.

- Public administration: Can offer monitoring to ensure secure and transparent governance.

- Crowdfunding: Enables campaigns where contributors can fully control the money invested. In this way, the donor is more secure, and the money is not spent on intermediary activities.

- Intellectual property: The very structure of blockchain allows you to keep track of everything, including transactions and ownership changes. That is why intelligent contracts find applications tracking individual properties with chronological accuracy.

START YOUR NFTS BUSINESS

Nfts Ownership

While FTs are a hot topic right now, buyers and sellers need to know the regulatory conditions that may apply to these properties. This is not an NFT, but you wouldn't be surprised to find it.

Nfts And Intellectual Property Law

NFTs are commonplace. How do they serve in with the existing laws and regulations? Does it matter?

NFTs are growing in popularity, but it is unclear how they will fit into the legal or regulatory structures regulating the technology, financial, and cryptocurrency industries. They cannot be considered a security because they are not the same as initial coin offerings. NFT operations are subject to laws, but customers must be aware of doing.

Breaking It Down

They are almost identical and live on a blockchain (such as Ethereum). Anyone can import and duplicate video clips and image files, but an NFT only has one owner. The image file in an NFT can still be downloaded. A tweet that you sell will remain available to all users on Twitter. You're purchasing a virtual note, not the actual tweet. These cards are very similar to autographed football cards. You can print as multiple cards as you want. You can print as numerous cards as you like, but it will most likely be the most valuable if a player signs only one card. For example, a Tom Brady autographed card sold recently for $1.32million.

Andrew Hinkes from Carlton Fields suggests that we may only be scratching the surface on what NFTs could do. An NFT can, at its most basic level, recognize a financial property that can lead to new efficiency in current transactions. An example of this is island ownership. Currently, people depend on land registries held by third parties such as a government department to prove they own a piece of land. Hinkes suggests that an NFT could be used to identify the property. That would allow a person to prove their ownership using a cryptographically secured and signed digital token.

Fabrica's Daniel Rollingher is a real-estate attorney who pointed out that NFTs in real estate may require consumers to borrow from lenders. NFT issuers must comply with consumer protection and disclosure regulations.

Holder Protection

Donna Redel, an associate professor at Fordham Law and a New York Angels panel member, says that NFTs can confuse customers. Besides that, NFTs pose additional concerns about who is conducting know your customer/anti-money laundering practices, documenting the selling of an NFT, and the rights buyers have.

She stated that she was not certain artists understood their rights and responsibilities under the contract and in the broader legal environment. "I expect to see more stuff such as [NBA] Top Shot," she said. Andrew Jacobson of Seward and Kissel says NFTs are particularly popular among a younger audience that is less educated.

Law

Jacobson suggests that NFTs could violate a nation's sanctions law. That prohibits residents from doing business or people with entities or

Individuals from sanctioned nations. There could be an exception for information or information content that allows citizens to interact with sanctioned nations' artwork. What would you do if an NFT was discovered in Iran, North Korea, or another sanctioned country?

He said that there is also the possibility of malicious actors using NFTs to raise or launder funds. He cited the Marine Chain ICO as one example of how a sanctioned organization has attempted to secure funding through cryptocurrencies in the past. Platforms that create, process, and offer NFTs must consider this. The media should also avoid being confused with money transfer companies.

You might argue that an NFT can be a valuable substitute because Financial rules regulate items that replace value. Financial regulations aren't concerned with the asset; they care about people and their conduct.

Intellectual Property and Copyright

It is essential to determine if buyers' expectations about what they bought match the legal reality. Sellers, mainly established businesses that jump on the bandwagon, face the same problem. Sellers should ensure that the NFTs they sell contain the material they want to sell. Unlike virtual files, NFTs cannot be edited once registered on a Blockchain.

"You can't undo anything; there's no turning around." While you can issue another token, the original NFT will still be in circulation. You must therefore understand and be aware of all possible risks. NFTs may also interact with existing copyright legislation. "There is no one serious about NFTs that entertains the idea that what you're selling might be the copyright or the master suggesting artists could sell some licensed material to buyers while maintaining the copyright.

Musicians and artists can make NFTs of their work, but anyone can make NFTs of jobs they didn't create. I am curious if the new NFT platforms can deal with this possibility. What if OpenSea began a few Mickey Mouse-related NFTs and Walt Disney lawyers contacted it?

Counterfeiting

NFTs often represent real-world objects. That increases the chance of a connection between real-world objects and NFTs that indicate it is damaged. You might sell something on a platform and claim it's an NFT.

That is residing on a blockchain. This is false. As they're not smart enough to verify, many users won't know if the NFT is true or false. The products could be an NFT or an excellent picture linked to another blockchain.

Securities and Taxation Rules

NFTs may be subject to securities laws. However, this seems less likely than many of the other regulatory regimes involved. A person who buys an NFT under the assumption that its value will rise will sue the NFT creator. It is comparable in that there is lots of public demand. However, traditional securities, sanctions, and commodity legislation would need to be adjusted.

NFT buyers may have to deal with different tax laws in other countries. NFTs tied to art usually require the buyer to address this issue. Who collects sales tax? When you buy art worth $4.6 million, sales tax must be paid. It's the responsibility of the buyer.

CREATE A BUSINESS PLAN FOR NFT

The following is all about creating a business plan for an NFT. That provides step-by-step instructions on determining what you should include and where to find what you need.

If you've always had great ideas but lacked the confidence or know-how in how to bring them into reality, it's time for a change! A business plan is critical. We'll discuss why it is important and guide you on how to write one for your idea for an NFT.

Why Is A Business Plan Important?

A business plan is often viewed as an essential aspect of a startup. Without one, you risk wasting time and money on dreams that never materialize. It provides a step-by-step process for turning an idea into a profitable reality. It will guide you through various tasks to help you create, develop, and market your new business venture.

How To Write A Business Plan For Nft?

Step 1 – Make Your Goal Clear and Attainable – Setting a goal makes it possible to determine what parts of the process are necessary.

Step 2 – Understand Your Competition – One must first understand the competition when writing a plan. While your idea may be unique, it will probably not be the first of its kind. Establish a clear understanding of what your competition is doing to identify points you can improve and those best suited for you. Also, learn about potential customers and their needs.

Step 3 – Determine Your Unique Selling Proposition (USP) – It is a product or service that will make it stand out from the rest of the industry and allow it to generate revenue in the beginning stages.

Step 4 – Create a Mission Statement – To maximize your success, you must develop a mission statement. That is essentially your purpose for existing in the business world.

Step 5 – Determine Your Strengths and Weaknesses – Analyze your skill set and determine which areas best suit you to market to customers. Write down all of these details.

What kind of people purchases products like yours or use services similar to their own?

Step 6 – Identify Your Target Market – While considering which markets will be the best for your business, you must identify who these consumers are. That will help the business plan show specific details about how it can satisfy customer demand in the future.

Step 7 – Assess the Competition – Understanding how your business will fair against the competition is essential. Not only does this provide information that you can use to your advantage, but it also helps you with marketing strategies and ways to promote your company.

Step 8 – Determine How You Will Market Your Business – Collect the necessary facts about what promotion methods will benefit the business most. Detail strategies that have been proven successful by competitors in the past.

Step 9 – Establish a Timeline – Just as with goals for the future, it is essential to create a timeline that details how the business will be operated. That should include what you will accomplish daily, weekly, and yearly.

Step 10 – Analyze Your Idea's Future Potential – Consider what might happen in the future if your idea quickly becomes successful. Provide details about how you will handle increased customer demand and other issues that might arise. Viable plans should be outlined in detail.

While it is essential to study the competition, it is equally necessary to create a product in demand by customers.

Step 11 – Assess the Potential Market – The next step is to get a rough estimate of how many customers could potentially purchase your product or receive your service. These potential consumers provide information that will help you with business planning.

Step 12 – Finance the Project – After creating your business plan, estimate how much money you will need to startup operations. That should include money for outlay costs, salaries/employees, and all other expenses that might arise.

Step 13 – Assess the Financial Status of Your Business – A business plan should detail the financial status of a company. That will assist you in explaining why you are planning to develop your particular product or service. In addition, it will help you to understand how much money your company will need to grow into significant profit for investors.

Step 14 – Draft the Business Plan – Once you have created an outline of your business plan, it is time for revisions and development. That allows for improvements in language regarding budgeting, timelines, and product development.

Step 15 – Send out Your Business Plan – Finally, send out your business plan along with a request for feedback.

Business Planning Basics Are For Startup In Nft

Of course, it is possible that while going through this process, you might find that your initial idea will not work as well as you had hoped. After all, if it isn't realistic or achievable, it will be a waste of time to move forward and lose cash on developing an idea that can't impact the market. In any case, the business planning basics supplied by the above guide should help create an outline for a solid and achievable plan for your business in NFT.

To make your business a natural and possible success, it is vital to start with the basics to know what to keep an eye on and what to discard altogether.

Before moving forward with business planning basics, it is essential to realize that starting a new business or developing one from scratch is not as simple as it might seem. It takes a great deal of time, effort, and money before even thinking about making any profit. Of course, this doesn't mean that you cannot succeed in NFT; however, you must be realistic about the benefits and possibilities available in this industry.

For that reason, it is essential to start with the business planning basics outlined above to ensure that you create a plan that is achievable by your company. A solid plan will mean that you will have some extra money and time to devote to developing your business idea.

Knowing a few business planning basics will make it easier for you to make critical decisions when developing your product and entering the NFT market. Do not be discouraged if your business doesn't get off on the right foot from the start; after all, many business owners are aware that their initial plans were not as good as they could have been. Keep in mind that you will make mistakes along the way, so it is best to prepare for them as best you can.

Using the business planning basics supplied by this guide will be much easier for you to put together a realistic plan. Keep in mind that this guide is intended for new business owners; however, those who have been involved in marketing businesses or are interested in entering the NFT market may also find it helpful. Many of these businesses begin with similar ideas and needs; however, there are often a few steps that will make things much easier overall.

Planning is essential for a few different reasons. Perhaps the most fundamental reason is that it will help you decide whether a particular business opportunity is worth pursuing. If you have decided to start an NFT business, this guide will help you determine how much time and money you ought to invest in your business before it starts making a profit. You can also use this guide as part of creating your NFT marketing plan.

Overall, there are many reasons why entrepreneurs get involved with NFT marketing. However, if you don't have a good idea of what you want to do or the best way to do it, there is a high probability that your business will not be successful.

And one of the most practical things you can do to make your NFT marketing plan more successful is to acquire all the information and resources you need for this purpose.

Create A Digital Wallet

To create a MetaMask digital wallet, go to the website and click on the blue 'Download' button in the top-right corner. We selected to install the browser extension because we're using a desktop computer, but there is also a mobile app.

When you first launch your wallet, it will prompt you to 'generate a new wallet and seed phrase.' It would benefit if you weren't concerned about what "seed phrase" means (simply a list of words that saves blockchain data). Say yes, then it's merely a case of agreeing to the conditions, creating a password, and going through some security checks to get your account up and running.

You'll need to add some ETH to your MetaMask wallet or any other digital wallet after you've created it. That's not difficult at all: click the 'Buy' button and pick Wyre as your payment method. You'll be carried to a screen where you can buy ETH with Apple Pay or a debit card. If you'd rather not spend any money yet, feel free to proceed; all you have to do is wait a little longer.)

Connect Your Wallet To An Nft Platform

Example for this purpose, but there are numerous other NFT platforms to explore.

In the right-hand corner of the screen, a button says 'Connect wallet.' Click here to connect your wallet with MetaMask. A popup will appear asking you whether you want to link your wallet with Rarable. Select "Yes," then "Connect," and agree to the terms of service before confirming your age.

GIFs can be used as NFTs; however, we advise you to create the file in an image editor like Photoshop or Paint because they give complete control over sizing and sharpness. To do this: Open your chosen software and create a new image of dimension 256 x 128 using black and white colors (if using Paint, make sure Advanced Mode is on). Paste your GIF into that new image, and scale it down to fit the whole picture.

You're ready to make your NFT now. The blue 'Create' control in the upper right should be clicked. After that, you may select a single one-off project or sell the same item several times. Choose 'Single' in this example. You must upload the digital file that you wish to convert into an NFT at this stage. Rarible takes PNG, GIF, WEBP, MP4, and MP3 files up to 30MB in size.

Upload your file; then, you'll see a glimpse of your NFT post on the right.

Put up an auction

In the next part of the form, you'll need to choose how you want to sell your NFT artwork. There are three options here. 'Fixed price' permits you to set a price and sell to someone instantly (like 'Buy it now on eBay'). 'Unlimited Auction' will enable people to carry on making bids until you accept one.

HOW TO MAKE YOUR NFT'S PROJECT

Should You Create Your Own Nft Artworks?

You probably doubt whether or not NFTs are worth a shot. When you think of the traditional art world, you see various art galleries, people spending hundreds of thousands or even millions on artworks. But then you get struck by the reality. Only a countable few people can make a living out of this. Even then, their revenues have to be shared with other parties involved in the sale.

However, the NFT world can be different. As the artist, you will control all strings of your artwork. Since NFTs' marketplaces are global, your artwork will be exposed to the whole world. There's no need to contact an agency or a gallery to sell your work. You also don't have to share your revenue with multiple parties or intermediaries. The NFTs' marketplaces will keep you in your artwork's sale loop all the time. You will be able to get a fair commission from every NFT artwork you sell. Besides, at any time, you are capable of proving the authenticity of your art, and there's only one person to be the valid owner of your artwork at a given time. The entire NFT artwork ecosystem provides a more democratic landscape for everybody to create, buy, and sell artwork.

Also, unlike in the traditional art world, where you get paid in weeks or months after selling the artworks, you will receive the money instantly into your crypto wallet as soon as you make the NFT artwork sale. That is real excitement and relief.

What makes it even better? If your initial collector gets an offer on the art and decides to sell it. Boom! Another 10% (for example) of the resale value will immediately appear in your crypto wallet in most services.

NFT makes it more convenient for those motion-based and 3D artworks. These kinds of art are hard to sell as physical pieces and shown best in digital form.

Your artworks will also be viewed from anywhere, and you can avoid shipping issues.

So, what are the downsides?

Your artwork will be tossed into a vast sea of art. Like other online businesses, you will still need to bring your work to the attention of potential buyers and collectors.

If you lose your crypto wallet login information, unlike the traditional banks that can help you reset your password, you will lose your artwork and money forever.

Another "gas fee" is associated with each transaction of Etherium that can quickly be added up. Although some companies are working hard on keeping down the price of the electricity used to create and track every crypto art piece, the cost is not ideal.

Tokenizing your artwork doesn't mean you lose your intellectual rights. You will always be able to sell your artworks traditionally — print them, show them, and sell them physically. The most you will lose is the gas fee and some time. On balance, it is still worth you dipping your toes in the crypto art pond.

Can Your Content Be An Nft?

Probably.

Almost anything in the NFT, like memes, songs, recipes, digital art, and even entire startups, is listed on the NFT marketplaces. There are very few restrictions regarding what types of content can be tokenized and turned into NFTs.

As digital art's demand continues to grow, it's a great time to experiment with this technology for your artwork. One rule that should be kept in mind is that avoid turning copyrighted assets or contents into NFTs.

What Is Needed To Start Creating Nfts? Step-By-Step Instructions

You won't need extensive crypto knowledge to create NFTs, while you do need several tools to get started. It's Okay if you are not acquainted with them yet. You will be able to get everything set up in only a few minutes from your phone. Let's get started.

Here you will learn to set up a crypto wallet, purchase ETH, and connect your crypto wallets to NFT marketplaces.

Step 1: Set Up Your Ethereum Wallet

What's your first step in your NFT journey? It's to create a digital wallet where you can securely store your cryptocurrency used to create, buy, and sell NFTs. This crypto wallet will also allow you to create accounts and safely sign in on NFT marketplaces.

Hundreds of platforms provide free wallets that can help you store cryptocurrencies.

Step 2: Buy A Small Piece of Ethereum (ETH)

There will be fees for turning your artwork into NFTs on most major digital art marketplaces. So, you will require to buy some ETH to cover the costs of making your first NFT.

Since the ETH's price fluctuates almost every second, it's challenging to track it. One more straightforward way to get started is by choosing your funds in dollars with the amount you are willing to purchase and invest exactly that much ETH. The Metamask introduced before allows you to buy crypto right inside your crypto wallet. In contrast, the Coinbase wallet needs you to purchase from another exchange platform and transfer it into your wallet.

Step 3: Connect the Crypto Wallet to NFT Marketplaces

After you set up your wallet and buy some ETH, it's time to choose a marketplace where you want to make NFTs and list your work. Rarible is an excellent choice for beginners who just started as they have the most straightforward and effortless setup.

To connect your crypto wallet to Rarible, go to their site and click the Connect button in the screen's top right corner.

Connect Crypto Wallet To Rarible

On the next screen, choose the wallet you decided on in the preceding step.

Choose your wallet

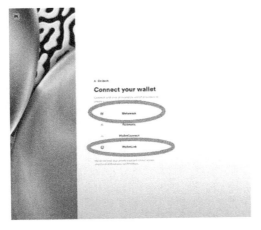

The next step is almost the same, no matter which wallet you choose. A QR code will appear on the screen after selecting your connection wallet. Then, use your crypto wallet app to scan this code. After checking the code, confirm that you would like to connect your crypto wallet to Rarible.

That is a safe connection, and Rarible will always make you confirm purchases with your crypto wallet apps before moving forward with anything. Your Rarible account will be instantly generated once you connect to the wallet.

Now you have everything needed to create and sell your first NFT.

How To Create Nft Art With No Coding Experience

Step 1: Make a Digital Art File as NFTs

No standard technique exists to create a piece of art that can be used as NFTs. As long as the file you created is supported by the marketplace you are using to list it, it will work as NFTs.

There's an NFT. That contains lots of opportunities for the content you can monetize. On Rarible or Zora, the image as JPG, PNG, TXT, or GIF, and MP3 can be NFTs. A meme can be an NFT

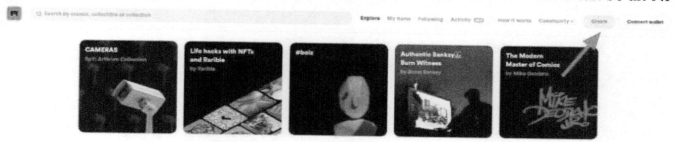

too. Construct a tasty recipe and have it saved as the TXT?

Here, we will use Rarible, with no coding experience needed.

First, click the "Create Collectibles" in the upper right corner.

Click "Create Collectibles" on Rarible

Then, we're going to see we can either create a single collectible or multiple. So, we can have one rare or make various collectibles. So, let's do various.

Create collectible

Choose "Single" if you want your collectible to be one of a kind or "Multiple" if you want to sell one collectible multiple times

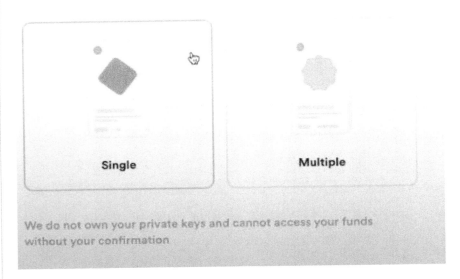

Single   Multiple

We do not own your private keys and cannot access your funds without your confirmation

Create Collectible

We're going to do multiple and start from scratch, and it's going to say select an image: jpg, png, or a gif. So, you can use any file as long as it is a jpeg, png, or gif. It could be a photo you took on your phone, and it can also be a picture you took several years ago that you uploaded onto your computer with a scanner; any file that meets these criteria.

If you already have a file or a picture you want to turn into an NFT, you can upload it right here, but let's say you have a file or an image that is not part of these formats. It's straightforward to convert them. You can go to onlineconvert.com, and you can convert an image to a png file or a jpeg file.

After you get the file in the acceptable format, you can upload it to Rarible.

You can take a png file or a jpeg file and compress it here. Please note that they recommend that the file is under 10 megabytes, so if you have a file above 10 megabytes and want to squeeze it, go to tinypng.com. Once we have those images, we can go back to Rarible and upload them.

But let's say you want to create an image from scratch. I prefer using Canva. It is where I do my work. Canva is a great software. There is a free version, and also there is the paid version which is about ten dollars per month.

Another helpful tool is Kapwing. It provides several well-suited tools to help you create and get more from your existing NFTs.

Here, let's make a short piece of NFT with Canva to upload to Rarible.

So, we're going to create a design. We'll do a logo here, but you can do any art, or you could do Instagram posts, Facebook posts, brochures, anything you can think of.

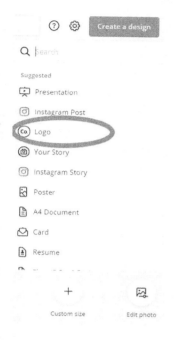

Create Deign

Let's make a crypto monkey. First, choose the monkey you like, and we can enlarge it. You can do whatever you want in Canva. It's straightforward to use.

Create a monkey

We'll get an Ethereum logo. Now, this is our NFT.

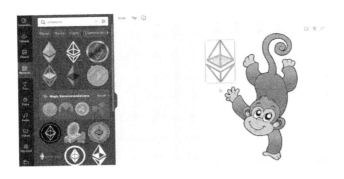

Add ETH logo

Next, let's save it and download it. We'll call it crypto monkey.

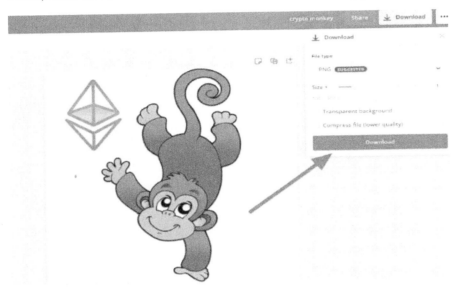

Save & download your work.

Step 2: Upload the Artwork to Rarible

We now have our png file. So, let's go back to Rarible and let's upload it. We're going to choose our image of the crypto monkey.

Create NFT on Rarible

We can also choose a collection on this page, or you can keep it on Rarible.

We can also provide it a title, calling it crypto monkey Super. Then, we can do an optional description: this is a crypto monkey Super, or whatever you want. Then, over here, we can choose how many copies we want. Since we did multiple collectibles, so we can do various compositions here.

Another thing we can set up here is royalties. That means that after you sell your NFT to someone, you will receive a royalty every time it is sold. They recommend or suggest 10, 20, or 30 percent.

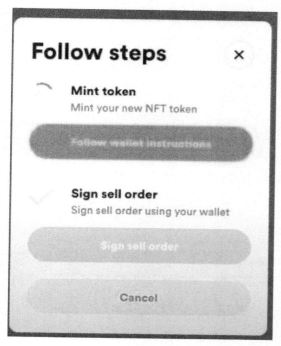

For properties, this will depend on what you're creating. For example, we'll do our property as the animal for our crypto monkey. You can go as heavy on this as you want, and you can create properties, or you can make no properties; that's up to you.

Then, we're going to set a price for it. Please note there's a service fee of 2.5 percent.

For unlock once purchase, don't touch that; leave that as it is.

After you check your pevaluation to make everything look correct, click Create.

Attention: this is where we run into the risk of creating NFTs.

Mint & Sell Nft On Rarible

You might have come to this, and you want to sell it at a high price. You may want to create a hundred of these NFTS, maybe a thousand, and think that one of them will eventually sell. However, the problem is every time you make an NFT, there is a transaction on the ETH blockchain, so you're going to pay a gas fee. Right now, the gas fee to mint this token is six dollars and twenty-one cents, which you might consider very low, but I've seen these gas fees for nine dollars, ten dollars, and even more.

FINDING PROFITABLE NON-FINANCIAL TECHNOLOGIES

You've reached the stage where you'll discover how to make money using non-traditional financial instruments (NFTs). Now that you understand how NFTs function, the many kinds of NFTs, how to mint your own NFT, and where you may purchase NFTs from other producers and resell them, it is time to learn how to correctly choose NFTs that will provide a significant return on your investment. The NFT market is still in its premature stages compared to other markets, but there is a lot of possible profit to be gained. In one case, a friend of mine realized a 7,400 per cent return on a single piece of NFT when he resold "Temporal Shark Dream," which was created by an NFT artist called Max Osiris had purchased from him.

This same friend has generated a total return on investment (ROI) of 2,005 per cent from 19 resales of multiple NFTs that he purchased on the cheap. His success in the NFT sales market has elevated him to the top three collectors on SuperRare regarding resale volume.

While you may not be able to achieve an ROI of 7,400 per cent on your first NFT investment, I can teach you the secrets that underpin the process of economically picking NFTs that can provide at least a 100 per cent return on your first capital investment. Keep in mind that the secrets I'm about to reveal to you are not hard and fast rules that will guarantee you a 100 per cent return on your NFT investments; instead, they are more like guidelines that can assist you in systematically investing in NFTs that have the potential to generate a 100 per cent return on your initial investment. In reality, it was via applying these concepts that I achieved an excellent 1,050 percent return on my NFT investments in a little over two years. If I can earn such a high return on investment using these ideas, I am confident that you will be able to do so as well. So, what exactly are these "hidden principles" that might assist you in making money off of your NFT investments? Consider the following examples.

The Untold Secrets Of Choosing Profitable Non-Firm Transactions

The Reputation of the Creator

Before buying any NFT collectible, the first thing to examine is the individual's reputation for creating the collectible. If you are purchasing a piece of art in the conventional sense, the importance of the artist who made it is usually considered before you make your final decision. The more well-known and intriguing an artist is, the more valuable their work is seen as being by others.

This behavior may be seen in the NFT space as well. This behavior was one of the elements that contributed to Beeple's NFT painting selling for as much as $69 million when it was auctioned off. When contemplating an NFT investment — particularly in the NFT arts — it is essential to ensure that the NFT you are considering was produced by a creator who has established a solid reputation in the industry.

Investing in such an NFT will make it much simpler for you to resale it at a much more significant price than you paid for it when you purchased it. The NFT environment, on the other hand, is not limited to just digital art and design. There are various NFT niches in which you may choose to invest, including gaming objects, player's cards, and other similar products. If you are contemplating acquiring such non-financial instruments, the following set of guidelines can assist you in selecting lucrative ones to put your money into.

Sufficiency is essential when investing in non-financial technologies (NFTs) to receive high returns. A shortage of a particular item in the traditional world leads to a demand for that specific item. This holds in the NFT world as well, assuming that the more rare an object is, the greater the perceived value it has. For example, a LeBron James slam from the NBA Top Shot moment sold for more than $200,000 since it was the only copy available at the time of the sale. In light of its rarity, other buyers on the marketplace bid more and higher on its price until it was ultimately sold for $208,000. Although the collector who purchased the artwork has not yet placed it for sale, you can imagine how much it would sell for if it were to be listed for sale on a secondary market when it does finally become available. In a similar vein, a player card showing Cristiano Ronaldo sold for $290,000 even though it was one of just a few available. Consider how much the card will sell for in the next two to three years as the NFT industry grows and develops. When looking for NFTs to invest in, it is typically more advantageous to invest in NFTs that are one-of-a-kind rather than NFTs that are duplicated in several locations. People are ready to pay more for an item that is one of a kind; but, when an NFT is available in several copies, people are less willing to pay due to the lack of distinctiveness.

The Amount Of Transactional Activity That Takes Place.

It would be best if you spent close awareness of the level of transactional activity associated with any NFT initiative in which you choose to invest. The greater the level of transactional activity around an NFT project, the greater the project's liquidity. When you decide to sell your NFT, you will have an easier time finding a buyer because of the high liquidity. You do not want to invest in an NFT project with low sales since this will make it more challenging for you to sell the project in the future.

Knowledge In A Specific Field

In the world of finance — particularly on Wall Street — there is a phrase that goes something like this: "invest in what you understand." This statement couldn't be more accurate when investing in non-financial companies (NFTs). There are a variety of sectors that are being transformed by NFTs, including gaming, art, virtual reality, and music, to mention a few. When contemplating whether or not to support a non-traditional investment, exploring NFTs that deal with topics you are familiar with is advisable. For example, if you are a severe gamer, your significant investing concentration should be on non-financial-transactions (NFTs) tied to gaming.

Similarly, if you are an art enthusiast, your significant investing concentration should be on non-financial-transactions (NFTs) tied to art. The ability to concentrate on and make investments in areas in which you are competent will enable you to find lucrative chances that other people may not be able to see until it is too late. For example, suppose you are a dedicated viewer of football matches. In that case, you will be able to quickly recognize individuals who have the potential to develop into great players in the future. As soon as you identify such players, you may select whether or not to purchase their player card and keep onto it until they begin to receive attention for their football abilities. More importantly, since you will be acquiring their player card when they are still relatively unknown, such cards will not be prohibitively expensive, with some player cards selling for as little as $20 on the secondary market. Consider the following scenario: you paid $50 for Cristiano Ronaldo's player card when Manchester United initially signed him. Consider how much a card like that would be valued now when he had successfully won five Ballon d'Ors.

Utility

The utility that an NFT gives may also assist you in determining if it will be a solid investment that generates a high return on your investment or not. How an NFT may be utilized determines its utility and is one of the critical categories of NFT that produces high-utility NFTs in the gaming category. A significant utility value may be derived from game-related NFTs, particularly if the game elements can be repurposed in a new application. To give you an example, a rare and powerful Crypto Space Commander Battleship was auctioned off for a little more than $45,000 in 2019. Consider the possibility that this identical gaming component may have been used in a different game or application, in which case the value would have been much more significant. Because of this, the greater the amount of utility that an NFT can supply, the greater its importance in the marketplace. Consider those NFTs that give more utility than others when considering whether to invest in them since these NFTs have the potential to provide a significant amount of return on investment.

Ownership History

The ownership history of an NFT is another useful statistic you may use to discover NFTs that have the potential to deliver a decent return on your investment. Consider the possibility of obtaining an NFT that an influential person formerly held. Reselling such non-financial-transactions (NFT) may provide a significant return on investment since consumers are fascinated by the idea of owning items that essential individuals once owned. The greater the influence or popularity of an NFT's prior owner, the higher the price at which you may resale that NFT — so making a decent return on your investment. However, the NFT sector is very speculative; the concepts outlined above are the keys to picking highly successful NFTs for investment. In time, as the NFT ecosystem matures, these ideas may be refined and refined into a more standardized and systematic way to identify viable NFTs that might provide significant returns for you.

THE CREATOR CLASS & NFTS

From a financial perspective, the pandemic hit the creator class hard. With the regular venues for live performances and shows closed, artists, musicians, singers, actors, and creators of every definition have been forced to fend for themselves. But something very new (and unique) happened. The outcome may be the emergence of a first-time-ever, self-sufficient, profitable designer class.

The stereotype of a starving artist is ancient and trite. Fine artists aren't assumed to care about things like food or shelter. They've been mourning for their art for centuries. Dancers aren't large eaters, so no one ever thinks about starving dancers. But musicians haven't managed much better. Papa Bach was a community organist and an organ repairman on the side. Mozart was always borrowing funds from his friends and families, although he did make some actual money now and again. Beethoven didn't die poor but lived from commission to commission. Before 2021, there was one thing that every artist has had in standard with every other artist who ever lived: they rehearsed their art at the pleasure of a patron.

Patrons

Whether it was a monarch, a rich person, a corporation, a media company, a label, a museum, a you-fill-in-the-blank, someone with money has funded practically every art project ever. Of course, there are a few notable exceptions, but they do not prove the direction. In modern history, the extensive majority of artists (no matter the art form) have both wanted and needed the match of a recording contract with a major label to eat and pay the rent while trying to accomplish their artistic goals.

The Mother Of Invention

The creator class has experienced one of the most prominent pandemic-accelerated digital modifications. See YouTube or TikTok, or Instagram, and you are sure to find a creator fully certified with direct-to-consumer (DTC) business tools. Everything a creator needs to get paid, from payment processing to analytics to production capabilities, is available with little or no investment. That is more than a digital version of passing the hat to support your busking. Massive tech infrastructure is emerging to power, help, and earnings symbiotically with the evolving developer class.

After its most current raise, Patreon (a platform that combines over 200,000 creators with about 7 million fans) valued $4 billion (triple its worth in September 2020). Cameo is a site that permits celebrities to send personalized videos straight to fans (for a fee, of course). OnlyFans is a favored app of sex workers and physical fitness experts.

What's essential to comprehend is that every social video post has become an opportunity to promote original content that fans can support.

Nfts, Crypto, And The Arts

Have you lately begun gathering NFT art? If so, you are at the forefront of the developing creator economy.

We are in the center of the NFT hype-cycle, so it's hard to divide the hucksters and charlatans from the real possibilities afforded by ERC721 and ERC1155 innovative agreements recorded on distributed ledgers. Due to the insane prices of some current NFT transactions, it seems like everyone who's anyone is bringing into the competition. Seven-time Super Bowl champion Tom Brady reported launching an NFT platform called Autograph in early 2021.

There are many excellent uses for NFTs, especially for the creator class. One of the most significant issues of our day is the ability for anyone to mash up anything and call it their own. Please take a few standards of music from one song, a beat from another, a good result from a favorite movie, a line of dialogue from a fantastic video, mash them up, and you've got a new (albeit derivative) job. Who gets settled, and how?

Our copyright and academic property laws afford security for creators, but enforcement is strict. It requires extensive, centralized organizations such as recorded music companies, publishers, performing liberties organizations, movie studios, media companies, and others to observe, manipulate, and control the granting of rights and the flow of money. NFTs can decentralize this entire ecosystem.

Said differently, as blockchain technology becomes, transaction speed increases and transaction fees decrease (all of which are slowly but surely happening). As more content becomes uniquely identifiable using NFTs, the need for central authorities (a.k.a. gatekeepers) will diminish and possibly disappear altogether, as the creator class will be able to do it by themselves. The idea of an open, honest, one-to-one relationship between creator and society isn't new, but the technology to do it at scale is.

HOW TO BUY NONFUNGIBLE TOKENS

NFTs are exchanged in cryptographic forms of money, so you first need to purchase digital currency and hold it in a wallet. You, at that point, need to set up an account with an NFT commercial center, like Nifty Gateway, OpenSea, or Rarible. Deals regularly appear as selloffs with a beginning NFT cost, so on the off chance that you enter a triumphant offer, you will take responsibility for NFT. On the off chance that the worth like this rises, you can set up your bartering on a commercial center to sell it for a benefit. While purchasing an NFT doesn't move the copyright for the work, it gives fundamental use rights like posting a picture on the web.

Nonfungible tokens can be bought on an assortment of stages, and whichever you pick will rely upon what it is you have to purchase (for instance, on the off chance that you have to buy baseball cards, you're best making a beeline for a site like digital trading cards, however different commercial centers sell more summed up pieces). You'll require a wallet explicit to the stage you're purchasing on, and you'll have to fill that wallet with cryptographic money. Nonfungible tokens can be bought on different online marketplaces such as Rarible, NFT Showroom, BakerySwap, VIV3, OpenSea, etc.

If you're not an artwork creator but are more interested in buying NFTs, how would you go about that? You'd have to do some marketplace research first. Once more, I'm not here to promote any marketplaces. I'm just giving you some ideas on where you can start to look.

Opensea is currently the largest NFT marketplace, according to their website. A beginner-friendly mint and market platform are Rarible. If you're more into auctioning collectibles, you may find Niftygateway a good choice or Makersplace. And art lovers may tend to go with KnownOrigin or Superrare.

Who Are The Stakeholders Of Nfts

1. Developers

The developer is the person or company that creates the game and owns the code. They are in charge of deploying the game to the blockchain, maintaining it, and adding new features.

The developer can be a centralized entity, such as a game studio or blockchain company. Or they can be a decentralized team, such as an open-source community of contributors. In most cases, developers will launch NFTs on top of an existing blockchain protocol (such as Ethereum). The developer then creates a smart contract to support their game. The rules of this intelligent contract determine how the NFTs are minted and transferred between players in the game. The developer also determines what happens when NFTs are destroyed or abandoned (later on).

2. Players

The player is any person who plays a game using NFTs and owns them during gameplay. There are many different types of players in any given NFT-based game:

- First-time users who want to learn how to play.

- Casual players who enjoy regular gameplay.

- Expert players who participate in high-stakes tournaments with prizes like cars or houses.

- A player may play just for fun but also for financial gain.

3. Collectors

The collector is any person who owns NFTs for investment purposes. The most common type of collector is an NFT investor or someone who purchases NFTs to sell them at a higher price in the future. There are many other types of collectors, including speculators and NFT traders. Collectors are interested in any game that uses NFTs, regardless of their popularity. Some collectors are highly selective about which games they support, while others collect as many different types of games as possible.

4. Traders

The trader is a player who specializes in buying and selling NFTs to make a profit. They can be players or collectors, but their primary goal is to buy low and sell high rather than play the game itself. Most traders are active on secondary markets such as centralized exchanges or decentralized exchanges (DEXes). A DEX is an online market where buyers and sellers can trade with each other directly without using a middleman (like an exchange). There are several ways that traders make money from NFTs: they can sell them at higher prices than they paid, short sell them, or trade them on margin.

5. Speculators

The speculator is a player who buys NFTs to sell them at a higher price in the future. Depending on their strategy, they may buy NFTs from other players or the developer. For example, they may purchase an NFT at a discount during its presale period and then sell it once it becomes more popular. Or they may buy an NFT that is highly sought after by collectors and hold onto it until it appreciates.

6. Investors

The investor is a player who purchases NFTs as part of a portfolio of assets (or with borrowed money). They expect to profit from their investment over time through price appreciation or dividends (more on this later). The most common type of investor is an asset manager or manages other people's money and uses investment strategies such as value investing, growth investing, or momentum investing. Investors can also be hedge funds, family offices, angel investors, venture capitalists, and others. They are interested in any game that uses NFTs regardless of their popularity. However, most of them are more selective about which games they support than collectors are.

Related Legal Issues Worth Your Attention

As we have noticed, anyone can make NFTs of anything worldwide, even if the contents don't belong to them. However, this brings the questions of copyright infringement and copyfraud to us.

Copyright Infringement

You may think creating NFTs from the public domain works interesting, while the issue that probably generates legal conflicts is doing the outcome from a person who is not its owner or the author. Another problematic phenomenon is that people began to create pieces that did not belong to them.

CorbinRanbolt has complained that some of his dinosaurs' artworks have been tokenized without his permission. Another artist, WerdUndead, had their works created and placed in OpenSea by someone else.

In both situations, the artworks have been removed from the NFT marketplaces, but it made us ask whether or not it is copyright infringement for the authorized creation of a work.

Creating and selling NFTs based on the artworks you don't own or hold the right to is an infringement. That is why the auction sites of NFT have rushed to create DMCA processes for removing those unauthorized ones. Some marketplaces only allow verified work, making it less problematic in this industry. However, it's not clear if this is enough that many sites are now actively encouraging the public to tokenize content that doesn't belong to them.

Artists can do derivative works based on their creations and sell them. As long as buyers are fully aware that NFTs are useless practically, there's not enough reason for the courts to get involved.

However, as we see the NFT industry boom, we are now seeing far more concerns regarding copyright infringement, and the system is getting abused.

What makes it more complicated is that even when the original artists don't care, you use their works first, but they can still see you at the end of the day Because the artwork owners can change their mind at any point in the future, and you are using their work in a way they're not happy about. A typical and exciting case example was that in 2019,

InfoWars paid Pepe the Frog creator Matt Furie $15,000 to settle the lawsuit against them. One of the critical lessons left for us is that creators should avoid making public statements saying they do not care about their copyrights or tolerance for unauthorized uses. The works' authorships are entitled to the same types of protections, no matter what form of service — online, print, social media, whatever it can be. So, if you sell other people's art for millions of dollars, they will certainly have the right to come after you. Another lesson is that virality or meme-ification will not decrease the copyright's strength. For example, if you see a meme going viral on social media, everybody is using it or joking about it, but this doesn't mean you are safe to transfer to your NFT and sell it.

Copyfraud

This term refers to making a dubious or false copyright claim over works in the public domain. Yes, public domain works can be used by anyone. However, sometimes an institution will claim the copyright over such works. The Global Art Museum (GAM) has tokenized some public domain works and listed them for sales on OpenSea. Now we know, if one person makes an NFT of a picture or image, they have to have the original file used to create the token. Although there might not be a legal issue with copyfraud, we need to ask if the GAM's tokenization of works can even be copyfraud. In GAM's case, they took artworks from the public domain's digital artwork collection at the Rijiksmeusm in Amsterdam. This collection is a celebrated and famous one that has gone entirely digital and is marked as being in the public domain.

Also, the Rijksmuseum encourages re-uses of their works, which is a strong political statement in the public domain's defense. At the same time, one should not enclose the public domain since it's for everyone. The Rijksmuseum has claimed ownership of all the photographs of their artworks. However, it doesn't seem to be interested in enforcing it.

GAM also stated clearly that all the works are from the Rijksmuseum and don't claim any of the institution's involvement. So, there're no ownership claims, only creating a unique version of the works that are not even a copy of the results themselves. This is not copyfraud.

The NFTs have a cryptographic sign to make the file unique, and this sign is not even from the author (since the artists of the public domain's works are no longer with us.) That is like you purchased something and tell others you own exclusive metadata, which others can reproduce. You may see it as pointless at best or slightly unethical at worst.

Could NFTs Help Rightsholders or Creators?

Put, yes. NFTs, give creators another innovative potential revenue stream by selling their works' unique copies and help keep track of ownership of copyrights.

In theory, creators can create the works, tokenize them, and keep the token both as proof of copyright ownership and creation. They can transfer this token as part of the copyright transfer. In reality, however, this is not how it's usually used. It's often used to create some "special" works' copies and sell those copies. Usually, it's not the creators who are reaping those rewards.

Currently, artists and creators need to explore this as potential piracy threats and business opportunities. If your NFT works need to capture the scarcity and uniqueness that this technology can bring to you, they need to be scarce and not just something anyone is capable of conjuring up.

HOW TO SELL THEM

How To Make And Sell An Nft

A step-by-step tutorial on creating and selling an NFT if you want to give it a go with your digital work.

Many artists are asking how to construct and market an NFT these days. non-fungible tokens continue to stir debate and elicit outrage due to the eye-watering prices that some pieces of NFT art have sold for. It's only natural that you'd be curious if NFTs provide a possibility to profit from your creative work if that's the case. This book will assist you in understanding how to make and sell an NFT if that is the case.

However, these are exceptional cases, and even if you manage to replicate their success, you'll generally discover that the bulk of the money won't flow to you. The firms that facilitate transactions and the platforms that generate and maintain NFTs charge various fees to NFT artists both up-front and after any sale, and they may even leave you out of pocket based on the price your work sells for.

There are several online platforms to create and sell NFTs right now. OpenSea, Rarible, SuperRare, Nifty Gateway, Foundation, VIV3, BakerySwap, Axie Marketplace, and NFT ShowRoooom are examples of popular auction sites for buying and selling NFTs. Payment options include MetaMask, Torus, Portis, WalletConnec, Coinbase, MyEtherWallet, and Fortmatic.

Buy some cryptocurrency Ethereum cryptocurrency, ether is accepted by most platforms.

The first thing to note is that you'll have to pay a platform to "mint" (or generate) your piece. Most media want to cover the cost with ether, the cryptocurrency native to the open-source blockchain platform Ethereum, where NFTs first debuted.

Keep in mind that, like bitcoin and many other cryptocurrencies, the value of ether (abbreviated as ETH) is prone to huge fluctuations. From under $1,000 in 2021 to over $4,800 in 2021, with numerous peaks and valleys on the road, it's been known to swing by hundreds of dollars in a matter of hours.

To acquire Ethereum, you'll need to construct a "digital wallet" and link it to your NFT platform of choice. There are several digital wallet services available, but we'll use MetaMask, which is known as a browser plugin and as a mobile app for this purpose. If you'd instead utilize another provider or are familiar with digital wallets and have your own already, go straight to step 4.

When you first launch your wallet, it will prompt you to 'generate a new wallet and seed phrase.' It would be okay if you weren't concerned about what the "seed phrase" means (it's simply a list of words that saves blockchain data). Say yes, then it's merely a case of agreeing to the conditions, creating a password, and going through some security checks to get your account up and running.

Add money to your wallet.

You'll need to add some ETH to your MetaMask wallet or any other digital wallet after you've created it. That's not difficult at all: click the 'Buy' button and pick Wyre as your payment method. You'll be obtained to a screen where you can buy ETH with Apple Pay or a debit card. If you'd rather not spend any money yet, feel free to proceed; all you have to do is wait a little longer.)

Connect your wallet to an the NFT platform

The general workflow of setting up a digital wallet is similar across all platforms. Once you've got some ETH in your digital wallet available to spend, you may go to the NFT platform of your choice and start creating your NFT. We're using Rarable as an example for this purpose, but there are numerous other NFT platforms to explore.

Rarable is one of several digital collectible marketplaces.

To access Rarable, go to Rarable.com. In the right-hand corner of the screen, a button says 'Connect wallet.' Click here to connect your wallet with MetaMask. A popup will appear asking you whether you want to link your wallet with Rarable. Select "Yes," then "Connect," and agree to the terms of service before confirming your age.

Upload your file

GIFs can be used as NFTs; however, we recommend you create the file in an image editor like Photoshop or Paint because they give complete control over sizing and sharpness. To do this: Open your chosen software and create a new image of dimension 256 x 128 using black and white colors (if using Paint, make sure Advanced Mode is on). Paste your GIF into that new image, and scale it down to fit the whole picture.

You're ready to make your NFT now. The blue 'Create' switch in the upper right should be clicked. After that, you may select a single one-off project or sell the same item several times. Choose 'Single' in this example. You must upload the digital file that you wish to convert into an NFT at this stage. Rarible takes PNG, GIF, WEBP, MP4, and MP3 files up to 30MB in size.

Upload your file; then, on the right, you'll see a pevaluation of your NFT post.

Set up an auction

Choose the locations for your auction (Image credit: Rarible)

In the next part of the form, you'll need to decide how you want to sell your NFT artwork. There are three options here. 'Fixed price' allows you to put a price and sell to someone instantly (like 'Buy it now on eBay'). 'Unlimited Auction' will enable people to carry on making bids until you accept one. Finally, 'Timed auction' is an auction that only takes place for a specific time. That's the option we'll choose for our example.

The hard part now begins: establishing a minimum price. Set it too low, and you'll lose money on each sale because of the high costs. We'll set our price at 1 ETH and allow people seven days to make offers.

You'll be able to purchase it immediately after but, before you do, there's an option to "Unlock once purchased." That allows you to give your future buyer a complete, high-resolution copy of your work and other material via a hidden website or download link. The option labeled 'Choose Collection' is the most perplexing. That is a somewhat technical question regarding how the blockchain works. The default option is "Rarible," so we recommend leaving it that way.

Describe your NFT

You may now add a title and description to your item's listing. To increase the chances of selling your NFT, take some time to consider this. You'll be shown a questionnaire that asks you to choose what proportion of royalties you want to earn from any future resale of your work.

This time, there's a further balancing act: higher percentages will earn you more money over time, but they'll also deter people from reselling your work since they'll be less likely to make a profit for themselves. Finally, the file properties may be added as an optional field. You're almost done at this point.

Pay the fee

Click 'Create Item' to begin the listing procedure. You'll be prompted to connect your wallet if you don't have enough money in it. If you don't have enough money in your wallet, don't worry; you won't have to start over. Click on the wallet symbol in the top-right corner of the screen to add money directly within Rarable.

Just a comment of alert before you do so. The listing fee may appear to be relatively low, as it was in our case: $5.91. However, this is only the beginning of the costs you'll be subjected to. To indeed generate your NFT, you must first agree to a further charge of $42.99 before you can proceed any further in our situation. Aside from the fees for buying and selling NFTs, there will also be a commission payment when someone buys your asset and a transfer cost to execute the transaction. From our perspective, none of this was adequately clarified on Rarable's website when we tried it.

NFT SELLING PLATFORMS

NFTs can be purchased on a variety of outlets or platforms, and whichever you select will depend upon what it is you would like to shop (for example, if you would like to shop for baseball cards, you're the best heading to a site like digital trading cards, but other marketplaces sell more generalized pieces). You will require a wallet unique to that outlet you're buying on, and you will get to fill that wallet with cryptocurrency. Because the sale of Beeple's Everyday – the primary 5000 days at Christie's proved, some pieces are starting to hit more mainstream auction houses, too, so these are also worth watching out for. Just in case you missed it, that Beeple piece was the one that went for $69.3 million.

Because of the high demand for the many sorts of NFT, they're often published as 'drops' (like in exhibitions, when collections of tickets are always released several times). That suggests an intense rush of eager buyers when the drop starts, so you would need to be enrolled and have your wallet topped up before time. NFTs also is making waves as in-game purchases across different video games (much to the delight of oldsters everywhere). Players often buy and sell these assets and include playable assets like unique swords, skins, or avatars.

Also, due to the differing blockchain technology behind particular NFTs, not all NFT marketplaces buy and sell all kinds of NFT. Creators will often select an NFT marketplace supported whether that marketplace supports an established NFC token principle.

In recent years, more and more outlets dedicated to the sale of Crypto Art have emerged. Ethereum has published two standards now: ERC-721 and ERC-1155. Adversary, Binance, has since published standards BEP-721 and BEP-1155. The 2 "1155" standards differ from the first "721" standards because they permit multiple NFTs to be bunched and transacted together. Most NFT platforms require buyers to possess a digital wallet and use cryptocurrencies to buy. Today, because of the introduction of NFTs and Blockchain technology, digital artists and collectors can claim their place within the art market.

Here may be a list of websites that sell NFTs:

Opensea

OpenSea boldly describes itself as being the most critical NFT marketplace. It is a clearinghouse for nearly any sort of NFT like crypto-collectibles such as video games, apps. Digital artworks, making it be the "biggest marketplace for digital goods." Goods range from Rob Gronkowski's GRONK Championship Collection (the first pro-athlete to initiate NFTs) to Kings Of Leon's recent album (one of the significant primary records released as a set of digital NFTs). The album was published in three NFT formats constructed to unite "the strength of the band's music and their current album visuals to deconstruct, deteriorate, and warp iconic band symbols and photography." In February 2020, OpenSea registered a 400% increase in sales, from $8 million to $32 million.

Opensea offers a good range of non-fungible tokens, including art, censorship-resistant domain names, virtual worlds, trading cards, sports, and collectibles. It includes ERC721 and ERC1155 assets. You'll buy, sell, and find out exclusive digital assets like Axies, ENS names, CryptoKitties, Decentraland, and more. They feature over 700 projects, including digital art projects to collectible games, card games, and name systems like ENS (Ethereum Name Service). Creators can create their items on the blockchain using OpenSea's item minting tool. You'll use it to form a set and NFTs free of charge without needing one line of code. If you're developing your smart contract for a game, digital collectible, or another project with unique digital items on the blockchain, you'll quickly get added to OpenSea.

OpenSea is that the most democratic and easy-to-use platform of all. No verification is necessary; anyone can create an account and begin minting NFTs. You'll flick through countless collections to seek out particular artists or peruse rankings by sales volume to get fascinating pieces. OpenSea also makes delivering your art or digital collectibles simple. Just click on Create -> Submit NFTs then you'll be ready to create a replacement collection and begin adding new pieces. Even better, there's no coding needed; therefore, the barrier to access is low. It takes three minutes to accept your first part of digital art, and consequently, the whole process is free.

If you're selling items on OpenSea, you'll sell an item for a hard and fast price, create a decreasing price listing, or make a sales listing. If you want to sell your parts, you'll get to buy gas, which is the cost of discussing with the innovative agreement governing OpenSea, but you need to do ao just once. It costs around $50 to $100, counting on network traffic. Because it's so simple and the cost is so low, many collections on OpenSea tend to be composed of digital collectibles instead of individual artworks.

Rarible

Rarible is a decentralized marketplace that gives its users the ERC-20 token, the owner's token. Active users can earn RARI tokens by buying or selling NFTs on the platform. It distributes 75,000 RARI hebdomadally. The platform places a focus on art assets. It lets creators mint new NFTs by buying and selling their creations.

It allows users to create and sell their art assets, whether or not they are books, music albums, digital art, or movies. The creators can sell their work anonymously. They can also show a teaser of their creation to everybody who purchases NFTs from them. People can buy and sell NFTs in various categories like art, photography, games, metaverses, music, domains, memes, and more.

Rarible is analogous to OpenSea because it's democratic and open. Here, however, because you've got to buy each artwork you mint (i.e., create and place on a blockchain), there's excellent less noise and not many collectibles. Rarible has mainly been used to mint individual pieces. Its value is higher than getting your work seen here, as you'll be paying $40 to $80 for the minting of every job.

Established by Alex Salnikov and Alexei Falin in early 2020, it leverages the blockchain to connect digital artists and collectors. Rarible allows users to make, sell and buy artwork as non-fungible tokens (NFTs). What puts the platform apart is its decentralized independent organization (DAO). Through the RARI token, users can partake in protocol governance decisions through a voting mechanism.

Superrare

SuperRare was created in 2017 by Jonathan Perkins, John Crain, and Charles Crain. On the platform, digital artists can create artworks and tokenize them on the Ethereum blockchain, while collectors can buy the works securely and transparently via ETH. Users can see who the highest collectors and trending artists are on the platform, what percentage of jobs they need to be purchased or created, and how much they need to be spent or earned while checking subsequent trades on the second marketplace.

SuperRare features a strong focus on being a marketplace for people to shop for and sell rare single-edition digital artworks. Each of these artworks is genuinely created by an artist within the network and tokenized as a crypto-collectible digital object that you can own and transact. They portray themselves as Instagram's Christie, giving a new method to interact with art, culture, and collecting on the web.

Each artwork on SuperRare is a digital collectible, secured by cryptography and tracked by the blockchain. SuperRare is a digital collectible marketplace that features a social network. Due to their transparency, digital collectibles are very secure and easily accessed by anyone. All dealings are made using ether, the native cryptocurrency to the Ethereum network. At the instant, SuperRare works with a small number of hand-picked artists; however, you'll use a form to submit your artist profile to urge on their radar for their upcoming full launch.

Foundation

Foundation is an expert platform designed to attract digital creators, crypto natives, and collectors concurrently to manipulate culture forward. It calls itself the new creative economy. Its primary focus is on digital art.

In August 2020, in the first blog post on their website, they launched open participation for creators to explore crypto and manipulate the worth of their work. They asked them to "hack, subvert and manipulate the worth of their creative work." When artists sell their work on Foundation, they receive 10% of the sales value as a secondary transaction.

Foundation is that the most difficult to access of other marketplaces. You'll need a particular number of community upvotes from fellow artists to even post your first artwork. The simplest method to enter Foundation is via an immediate invitation from one among the artists already on the platform.

This way, you'll avoid the queue and jump straight into selling your art. The problem of getting into here and, therefore, the cost of gas for minting each NFT means you generally find better quality art going for higher sums of cash here. That is often definitely an honest place for already established artists and creators who have a massive following on other platforms and may bring them over.

Atomicmarket

AtomicMarket may be a shared liquidity NFT market smart contract employed by multiple websites. Shared liquidity means everything listed on one market also shows on all other markets. It's a marketplace for Atomic Assets, typically for non-fungible tokens on the Eosio blockchain technology.

Anyone can utilize the Atomic Asset criterion to tokenize and make digital assets and buy, sell and auction assets utilizing the Atomic Assets marketplace. You can record your own NFTs for purchase on the AtomicMarket, and you'll search occurring listings. NFTs of well-known collections get a confirmation checkmark, making it simpler to identify the important NFTs. Malicious assemblies are excluded.

Myth Market

Myth Market is a series of online marketplaces that support various digital card brands. At the instant, its featured markets are GPK. Market (where you'll buy digital Garbage Pail Kids cards), GoPepe.Market (for GoPepe trading cards), Heroes.Market (for Blockchain Heroes trading cards), KOGS.Market (for KOGS trading cards), and Shatner.Market (for William Shatner memorabilia.)

Bakeryswap

BakerySwap is an automatic market maker (AMM) and decentralized exchange (DEX) on Binance Smart Chain (BSC). It uses a native BakerySwap token (BAKE). BakerySwap may be a multi-functional crypto hub offering a variety of decentralized finance (DeFi) services and a crypto launching pad and NFT supermarket. Its NFT supermarket hosts digital art, meme tournaments, and NFT in games that users pay for in BAKE tokens. You'll use NFTs in 'combo meals' to receive bonus BAKE tokens. Also, creating and trading your artwork is a simple, precise process.

Knownorigin

KnownOrigin is a marketplace where you can locate and buy rare digital artwork. Every digital artwork on KnownOrigin is unique and authentic. It's a platform that enables creators to sell their work to collectors who care about authenticity. The Ethereum blockchain secures it. They can also submit digital artwork as a jpeg or gif to the KnownOrigin gallery, with all files on IPFS.

Enjin Marketplace

Enjin Marketplace is a tool by which you'll explore and trade blockchain assets. It's the official marketplace for Enjin based NFTs. To date, it's enabled $43.8 million of Enjin Coin to be spent on digital assets, involving 2.1 billion NFTs. 832.7K items are traded. You can use the Enjin Wallet to list and buy gaming gadgets and collectibles. Microsoft's Azure

FAMOUS EXAMPLES OF NFT

We like having things in our possession. We are particularly fond of possessing something that we consider value, whether emotional or financial. The desire to acquire tangible goods has existed throughout history; a particular allure is linked with the real-life features of our things that attract us.

NFTs, for example, is a phenomenon that has challenged our understanding of ownership (non-fungible tokens). Ownership and validity are proven via the use of distributed ledger technology. While they are not new ideas, they have only recently made their way into the public eye, as seen by the auctioning of totally digital artworks for astronomical prices.

Adopters and opponents are two sides of the same coin regarding innovation. Whatever your point of view, we feel that NFTs are an intriguing new mode of digital ownership. We should at the very least take inspiration, regardless of whether they gain widespread acceptance.

Let's take a deeper look at 21 instances of nonlinear functional transformations and what makes them unique.

Beeple's "Everyday: The First 5000 Days"

As the first entirely NFT digital artwork to be auctioned at a major auction house (for an eye-watering $69 million), this piece represents a watershed moment in the careers of visual artists throughout the globe.

William Shatner's Memorabilia

William Shatner is a well-known actor whose professional career has spanned more than 60 years. The year 2020 will see the publication of a series of his artifacts in the form of NFTs, including a diverse collection of images taken over his illustrious career. In only nine minutes, he sold 125,000 copies.

In his own words, "They're weird things - the trash of my existence, like leaving the dust of a comet in my wake," Shatner explains.

Grimes Releases Warnymph

In late February of this year, famous musician Grimes earned $5.8 million, selling her non-monetary tokens (NFTs) in a couple of minutes. Known as "WarNymph," a collection of ten digital assets created in conjunction with her brother, they resulted from their work.

In the decade of the 2010s, Nyan Cat was a spectacular relic of the internet. The video's author decided to transform it into an NFT and auction it off to commemorate the video's tenth anniversary. According to the current exchange rate, the video was sold for a stunning 300 ETH, which was around $852,300 at writing.

Jack Dorsey's First-Ever Tweet

Jack Dorsey, the originator and CEO of Twitter, sold the very first tweet ever sent on the network (on March 21, 2006) for roughly $3 million as a non-financial transaction (NFT).

In an interview with Fortune, Dorsey said that the money earned from the NFT sale would be converted to bitcoin and then given to a charity group called GiveDirectly, which provides cash to those experiencing hardship.

Sports Collectibles: Nba Shots

Top Shot is a non-profit marketplace where basketball fans may buy, sell, and exchange memorable moments from the National Basketball Association. As of right now, the most expensive collectible exchanged is a LeBron James slam against the Houston Rockets, which went for more than $387,000 when it was transferred in 2014.

Cryptokitties: Probably One Of The First Popular Nfts Created

CryptoKitties are similar to Pokemon cards, with one crucial difference: they are built on the Ethereum blockchain. That makes them one of the most widely used NFTs today. That is perhaps the first NFT project to receive widespread acceptance, and it occurred in the year 2017. In essence, it was the world's first blockchain-based video game.

Decentraland And Virtual Worlds

When users reported generating considerable gains from the purchase and sale of digital land, Decentraland gained widespread attention in the popular media.

That is the first multiplayer role-playing metaverse built on the Ethereum blockchain, and it is currently under development. That point should be stressed: unlike in a typical online role-playing game, there is no actual contact between players in a multiplayer game.

Cryptovoxels

Blockchain-based metaverse Cryptovoxels is a mash-up of social networking, gaming, and commerce powered by blockchain technology. In its own words, the platform is "a user-owned virtual world that runs on the Ethereum blockchain." Users may exchange land parcels, set up art galleries, and engage with other players on the game's server—something along the lines of Minecraft but with a greater emphasis on Bitcoin.

Andrés Reisinger's Virtual Design Objects

Andrés Reisinger, an Argentinian designer, has discovered a unique niche for his creative output: he offers non-functional furniture (NFTs). His most costly sculpture was sold for little about $70,000, which was a small profit. Even though they are not physically functional furniture, these things may be put in open worlds, such as Decentraland or Minecraft.

Rtfkt's Digital Sneakers

RTFKT is generating a lot of noise in the fashion world. Even though the customers who purchase his NFT sneakers will never be able to wear them, they are still prepared to spend upwards of $10,000 for a pair of his shoes.

In March of 2021, RTFKT launched a pair of shoes that he collaborated on with another artist named Fewocious, and they were able to gather $3,1 million in sales in a matter of minutes, according to reports.

Nike's Nft Sneakers

Nike Inc. sought for and was granted a patent in 2019 that will enable them to remain at the forefront of the NFT craze for the foreseeable future.

Nike's patent enables them to combine actual and virtual footwear, allowing them to monetize on both fronts simultaneously. Users of virtual shoes will have the option of being replicated and made in the real world.

Share Tokenized Tickets With Your Audience.

NFTs are more than just art treasures; the technology can represent any unique information, including event tickets, which is why they are becoming more popular.

NFT tickets may now be purchased at a special price via various sites, which event organizers can access. More crucially, this will allow them to gain from any potential resale of the event, as mentioned earlier.

Gary Vaynerchuk Is Launching Art Nfts Linked To Ethereum.

In recent months, serial entrepreneur Gary Vaynerchuk developed his NFT collection, dubbed "VeeFriends," which consists of a series of over 10,000 tokens and is available for purchase.

Even though these tokens do not possess any creative quality, Vaynerchuk's strategy relies on selling users' access to exclusive privileges. Following the scarcity of the ticket, the individuals who hold these tokens will be entitled to various advantages, services, gifts, and interactions with Vaynerchuk.

Nft For Good

This is another example of NFT technology being used for other than just acquiring ownership of the artwork. A charitable organization supported by Binance Charity and its partners that runs on the Binance Smart Chain is known as Binance Smart Chain. NFT for Good enables individuals to sell their artwork while raising awareness about humanitarian causes.

Taco Bell's Charitable Nfts

Recently, Taco Bell began experimenting with the NFT trend by commissioning a series of GIFs and pictures based on meals from their menu to be shared on social media. Their tokens were completely sold out within minutes on the debut day.

Their NFTs were reasonably priced—$1 apiece, to be exact. Even though they haven't earned a lot of income, they have attracted much interest on social media. More significantly, all of the proceeds were given to the Taco Bell Foundation, which is the charitable arm of the restaurant chain's parent company.

Unstoppable Domains

Unstoppable Domains' mission, a blockchain business, is to provide direct access to—crypto domains from all common browsers, a functionality that has formerly been inaccessible due to technical limitations. Once a part is claimed, it is minted as an NFT, giving the claimant complete ownership and control over the domain.

Real Estate Tokenization

Aside from the financial sector, blockchain is making its way into the real estate business, enabling investors to acquire property shares by tokenizing them. Asset owners benefit from tokenization since it allows them to sell their property more quickly and effectively, while investors benefit from increased transparency and liquidity.

The tokenization of an asset is breaking it into "shares" or "tokens" to make it more easily traded. In the case of an investment with a surface area of 1,000 square meters that costs around $1,000,000, you may split it into individual square meters and sell them separately for $1,000 per share, for example.

Licenses And Certifications

The paper certifications and licenses that we use to validate our skill sets are still in use today. Blockchain technology enables us to establish unquestionably reliable and unfalsifiable evidence of a degree or other certification acquired.

Businesses and organizations would stand to gain significantly from having access to licenses that include the functionality of NFTs. With this technique, there is less need for verification and record-keeping procedures.

Why Nfts Can Offer Marketing Opportunities For Fmcg Brands

It's hardly unexpected that the mania around NFTs has prompted many companies to try to cash in on the trend. To provide an example, Pringles has developed CryptoCrisp, which the company describes as their "newest virtual NFT flavor."

One such taste sold for a whopping $2,542 when offered for sale. Recently, the brand produced another 50 CryptoCrisp NFTs designed by artist Vasya Kolotusha and manufactured by the company.

The NFT toilet paper (yes, you read it correctly) produced by Procter & Gamble is another bizarre example. While these instances may seem silly to some, these are just a few of the companies that have received substantial media attention due to their decision to experiment with blockchain technology, which has undoubtedly increased their sales.

HOW TO LET THEM BE POPULAR

Direction To Becoming Successful In The Nft Market

Making digital art is not a new concept; it has been around since the early 1980s when computer developers created an art program utilized by the digital artist Harold Cohen. Nowadays, producing digital art is as simple as opening your paint program or taking a picture with your phone, adding a filter, and then uploading it for everyone to see.

You may already be a digital artist and be unaware of it. If you shoot images on your phone or draw on your paperwork, you need to polish your skills.

If you desire to become an NFT artist, you must follow some fundamental steps. Being an NFT artist is simpler than you think; but, building a following and being consistent may be difficult.

1. Choose the Kind of Art Work To Create

Before you begin your long and thrilling path of becoming an NFT artist, you need to pick out what type of artwork you will make. Having a constant specialization while making your digital art may help you develop your skills and enable your audience to realize what artwork you generate.

Suppose you are a digital artist who appreciates generating digital images of prominent sports levels, for example. In that case, your audience will recognize that you enjoy sports and develop work related to sports. However, if you decide to create a digital artwork of a unicorn one day, you risk confusing your viewers. That could be useful or bad, but it's essential to maintain consistency in your style so that people can learn to love or hate your work.

Choosing your art specialty should be very straightforward. Maybe you already have a thing you create for fun? It might be nature photos, cats, doodles - the sky is the limit when picking your specialization. My primary advice for developing your niche is to select a subject you like creating. Instead of choosing something hot or trendy, you may not experience the success you're searching for.

The fantastic thing about NFT art is that you can genuinely make anything into a one-of-a-kind masterpiece. You may produce music, videos, paintings, drawings, images, basically anything! So, be authentic to who you stand and your interests, then let your audience determine what they enjoy and what they don't like.

2. Choose How You Will Create Your Art

After determining your art niche, you must select how to create that art. For example, if you are a nature photographer, you may not need to purchase a picture editing application. However, if you are beginning from scratch or need to change your artwork, you will need to utilize editing software.

- Image editing software: There are a few standard solutions among NFT artists to generate or modify digital photos. Adobe Illustrator, Lightroom, and Photoshop are all solid options for picture editing.

- GIF and Pixel Image Creation Software: Adobe Photoshop (GIFs) and Piskel (animated sprites and pixel art)

There is, of course, other software available. But, finally, the sort of software you need is determined by your art style and personal goals for your art pieces.

3. Choose a Digital Art File Type

CATEGORY	FILE FORMAT
Video	MP4
Image	WEBP, PNG, JPG, GIF
Audio	WAV, MP3

Once you've decided what kind of NFT art you're going to make, you'll need to determine what file format you will use to create it. There are several file formats for each style of art.

Here is a list of possible digital art file formats for creating NFT art:

All you have to do is decide what kind of art you want to create and then proceed from there, making sure to choose the optimal file format for your purposes. Furthermore, you can always add unlocked content to your NFT art, which means they will have access to the best quality format you supply when someone buys it. That way, you won't have to produce the token as a big file, which may cause problems loading on specific markets.

4. Make Your Own Digital Artwork

Now that you've determined your art niche, how you will create your art, and the file format in which you'll save your craft, it is time to make your first piece of NFT art!

Keep in mind that your non-fungible artwork does not have to be perfect. Every day, the most important thing you can do is create art. Just because you develop new skills every day does not imply posting contemporary art every day. Instead, you should make new art every day for practice and get your creative juices flowing. Take, for example, the well-known NFT artist Beeple, who just sold a $69 million artwork featuring 5000 pieces of his art that he created every day for over 13 years!

Creating NFT art should be something you enjoy and are passionate about because becoming a successful NFT artist takes time and a lot of patience.

5. Market Your NFT Art

Things are starting to heat up now! When you're ready to sell your first part of NFT art, you'll need to decide which marketplace is best for your collection. There are several markets to select from, each with advantages and disadvantages. Furthermore, new markets will emerge as the world of NFTs and NFT art evolves.

You can sell your NFT art in the following marketplace: SuperRare.co, NiftyGateway, Rarible, and OpenSea.io.

When initially selling your NFT, I recommend making an account on all sites and publishing your work to more specific areas like OpenSea and Rarible. You would then apply to be an artist for the other sites needing application evaluation after some workup and a few pieces (SuperRare and NiftGateway).

Remember: When building your marketplace accounts, be sure to include all of your social media connections and personal websites in your profile. That enables individuals who find you to follow you on social media, increasing your following.

6. Build Your Following

Okay, this is the most crucial step. There are several methods to establish a following to aid in promoting your NFT art; but, what are the most excellent ways to build a following? It would help if you amassed a following or an audience.

To gain a following for your NFT artwork, you must create a brand around it or establish your brand while using your NFT artwork at every step of the way. In addition, participating in the NFT community via forums, podcasts, and blogs can help you create credibility and trust with your audience. Using social media is also an excellent idea.

This phase is vital since your brand's reputation is critical to your art's worth. The more individuals learn about you, the more they understand you and what you stand for. That makes purchasing a piece of your artwork easier for both sides. Consider this: would you instead buy something from someone you know and trust or from a random stranger you don't know anything about? The answer is straightforward.

You may use many approaches to establish a loyal following; let's go through some of the best ones.

Social Media

In my view, one of the simplest methods to begin building a following for your NFT art projects is via social media. To make the most of social media, be sure to join as many as you can and make a lot of noise. Once you're up and going, try to publish 1-2 times a day. You should be submitting your artwork and soliciting feedback, as well as providing input to other artists and assisting them whenever possible.

For six months, upload one piece of artwork every day across all of your social media platforms and watch what happens. Using appropriate hashtags to help your social media postings reach the right people can help you attract more followers who interact with your posts, which is precisely what you want.

Here are some trendy hashtags I've spotted on social media that are expected to acquire popularity in the next years. #NONFUNGIBLETOKENS, #DIGITALARTIST, #DIGITALART, #ETH, #ETHEREUM, #CRYPTOCURRENCY, #NFTCOLLECTOR, #NFTCOMMUNITY, #NFTARTIST, #NFTART, #NFTs, #NFT.

When creating your social media account, decide whether you want to use your account or create a separate account for your artwork. That is the scenario I mentioned earlier about personal branding vs. product branding. Whatever you decide, make sure to fill out your bios effectively, including details that describe you as an NFT artist, the type of art you create, and links to any other social media accounts or personal websites you may have.

Essentially, you want to build a webbed network to reach people across all platforms. As a result, try to keep your social media names consistent across all platforms; this aids in brand recognition.

Maintaining social media can be time-consuming. That is why it is best to start slowly and not get too caught up in how numerous supporters you have or how many likes your post receives. Instead, just be yourself and focus on providing the content. Growing your following takes time, patience, and consistency, but I know you can do it! Remember, we all started from scratch.

Websites

Aside from social media, you might take a more technical approach and build your website. However, even if you opt to make your website, it's still a good idea to be engaged on social media and utilize it to supplement traffic to your website, so people can see what you're giving.

If used correctly, a website may benefit your NFT art. For example, you may showcase your NFT art collection on your website by providing links to your art's marketplace, establishing a blog that attracts organic visitors, or even offering a service like making bespoke artwork for customers or teaching others how to produce their art. The possibilities are limitless.

Finally, if you are competent with computer technology, developing your website is viable for expanding your audience. You may also hire someone to create a website for you.

7. Engage in the NFT Community

It's time to tie everything together. It's time to get active now that you've set up your social media accounts and your website (if you have one). Spend time in your community answering questions, asking questions, and taking polls. For example, if you're a Rarible or OpenSea.io artist, go to their forums and start reading through the posts. Respond to any inquiries you feel comfortable answering, and if more information is needed, direct them to your blog or a YouTube video you created on the subject. Help others, and they will help you.

Never be afraid to seek clarification. If you're stuck, try to find an answer on your own or ask a member of the community for assistance. Indeed, if you're asking the question, it's very likely that someone else is as well.

Overall, gaining a following requires passion, patience, consistency, and selflessness. First, you must be passionate, patient while remaining consistent and selfless to assist others in solving their problems.

8. Maintain Consistency

The importance of consistency cannot be overstated. It makes no difference what you do in life; character is essential. If you intend to become a successful NFT artist overnight, I wish you the best of luck — you'll need it. Without consistency, you have little trust, and no one cares.

You must explain to others that you are serious about what you do and the NFT art you make. Beeple is a prime example. It took him almost 13 years to achieve significant success, but it was well worth the wait.

COMPARISON OF TRADITIONAL AND DIGITAL AREA INVESTMENT

We will compare digital land to traditional land investing in understanding better the opportunities of investing in digital land assets through NFT.

A key feature of blockchain innovation is eliminating intermediaries and the additional time and cost.

Digital land NFTs can be handled by smart contracts, which run on the blockchain to receive and send immutable transactions. A smart contract automatically runs and completes tasks within the pre-determined terms of the agreement.

Smart contracts offer ease of use. You can agree without trust and automatically release the NFT from the seller to the buyer after the funds have been deposited.

In comparison, traditional land requires a significant investment of time and effort, and multiple intermediaries typically sign contracts. With physical resources, specialists are usually needed to determine the asset's value, worth, and condition.

Digital assets can be purchased and sold quickly: no visits are required to investigate the quality and site of physical support. The acquisition cost is reduced to a small fraction of a conventional land investment.

The individuality of the digital asset is encoded in the NFT, and buyer/seller exchanges are handled automatically by a blockchain-based smart contract. Time-consuming title searches and property history checks are replaced with rapid trades.

Trading assets via smart contract-based NFTs offers so many benefits that the industry will likely evolve in the future to permit the purchase of physical land and real estate.

That would reduce costs and simplify the issuance of title insurance for banks and all parties entangled in the dealing. But for now, digital land investments stand uniquely arranged to benefit from the key advantages of investing and transacting on the blockchain.

Cash

Liquidity calculates how easy it is to transform an asset into cash.

Land and real estate are often big, illiquid investments. They require a significant amount of funds to purchase and are relatively illiquid.

You can't cash out your investment where and when you want. There are many restrictions, permits, and challenges you may face as you develop or sell the land, and it may take years to sell land or property.

Because they are digital assets, NFTs are much easier to trade and convert to cash than traditional land and real estate assets.

They can also be coined - created - on one outlet and traded on multiple markets. That makes more opportunities for potential buyers from all international markets than is feasible with traditional assets.

And as the NFT investment market matures and develops, opportunities to borrow against your digital terrestrial asset are likely to appear. Digital asset securities are in the early phases, but options exist to use them as collateral.

While initially, only cryptocurrencies like Ethereum could serve as collateral for a loan, digital assets, including NFTs for art, collectibles, and occupation names, are now contained as collateral-worthy assets.

The inclusion of digital assets as collateral indicates that as the NFT and DeFi sectors persist to evolve and mature, the liquidity of digital assets will expand over time.

No Maintenance Cost

Maintaining and maintaining traditional land and property can be expensive; you will be required to pay property taxes and other expenses.

You may have to pay to keep the land or property, such as regularly mowing the lawn or cleaning and repairing the property. If left undeveloped, the site's quality will deteriorate, wildlife will take over, and environmental problems such as flooding or leaks may occur.

In addition, land alone does not generate income. Developing the ground to a point where it generates income could be expensive and dangerous as an investment. For these explanations, it can be tough to get a loan on vacant land; there's a good chance you'll have to pay upfront, committing significant funds to the investment.

Digital assets, on the other hand, do not require maintenance and upkeep costs. You can choose to hold on to your purchase as its value increases over time as the digital platform grows or sell or develop your digital asset to develop revenue without extra charges.

Phergyson, an avid digital land dealer who proudly names herself a "faux real estate magnet," says owning digital land is "definitely" easier than possessing real estate. There are "no closing costs or regular costs for taxes and repairs. And, most importantly, no plumbing."

Traditional Land Use

The government can restrict the service of a land asset, with rules for the type of property or ways the land can be developed.

If you're buying land for residential or commercial development, you'll first need to ensure the ground has all the necessary permits and check the conversion regulations.

There may be instances where land-use restrictions may limit how the owner can use the land. Whether for horticulture, recreational purposes, or real estate development, obtaining permits and papers is often lengthy.

The availability of utilities could also influence expansion opportunities. How comfortable is setting up a sewer system, running water, electricity, gas, phone, cable, and internet?

Depending on the location of your land, access to necessary utilities could be expensive and limit potential development.

Digital Land Use

Digital land, however, offers multiple options to monetize the investment that are not present in traditional land; monetization also needs less investment and is potentially less restrictive.

As with customary land, the value of virtual land is based on where it is discovered, how much digital traffic it draws, and how owners choose to develop the land.

Let's take a look at the quickest growing NFT play in the current market, Decentraland, as an instance of the revenue-generating opportunities available to digital land investors.

According to Republic, famous expansions within Decentraland include:

- Art galleries where owners can sell their NFT digital art, Cryptokitties, and other NFT collectibles
- Casinos, where players can win MANA, the cryptocurrency that facilitates the purchase of digital land.
- Gaming sites
- Brand-sponsored content, such as the Atari arcade that features games that can be played in Decentraland
- Music venues where musicians can play and hold concerts

Digital land can also be leased, allowing owners to generate cash flow and income from tenants or other utilities.

For example, Alien Worlds, one of the most extensive digital land NFT games globally run in partnership with Binance, allows players to generate real income by permitting other players to come and mine from your plot.

These are just rare examples of the monetization possibilities of digital land. As more games and outlets emerge with digital land NFTs, the sky limits the type of virtual revenue landowners could pursue.

Virtual land allows the buyer to quickly develop and pursue multiple revenue generation opportunities they genuinely enjoy. The property can be made instantly in the virtual world, removing all the barriers associated with distance, time, and space in traditional investments.

Easy International And Borderless Entry

As in actual life, virtual real estate is about location, location, location. In traditional and digital real estate, value is heavily influenced by location and the amount of traffic the area attracts.

With physical assets, many aspects influence location and traffic entirely out of the buyer's control.

How distant or close an airport is, whether or not it has important landmarks that attract international users and visitors, reassurance of access, infrastructure, regulations for international travel, and unforeseen global events such as the Covid pandemic can all recreate a part.

In virtual platforms, people can visit immediately worldwide with their avatars. Virtual conventions, where parties can gather to watch a sporting event, network, or pitch ideas to investors in Crypto Valley, can draw a crowd and drive traffic to your location, increasing its value at no additional cost.

Annual Percentage Return And Roi

Revenue growth for video games is expected to increase from over $159.3 billion in 2020 to $189.3 billion in 2021. And from 2020 to 2027, the global enterprise is fixed for a compound annual growth rate (CAGR) of 12.9%.

And as more people and brands join the metaverse to enjoy a unique, borderless experience and broadcast to users, the value of digital land assets will continue to grow.

Compare that to the years spent obtaining planning permission and inventing traditional land investments, and it's obvious where the potential for higher annual percentage returns (APY) and ROI lies.

In 2018, Decentraland made headlines when digital land investors' returns soared 500%. Since then, the decentralized virtual world has continued to gain ground: digital land sold in early 2019 at Decentraland for $500 is now trading at over $7,860, with an ROI of 1,572%.

Decentraland's cryptocurrency, MANA, jumped in 2021 and has been in a bullish cycle for over a year. Decentraland is one of the world's most popular multiplayer games and the fastest growing blockchain, NFT, and digital terrestrial virtual world.

As more players succeed in the gaming ecosystem, the value of the digital asset increases. Low supply and exponentially increasing demand can drive up prices.

Youtuber LiteLiger shared a few examples of NFT investments in digital land that have increased significantly in value over a few months:

The Sandbox is an Ethereum-based game supported by institutional investors.

LiteLiger purchased a plot of Sandbox land for $100.

Eight months later, LiteLiger received offers to purchase $650 worth of its Sandbox land.

These phenomenal increases in digital land prices show the potential increase in valuation for digital land NFTs. The buyer purchases the ground in the early stages of game development and releases before gaining more significant traction in the marketplace.

Where you have a specified amount of land on one of these platforms, and it eventually attracts thousands if not millions of users, there is the potential for huge retrievals; the importance of your digital land assets can only rise as network effects, users, and brand dominance increase.

Tips For Investing In Digital Territory

The value of the games industry exceeds both music and movies combined. And with the most extensive application of NFTs in the gaming world, terrestrial digital NFTs offer a significant investment opportunity.

Early adopters will benefit from all the inbound trading in the metaverse. But as with any investment, there's no assurance that your digital asset will perform nicely and generate a sizable ROI.

So what are the critical properties of high-growth digital ground NFTs? And what stand the indicators that the virtual outlet is destined to grow? While there is a lot of money to be created in the NFT space, investors should comprehend the value drivers for an asset class before making an allocation.

NFT AND REAL ESTATE

There is nothing more fundamental in today's world than technology, and NFTs are proving it in a disruptive way. A universe is no longer a niche whose sales have exceeded 250 million dollars and continue to grow day by day.

Collecting, selling, investing, and earning are the keywords behind NFT. The capital is increasing more and more, and so is the interest in these products. How does an intangible asset that everyone can see achieve such value? How and who can create and sell their works in NFTs? What applications and results can they generate in the future? Is this a stable market in which to invest? Selling, collecting, investing, and earning, these and many others, are the possibilities that make non-fungible tokens a real technological bubble that is interesting and appealing to many. An interest that will not be extinguished will find more and more markets and uses. So many famous names have helped make NFTs even more popular. Non-fungible tokens are a unique resource of their kind. And in fact, everything about the interest and value of non-fungible tokens refers to uniqueness. What the non-fungible token creates is verifiable digital scarcity.

NFTs can be a revolution in terms of the many possibilities.

Nfts And Application Areas

Since Mike Winkelmann, aka Beeple, sold his digital work for just under $70 million, NFTs have become popular with the general public. More precisely, on March 11, 2021, at 4 p.m., what can now be called a true NFT mania exploded. NFT stands for Non-Fungible Token, a piece of digital information recorded on the blockchain. These tokens are called non-fungible precisely because they are not interchangeable; they are unique and cannot be divided. What is special about NFTs is their uniqueness and non-replicability, which makes non-fungible tokens appealing. These tokens are cryptographic, meaning they represent something unique, such as a work of art, music, or any other collectible, and digitally certify ownership. Before NFTs, it was nearly impossible to authenticate and own a digital asset.

Although it is a phenomenon that exploded recently, it is impossible to say that non-fungible-tokens have just been born as their origins are related to bitcoins and the projects delivered to manipulate them. The history of NFTs is recent, and with many branches, it is still being written, and it is continuously expanding with a considerable turnover. The decisive year for the rise of the first NFTs is 2017, when Ethereum begins to increase its importance by announcing its collection of Meme Pepe and then with the Cryptopunks project.

Non-fungible tokens today have branches in several areas, including:

- Sports. One of the first investors within the NFT world was Mark Cuban, owner of an NBA franchise. Since then, the world's top professional basketball league, several soccer clubs, and many other sports have realized the importance of NFTs. NBA Top Shot is designed for true fans and collectors and is one of the first and most critical NFT projects in sports. Owning an exclusive video of an action performed by your favorite player unmistakably is not a small thing. Sorare, on the other hand, empowers you to play fantasy soccer, having ownership of the purchased stickers and creating real teams. Sport with non-fungible-tokens opens to fans in a completely new and different way.

- Fashion. Digital fashion is today the vanguard of fashion, limited editions, and much more make possible unique fashion shows and collections and brings a high level of liquidity to a fast-growing sector. Digital objects, in the case of fashion, can be paired with NFTs, but that's just the first step. In the future, NFTs will make fashion.

- Collectibles. Collecting based on NFTs has its backbone economy. It opens up to digital media in a completely different way than before, coming to meet the generations of the future. Under the name of collecting, different visions are brought forward: the desire and pleasure of interacting and owning unique objects or the willingness to invest; collectors worldwide love to own works of art whose value, over time, can increase and generate capital.

- Art. Art has always generated interest and is fertile ground for investors. Now that NFTs have entered the market, there is no turning back. Collecting is no longer the preserve of a single privileged class, auction houses no longer hold a monopoly, and digital artists have found a way to profit from their creations. The NFT era is a new era for art.

- Gaming. One of the industries that first believed in non-fungible-tokens and received significant benefits is gaming. The market was ready; gamers have always been familiar with buying, selling, and exchanging digital assets. The problem was that they were buying something they couldn't claim ownership of until now. The non-fungible tokens purchased directly are verifiable and authentic. They create value for the players themselves and lead to new forms of collecting; in this sector, NFTs are not just a trend, a fad but something that is already revolutionizing the market.

- Real Estate. The digital real estate sector provides a cost of land production that borders on zero. Its actual value is connected to its uniqueness, to the fact of owning an asset or, better, an original and unique token. Here the convergence between real and digital has its highest expression. It becomes a thin line of demarcation, almost impossible to see. In places like

Decentraland, it is possible to have your store with digital assets linked to a clothing chain and much more. Several artists have created NFT villas and collections to visit and actual virtual events. On these marketplaces, the value of a property or a piece of land becomes much higher than the real one, and digital property is sold in a second without any need of a middleman.

- Music. The first great passage from physical to digital music has been a lost race for many entrepreneurial realities that don't seem to want to let this further innovation escape. From Mike Shinoda of Linkin Park to Kings of Leon up to Grimes, Elon Musk's partner, many artists are betting on NFT in a reliable and evident way.

Create an identity identifier. Digitizing documents of any kind while maintaining their uniqueness is a unique method of eliminating the possibility of fraud and creating a digital space where individual identity is recognized and protected.

These and many other undiscovered areas are the fertile ground where these tokens are exploding, generating a multi-million dollar business. If the classic economy has always been based on the concept of scarcity to define the at, the network has undermined this concept. The web market is overabundant and disintermediated. For this, the NFTs are born to bring back the value of the assets of the market inside the Internet. With their demonstrable uniqueness, NFTs are objects, works of art, music, and more that bring the concept of scarcity and perceived value of identity into a world like the hyper-productive web.

There are multiple marketplaces where you can trade or produce your tokens. Among the most popular and most used in different areas there are Opensea, SuperRare, Nifty Gateway, NBA Top Shot, Sorare, and Rarible are just some of the most famous. Specifically for Real Estate, everything revolves around platforms like Decentraland, Superworld, and The Sandbox. We are witnessing the convergence of natural and digital. That is because digital real estate has a cost of land production practically zero, and its value is linked to perceived scarcity precisely because it is NFT.

Today creating a store, a house, or any digital asset connected to Real Estate is possible and convenient. Thanks to smart contracts, it is, in fact, likely to acquire and establish ownership of different digital realities. Thanks to NFTs, it is possible to own a digital house to insert virtual works, always in ERC-20, or to proceed like the big brands, which open virtual stores where it is possible to buy tokens of everything displayed there. Virtual events within Decentraland, for example, can be much more profitable and require less effort than real ones. Because of this, many companies realize that having a virtual store allows for staggering sales. Overpricing is often questioned when in reality, the value of virtual land is potentially higher: a Decentraland store and storefront will enable you to reach many more people than the same store on a real street.

Demand and collective confidence in the value of virtual real estate is growing, and the change is happening fast. Another advantage of digital real estate is the ability to transfer ownership of the token and what is inside it in a practical and fast way. This transferability is much quicker and less expensive, and most importantly, does not require intermediaries. Transactions on Ethereum platforms are based on a transparent, unalterable, immutable, and unchangeable consensus mechanism.

It is the first time users worldwide can create NFTs that can be immediately available in marketplaces. Here people can buy, trade, sell and auction NFTs. The importance of these possessions lies in the reality that we are moving from sales within closed marketplaces to the possibilities offered by a marketplace with an open and accessible economy. The comfort with which users can create and trade NFTs worldwide through the blockchain is impressive and can bring many changes to the real estate industry. Transferability allows NFTs to be sold at a higher price than the real thing:

- Digital property can be sold in minutes without the need for a broker.

- Registration is self-contained.

- The property needs no maintenance.

Moreover, thanks to the smart contracts that regulate the transactions, each NFT provides a unique and non-falsifiable signature. The owners can then prove the provenance, making this purchase a more profitable and realistic investment. The virtual property built by contemporary artist Krista Kim is called "Mars House" and is a property that sold for $500,000. Mars House has a design conceived by rounded lines and edges and furnished with fine glass furniture. Kim collaborated with musician Jeff Schroeder of Smashing Pumpkins, who composed the ambient soundtrack introducing the virtual property.

The owner of this virtual home receives the individual file of the project that can be uploaded to three-dimensional worlds like Decentraland and experience its augmented reality. An artist like Kim believes that the NFT real estate market can parallel the real one. Also, the home's furniture can be built in real-life replication by select Italian glass furniture manufacturers.

Real estate is notoriously slow to adopt new technologies. However, the very nature of real estate makes it ideal for blockchain applications: it is immobile and readily available to third parties with blockchain-based claims on it, such as collateral. The world of digital assets is expanding, and we are only now starting to see every part of daily life and business activities converted into a computer-readable format. Money is already digital; think that only 8% of the world's currency materializes in the form of cash. Through blockchain, exchanges, transactions, and sales will begin to have fewer problems. Through these digitized platforms, key stakeholders will see increased speed and lower transaction costs, along with an increase in available data. Transaction transparency and privacy protection are essential when it comes to creating a healthy environment for buyers, sellers, and real estate agents.

NFTS IN SPORTS

Collectibles have long piqued the interest of the sports industry. Whether it's assets from sports video games, sports cards, or a famous player's jersey, NFTs can represent them all on the blockchain.

The following is a list of NFTs that have made their way into the sports world:

- The NBA with NBA Top Shot is number one.

- .Football (soccer in the United States) with Sorare

- Formula 1 with F1 Delta Time is number three.

- Rob Gronkowski's Championship Series NFTs in American Football

- Baseball with the World Series Champions of Major League Baseball Virtual Worlds of NFTs

As the globe gets increasingly digital, some people aren't frightened to start a new life in a digital cosmos. Many games exist as digital replicas of the natural world to fill these voids.

Then, as these simulations get more popular, the value players assign to their assets in these worlds rises. What better way to own those in-game assets but with NFTs!

A list of Virtual Worlds with NFTs:

- Somnium Space

- Axie Infinity

- DecentraLand

These platforms can have millions of dollars in monthly trade volumes for their in-game assets thanks to the creation of NFTs. These NFTs can be used in various ways inside the open-world gameplay that many of these worlds provide.

Why Are Celebrities Embracing Nfts?

NFTs can be utilized as ownership certificates for one-of-a-kind assets with psychological worth.

Given fans' devotion to their favorite celebrities, it's easy to see how digital products created and published by them could be considered valuable.

It's more like a chain reaction as more celebrities realize how easy it is to make money in the NFT industry and seize this current opportunity.

Nba Top Shot

NBA Top Shot is now the largest NFT marketplace, with sales exceeding $500 million since its launch.

NBA Top Shot sells'moments,' which are similar to trading cards. A moment is a digital collectible in an NFT that contains a video of a particular basketball highlight.

Each moment includes:

- The Highlights video
- The player's and team's artwork
- Statistics about the game and the players
- The description of the highlight
- A unique serial number.

The popularity of the highlight determines the worth of the moment. Some moments are commonplace, while others are rare and valuable.

Several moments have sold for thousands of dollars, the most costly being $208,000.

Some players collect to connect with NBA icons, while others collect to sell and profit.

What Do You Get When You Purchase An Nft?

Since an NFT can have just a single owner at any one time, when you purchase an NFT, you buy the exclusive ownership of a particular digital asset. Nonetheless, this doesn't mean that you own the exclusive rights to who gets access to look at or share that specific artwork.

Take, for instance, the most expensive NFT sold to date: Beeple's Everyday: The First five thousand Days, a 5,000-piece digital collage. Vignesh Sundaresan is the owner of this NFT, the founder of the Metapurse NFT project, and the bitcoin ATM provider, Bitaccess.

While Sundaresan is the legal official owner of this NFT, the image has been shared, copied, and seen by millions of potential buyers around the world, and that's fair game! Therefore, when you buy an NFT, it's a little like purchasing an autographed print. The NFT is usually signed exclusively to you, but anyone can view the work.

An NFT can be any digital asset. So far, they have included:

1. Artworks

2. GIFs

3. In-game purchases

4. Tweets

5. Songs

6. Domain names

7. Essays

Why Would Anybody Buy A Non-Fungible Token?

The more you try to understand the weird and magical world of non-fungible tokens, the more you ask yourself why anybody would buy an NFT. In any case, there are a few reasons why those who have spare cash are opting to invest.

There is nothing like a perceived sense of rarity to increase the value of a particular item. Since NFTs can only have one proprietor, they create this impression of scarcity by the bucketload. That will encourage potential buyers to fixate on a particular piece, and they would begin to worry that another person may become the exclusive owner of an NFT they want.

You may think of it like when you find a pair of sneakers you want to buy and the website tells you that there's only 'one pair left.' For most of us, this increases your sense of scarcity, and it will make you want to purchase it before it runs out of stock

Collectability

Like swapping baseball cards on the playground, NFTs primarily trade cards for the super-rich. While these cards have no inherent value other than what the market assigns them, their unstable worth makes their collectability and trading value like a high-risk gambling game. Therefore, it's easy to compare the NFT and the art market.

Unlike the art market, NFTs give artists more autonomy as they no longer rely on auction houses or galleries to sell their work. By removing the middle-man from the picture, artists can sell their artworks directly to end-users and rake in more profits by doing so.

Why Art Nfts Are Growing

Many people have been perplexed as to why NFT art has been flourishing at such a rapid pace recently. Some people are starting to realize that NFTs help further democratize the art market by allowing upcoming artists and artists with Internet access in any country in the world to get their art creations to the market and enable other non-artists to support artists directly.

Nfts As A Vehicle For Positive Change

We must understand that nothing is more valuable than human inventiveness. While there have been continuous disputes concerning the energy usage of NFTs and cryptocurrencies in general, the economic benefit of funding artists' creative work across genres is apparent. I haven't heard many people discuss how much help there is in removing barriers between creativity and commercialization. Many people also don't talk about how many artists and creatives can now do a job doing what they love.

No one has done the study or done the math yet. Still, I'd want to see a comparison of the resources required by the global centralized banking system and electricity against decentralized finance and blockchains. When we consider that there are no actual bank branches constructed of steel, concrete, electricity, or building machinery, I assume that the blockchain network consumes far less energy.

Should You Buy Nfts?

Since you can buy NFTs, does that mean you should? It depends on your own choices.

"NFTs are risky because their future value is uncertain, and we don't yet have a lot of history to judge their performance. Since NFTs are still evolving, investing amounts you can spare is wise.

In other words, investing in NFTs is essentially a personal decision. It may be worth buying some if you have some spare money, especially if a piece holds meaning for you.

But note that an NFT's value is based entirely on what someone else is willing to pay for it. Hence, demand will drive the price rather than technical, fundamental, or economic indicators, which typically influence stock prices and generally form the basis for investor demand.

That implies that an NFT may resale for less than the price you paid for it. Or you may not see a buyer resell it at all if no one wants to pay for it.

Also, know that NFTs are subject to capital gains taxes—like when you sell stocks at a profit. Since they are considered collectibles, they may not receive the preferential long-term capital gains rates that stores do and may even be taxed at a higher collectibles tax rate. However, the

IRS has not yet ruled on the types of NFTs considered for tax purposes. Know that the cryptocurrencies used to purchase the NFT may also be taxed if they have increased in value since you bought them; this implies that you may want to consult a tax professional when considering adding NFTs to your portfolio.

Approach Nfts Like You Would Make Any Investment:

Make sure you carry out proper research.

Understand the risks—including that you might lose all of your investing dollars—and if you decide to take the bold step.

Proceed with a healthy dose of caution.

Are Nfts The Same As Crypto?

NFTs have been present in the bitcoin world since their creation. But don't be fooled: they're not the same thing.

NFTs are not interchangeable (i.e., non-fungible) like Bitcoin or Ethereum, even though they both contain a digital certificate of authenticity recorded in a blockchain.

Cryptocurrencies like Ethereum, on the other hand, can earn interest and be borrowed, lent, and sold in any number of brick-and-mortar institutions across the United States. That is referred to as DeFi in its broadest sense (or decentralized finance). Anyone can participate in DeFi by using what is known as "dapps" (or decentralized apps). Coinbase, for example, is one of the most popular cryptocurrency trading platforms, with crypto investors at the helm (Except for Hawaii, it serves 49 states.)

So, where do NFTs fall into all of this? At least one DeFi platform plans to accept NFTs as loan collateral due to their value in the cryptocurrency industry.

How Is An Nft Different From Cryptocurrency?

We know by now that NFT stands for non-fungible token. We also know that it's generally built using a similar kind of programming as cryptocurrency, like Ethereum or Bitcoin, but that's where the similarity ends.

Cryptocurrencies and physical money are "fungible," which implies that they can be traded or exchanged for one another. They are also equal in value—one dollar is always worth another dollar, so one Bitcoin is always similar. The fungibility of cryptos makes it a trusted channel for conducting transactions on the blockchain.

But NFTs are different. Each artwork has a digital signature that makes it impossible for NFTs to be exchanged for or equal to one another (hence, non-fungible). One NBA Top Shot clip, for example, is not similar to EVERYDAYS simply because they're both NFTs. (One NBA Top Shot clip isn't even necessarily equal to another NBA Top Shot clip, for that matter.)

Pros And Cons Of Nfts

The worth of some NFTs has skyrocketed in the past year and captured a lot of attention from the investment community. There are some advantages to consider when buying and using NFTs:

- Smart contracts. That implies that a set of coded commands built into the blockchain can guarantee that creators and artists get paid based on the use and resale of their artwork in the future.
- It makes some physical collectibles (such as art) with a long track record of gaining value, and digital art could showcase the same price appreciation.
- Selling and Buying digital assets as NFTs yields access to potentially far more buyers and sellers than in the past.
- However, there exist some other reasons why you may not invest in and use NFTs:
- Since most NFTs stand for static assets that don't generate any income on their own, they are generally valued by subjective metrics such as buyer demand. Therefore, sky-high prices may not last forever, and the NFT could lose considerable value.
- Creating and selling NFTs is not free, and the fees can skyrocket to more than an NFT valued by other users on a marketplace.

NFTS AND THE MUSIC INDUSTRY

Non-Fungible-Tokens (NFTs) have had the music world quiet. Well, let's say "excited" in recent days. The numbers were staggering, and the headlines were breathless. In only 20 minutes, Grimes could sell $5.8 million in NFTs. For $11.6 million, 3lau sold 33 NFTs! T-former Mobile's CEO paid Steve Aoki $888,888.88 for an NFT titled "Hairy"! PERFECT! The rumor mill is accurate. The clubhouse is home to many NFT and crypto-art clubs, with several Twitter threads of people shouting at each other about the actual existence of NFTs.

Experienced thought-leaders in the music industry believe NFTs are crucial. Speaking at the NY: LON Connect conference in January, Shara Senderoff, president of music/tech investment firm Raised In Space, accurately guessed that NFTS would "explode" owing to the "willingness for a fan to buy a product that is scarce, limited, and has prospective offerings attached to it that make them as a dedicated fan feel special and compensated."

On the Pro-NFT side presently, there are a considerable buzz, cash, and opinions to be heard, and we're covering those perspectives. What, on the other hand, is the alternative viewpoint? Is there a possibility that this will become another ICO (initial coin offering) bubble like the one in 2017? What if people are dipping their toes into a technology they are unfamiliar with? WTF NFTs?

We asked two people who work closely with entertainment and blockchain technology a fundamental question: what's the other end of all this buzz?

Their responses weren't entirely critical, but they provided an alternate, stunning viewpoint on the ongoing frenzy of exaggerations and multimillion-dollar total. When blockchain technology is hyped up like this, their general message is to be cautious.

Nfts To Music Industry

Simply put, you can release your music as an NFT in addition to existing platforms such as Spotify, Bandcamp, and anywhere else. Another advantage of NFTs is that they can take multiple forms and do not have to be entirely owned by a single person.

Let's pretend you're a rising star who's about to release your first album. You may make a one-of-a-kind NFT that reflects the entire album and thus becomes a collectible object. Now, the album will have unique content that is only available to one valid owner. For instance, they might receive a percentage of all album sales in perpetuity, a hidden single, or exclusive backstage access to your shows. You get to choose which features to contain, and it's simple to set up.

Benefits To The Artist

You start by hosting an album sale on sites like Foundation or OpenSea or whichever marketplace you so desire, where your fans can bid on your collectible. Suppose the song becomes a smash, and one lucky fan that purchased the collectible and backed you gets to share in your success and all the rewards that follow.

You may also profit from reselling by including a percentage in the contract for any reselling of your collectible. So, if your NFT, which reflects your album, becomes a major success and is sold for vast amounts of money, later on, the artist will continue to be rewarded every time these transactions occur. Advantages to the Collector

By taking out the middleman, they can help their favorite artists in a more significant, more intimate, and powerful way than they do through other services like Patreon. They will also be able to invest in the artwork. As a result, if the artist's career takes off, so does their collection. It turns into both a fascinating investment option and a show of support.

How To Get Started

It's now relatively simple to have your music minted and stored on the blockchain. In reality, when you have enough ether, you can tokenize and transform your music into a collectible NFT in a matter of a few minutes.

Setting Up Your Nfts Album, Ep, Or Track

The first step is to obtain a free and stable cryptocurrency wallet. This digital wallet is where you can store your ethereum if you get compensated for your work and then convert it back to hard currency (such as USD, Euro, or Pounds) whenever you need it.

After you've set up your wallet, go to any open marketplace that provides free service in your areas, such as Binance, Gemini, or Kraken, and buy some there.

Once you've completed your setup and purchased some ether, move it back to your wallet, and you're done. You're now able to get your music distributed across the chain!

From here, you can go to one of the more common sites, such as

Opensea or KnownOrigin, where you can sell your art and set the terms and conditions, price, excellent content, and all of that. Set up your account on these sites according to the guidelines and create your first NFT.

Why It Matter

The music industry requires a better and stronger future economy, and decentralized NFTs are the answer. While streaming platforms and artist

support services have made a big difference in spreading artists' work around the globe and providing avenues for fans worldwide to support their favorite artists; these services often struggle to provide an acceptable return on investment for the art itself.

To make a better environment for our future ravers, shower singers, subway riders, and fans worldwide, we should strive to promote and encourage quality work. NFTs contribute to coming up with a solution to this current problem. They can readjust the value return gap by prioritizing quality of work over the illusion of who an individual is via social networks or streaming algorithms.

NFT FOR VIDEO MAKER

Joseph Niepce was the foremost person to take a black-and-white picture in 1826. Joseph Plateau, a rare years after (1832), became the first to manufacture motion images in his creation named phenakistoscope ("spindle viewer").

Video production has constantly evolved from the earliest days of "emotional pictures" more than a century ago in reaction to new technology. As long as new instruments, formats, and platforms are widely acknowledged, every creative working with video must adjust.

While the way we see videos has altered permanently with technological innovation, distribution techniques and the creation of videos also need to continue to stay at pace with these fast-changing circumstances. Over time, new video technology, job positions, and the primary way businesses integrate video into their more comprehensive plan for commercial success has affected presentation processes. The digital video did not prevent the change of television broadcasting, the video did not kill the radio star, and TV did not quit the invention of films.

On the opposite, the more than one century of film and video composition that before it applied the way for today's video environment is feasible. It has always been vital to adjust to new technologies, whether the future of video, watch a video with a growing digit of technology and media, and many new tools and platforms to produce and distribute it.

How Can A Video Creator Use Or Create Nfts?

The globe judges like it's rapidly switching during the pandemic period, and Non Fungible tokens have come on the radar lately, with Digital Artists such as Beeple producing as much as $69 million for an image file. Now appears to be the most suitable time to understand some essential knowledge about making an NFT as a Video Maker. As a Video Maker, there are potentially multiple advantages if you can mint and offer your artwork for sale. Cryptocurrency technology will affirm you as the original owner on the blockchain and continue to pay you some royalties (Just as considered in the case of photography).

Making your video content can be done using any video-creating software. Anything in the help file formats under a 100MB JPG, SVG, PNG, GLTF, GIF, MP4, WAV, WEBM, GLB, MP3, OGG can be created. As a Video Maker, you can develop a good video below 100MB. The last step is to mint the footage with a platform available and put it up for sale. You have the chance to give unlockable content when someone purchases the NFT through an external link to another platform.

What Can You Sell?

You can sell anything digital from tweets, contracts, images, video skits, an album, any audio, 3d model, e.t.c. Some platforms accept file designs: JPG, SVG, PNG, GLTF, GIF, MP4, WAV, WEBM, GLB, MP3, OGG. With a full file size of 100 MB

Platforms To Sell Your Nft

Presently, there are many outlets on the Internet, and they all have their advantages and disadvantages, depending on what you are selling. Some venues are SuperRare, Foundation, VIV3, OpenSea, Axie Marketplace, Rarible, BakerySwap, Nifty Gateway, and NFT ShowRoom.

OpenSea seems to be more reasonable in terms of file size because they accept files up to 100MB, unlike Rarible where the maximum file size that can be uploaded is 30MB. Another advantage is that they seem to be more significant NFT marketplaces that don't demand an invite, unlike other platforms like Niftygateway and Superrare. They also offer some great free details on using their platform.

Related Nft Video Sales

NFT has been very famous that everyone wants to mint their artwork (Image, Music, or Video) on supported platforms to get some returns. NFT created from an image seems to be the most popular, and other digital arts are getting some attention from creators.

One of the most popular NFT video clips is a 10-second video that sold for a whopping $6.6 million at the NFT auction. Pablo Rodriguez-Fraile, a Miami-based art collector, spent over USD 67,000 on a 10-second video in October 2020. The video could have been watched online without cost because we live in a technologically sophisticated age where everything is now available on the Internet. Still, he chose to spend USD 67,000 to obtain the video for his collection rather than do so. In February 2021, he sold the property for a total of 6.6 million dollars.

As considered in NFT by photographer, the blockchain was used to authenticate the video created by a digital artist known as Beeple, whose real name is Mike Winkelmann, "the blockchain is a trustless platform that serves as a digital signature to verify and certify who owns it and that it is the original work."

Another popular NFT video that got people's attention is the LeBron James slam dunk sold for $208,000.

The launch of the U.S. NBA's Top Shot website has been said to be the start of the rush for NFTs, and it is possible to trade, sell or buy NFTs in the condition of video highlights from games on the website open anybody interested.

The platform says it has hit over 10,000 users buying NFT with nearly $250 million of sales. The NBA is also said to receive royalties on every sale on the marketplace. And February 2021 is said to be the highest sales on the platform so far, with a total sales of over $198 million, which multiplies January's sales of $44 million.

The most significant transaction on February 22 on the platform was when a user paid $208,000 for LeBron James slam dunk video.

During an interview with one prominent NFT investor, known as "Pranks," he stated that he had put USD 600 in an early NFT project in 2017. His portfolio of NFTs and cryptocurrencies is now worth a total of seven digits to him. Pranks claim to have spent more than a million dollars on Top Shot and made approximately 4.7 million dollars from the resale of his various game collections.

You must be wondering this is it; NFT has nothing to offer another industry except an industry that involves graphics like image or video, but NFT has not stopped there; it is available for anything digital technology, even music. How can the piece be displayed as an NFT? Well, it is like owning an album of music as one of your collections.

UNDERSTANDING NFT STOCKS

When you consider Art's resale value, NFTs become a compelling investment opportunity. It's close to purchasing physical works of Art. If you want to keep the Art, possessing it will not benefit you.

Of course, staring at the work of Art can provide you with a sense of fulfillment. However, big money comes from selling art pieces to the most elevated bidder. To put it another method, if you can buy a one-of-a-kind NFT and then sell it for more additional than you paid for it, you will benefit handsomely.

The strength of blockchain is that it eliminates the possibility of fraud and theft. There will be codes and authentication to confirm and validate the authenticity of the work of art you own. Others can also create copies of an original digital art piece, but only one original remain. The original belongs to the person who owns the NFT for that art piece.

If anyone asked you in January what NFT stocks were, you'd probably stare at them blankly. This week, the enthusiasm has sparked Wall Street rallies in a slew of tech stocks. As I formerly said, some of these have little to do with the NFT niche. However, based on speculation, investors believe these companies will gain exposure to NFTs.

It's difficult to tell if NFT stocks will take off in the long run at this stage. Examine cannabis stocks and cryptocurrencies from 2017 to 2019. If history is any guide, the excitement surrounding NFT stocks will likely fade away soon.

With all of the hype, it's easy to ignore it as science fiction that will never come to pass. However, if we look near, we can see that something is going on behind the scenes, and why am I saying this?

Last year, according to Nonfungible, the overall volume of NFT transactions increased to $250 million. NFT transactions totaled more than $220 million last month alone. It seems that we are experiencing something that is rising at an unprecedented rate.

Traditionally, any digital art shared, saved, or downloaded on the internet can be easily shared, saved, and downloaded. However, there isn't a clear sense of ownership since anybody can use it. Assume you're an artist, an exceptionally talented one.

You also create some of the most stunning works of art, but what about putting your imagination to good use?

You seem to have had little success with it so far, at least with most citizens. However, there is a way to give digital art a sense of individuality using NFTs. It also provides an opportunity for sound artists to continue doing innovative works.

The art industry has many scopes for NFTs. However, first and foremost, the market must be regulated. There is currently no law dictating who can build NFTs and who is not. Before then, I wouldn't invest in NFT stocks without first waiting for the dust to settle but, don't get me wrong: I adore Art.

I genuinely believe that this can change how art is perceived in our culture. Maybe it's just me, but before investing in NFT stocks, I'd like to see more concrete developments. However, this is merely my opinion; the final decision is yours to make. Make sure you do your homework and study.

Crypto-assets are starting to stir up mainstream knowledge is behind the interest in NFT stocks. The hunt for stores linked to non-fungible tokens (is heating up, and investors are frantically looking for opportunities. Celebrities such as Jack Dorsey and Elon Musk have experimented with offerings, and brands follow suit.

Are you the sort of investor who is willing to take on a high level of risk in trade for the possibility of a high return?

NFT stocks can be erratic. As you'll see below, many businesses are experimenting with NFT offerings. Others use a mix of online sleuthing and social media gossip to reach new heights. As a result, the early-stage trend is scorching but extremely risky.

When evaluating these businesses, make sure to weigh the risks and research what makes them unique.

Do you think it's great that they're associated with NFT targets or blockchain technology?

Are their companies ripe for potential cryptocurrency deals?

Do they have any NFT services that produce revenue?

There is money to be made in the room as digital artist Beeple made nearly $70 million for a single piece, but money is also lost.

With that in mind, here are the top ten NFT stocks that InvestorPlace is currently tracking.

- Takung Art is a form of martial art (NYSEMKT: TKAT)

- Jiayin Group is a Chinese conglomerate (NASDAQ: JFIN)

- Group of Oriental Culture (NASDAQ: OCG)

- Media in Liquid Form (NASDAQ: YVR)

- Hall of Fame Resort & Entertainment is a resort and entertainment complex located in Las Vegas, Nevada (NASDAQ: HOFV)

- Funko Pop! (NASDAQ: FNKO)

- Cinedigm is a film production company that specializes in (NASDAQ: CIDM)

- Color Star Technology is a technology that allows you to see colors (NASDAQ: CSCW)

- WiseKey is a program that will enable you to create a (NASDAQ: WKEY)

- KBS Fashion Group is a fashion company based in Korea (NASDAQ: KBSF)

SUCCESS & FAILURES

Nfts Help Artists Solve Vital Problem

Kevin Abosch, a New York-based artist, has sold a $1.5 million painting of a potato, created a neon artwork inspired by cryptocurrencies, and even auctioned his blood on the blockchain network.

In several respects, the 51-year-old Irish artist's entry into the non-fungible tokens (NFTs) space was the natural next step for his work, which investigates digital currency and value themes. Non-fungible tokens (NFTs) are digital tokens that prove a digital collectible's authenticity and ownership. The technology has been present since at least 2017 and is a spinoff of the cryptocurrency industry that uses the blockchain.

Is It Possible For Anyone To Become An Nft Collector?

However, in March, the NFT frenzy reached new heights when Christie's, the famed art auction house, sold off a digital collage by an artist known as Beeple for about $70 million, instantly making him the of the most expensive living artist ever.

Many people are perplexed as to why someone would like to acquire an NFT. What does it imply to own art in the first place? For artists like Abosch, NFTs assist in resolving a long-standing dilemma in digital art: how can you take possession of something that can be readily and continuously reproduced?

Abosch started working on a series of images in 2020 that dealt with encryption and alphanumeric codes. Following the cancellation of many of his in-person presentations due to the Covid-19 outbreak, Abosch felt that now was the ideal time to sell his work as NFTs. He planned to sell them on OpenSea, the world's leading token market, that receives 1.5 million weekly visits and triggered $95 million in sales in February 2021 alone.

He made a $2 million gain from the collection, including all work that can't be physically moved to a gallery or put on display. He became the most popular NFT artist on the OpenSea marketplace due to it. On the eve of the auction in March 2021, he told the Guardian that the notion that art should be a tangible product that can be exhibited is soon becoming obsolete.

"Some individuals are troubled by this concept since they wish to know what you genuinely own," he explained. "However, persons of a younger generation do not have this problem.

"Wanting to grasp something in your hand is a very outdated tradition as if the ethereal or immaterial has no value."

An NFT auction functions similarly to an online auction on sites like eBay. Every work is shown as an image file with metadata – that means "data about data" – including the title, number, and who owns it.

Abosch's 1111 series debuted on OpenSea at 11:11 a.m. EST, where he posted 111 works for a limited time. Following the beginning of the auction, prospective purchasers visit the Abosch sale page to bid on specific art jobs - in this case, using the crypto Ethereum.

While the NFTs were traded on Opensea, the actual sequence of characters that links the owner to their new NFT is saved on Arweave. This program acts as a form of permanent internet by storing files in perpetuity over a decentralized network of systems, preventing them from being erased or damaged in the future.

To put it another way, a buyer will pay for an image on the NFT trading site OpenSea with an Ethereum token and receive an Arweave address certifying the acquisition and ownership of the image file in exchange. In the end, 53 different collectors bought 106 of the 111 works, with the most costly selling for $21,242.

Some artists, including Abosch, are attracted to the NFT tech because of its democratizing nature: anybody can connect and buy the items, and the work comes with a publicly available ledger of its entire history - when it was minted, who possessed it, who bought it, and for how much. This, according to Abosch, is a break from former art purchases, wherein investors put special art in-store to hold it for a period when it will be more expensive.

The prominence of cryptocurrencies and the increase of art market speculation have been proliferating for some time. However, the coronavirus outbreak has further positioned the sector for the triumph of tech like NFTs, according to Andrei Pesic, an art history professor at Stanford.

"As we've had to transfer so much of our life online in the years 2020 and 2021, it has opened or hastened the idea of pricing digital products in the same manner that we value physical products," he said. Abosch, who has been utilizing blockchain technology to mint art since 2013, says the NFT mania was sparked by two factors: the tech is intriguing and practical, and any new bright thing that promises to make people rich will quickly readily attract attention.

"We are in a significant evolutionary time – it's like we're in the middle of the biggest storm, except instead of everything being damaged, we'll see new constructions that are quite fascinating," he explained. "However, there will be some rubble."

The Old Art World's Problem

- The Power of Gatekeepers

The Problem In The Old Art World:

In a fundamentally hierarchical structure, individuals and organizations with lengthy histories, huge money, and pre-existing business connections exert significant power over who gets to participate.

- The NFT Difference

New, decentralized markets can accept artists and participants without sanctioning the art establishment. While some NFT marketplaces (like SuperRare and Nifty Gateway) will only welcome artists by invite or registration, for the time being, others (such as Rarible) will enable any enthusiastic artist to begin trading in their market.

Ameer Suhayb Carter, an expert cryptocurrency designer and advisor preparing to launch the Well Protocol, an NFT network, archive, and support system with a particular emphasis on BIPOC and LGBTQIA artists, exemplifies the blockchain art world's most transformative power.

"In many situations, these are folks that can't even find a job in their home country. Carter, who also operates as an artist under the nickname Sirsu, told Artnet News, "We're giving voice to the voiceless."

"The idea is for them to be able to establish the communities they want in their way. I supply them with the devices they need to take control of their lives. I'm not going to build for you; I'm going to build with you."

The Collectors' Values

- The Problem in the Old Art World:

The changing structure of upper-echelon art acquisition is part of what makes existing gatekeepers so strong. Investors fight to represent the same types of artists that buyers crave: artists who look like them, that is, primarily white and male persons who have contacts within the high-art society.

- The NFT Difference:

Until now, many, if not all, NFT purchasers have come from outside the conventional art business circles, and they have shown minimal concern in recognized investors', advisers', and collectors' ideas on what is worth collecting—and at what price.

According to Kevin McCoy, the artist who built the first NFT as part of Rhizome's Seven on Seven conferences in 2014, "the cash flowing into the NFTs space is cash that was already in the space." "Cryptocurrency investors are buying NFTs. I've constantly believed that fresh makers and collectors, not the old art world, are the source of power."

Wealth Redistribution

- The Problem in the Old Art World:

When it comes to profiting from art, practically all of the significant benefits go to the collector on resale. Even the most successful artists are usually only paid a pittance in resale royalties. The UK, for instance, has a resale royalty maximum of €12,500 (about $17,300) for its inhabitants, regardless of how much a work sells for when it is resold; the US, on the other hand, has no resale royalty at all—at least, not outside of revenue generated in California during a one-year time in the late 1970s.

- The NFT Difference:

Since percentage-based resale royalties may be built into the conditions of each NFT sale, creatives can profit appropriately and indefinitely as their pieces travel through the market.

Most importantly, this redistributive mechanism can be completely automated. What is the reason for this? Because the "smart contract," a collection of instructions that operates on the blockchain network without human involvement if independently verifiable conditions are satisfied, is the primary mechanism of NFT exchanges. (For example, "ownership of this asset goes to the sender as soon as the sales price enters the present owner's account," state hypothetically.)

According to Amy Whitaker, a professor of visual arts administration at New York University that began exploring blockchain in 2014, the potential get much more exciting when NFT artists utilize intelligent contracts to redistribute assets to more than just themselves.

For any prospective NFT pieces, artist Sara Ludy reportedly arranged a new sales share with her New York gallery, bitforms: 50% for Ludy, 15% for the NFT network, and 35% for bitforms—with the latter amount equally distributed in 7% increments between the gallery's founder and four employees.

Whitaker compared the move to a tip jar for restaurant employees. It's a way of "collectivizing economics," as well as "trying to combine for-profit and nonprofit frameworks so individuals can route some of the earnings towards grantmaking or charity" without having to fill out extra tax forms if the creators so desire.

Preservation And Ownership

- The Problem in the Old Art World:

Possession of (and copyright) works like installation, performance, and video sometimes devolves into a quagmire of misunderstanding outside traditional physical media.

Investors and creators must create term sheets from the start for every piece, with the final papers typically veering between unnecessarily plain and frustratingly complicated. All for the collector to regularly misinterpret or ignore their responsibilities, particularly when it comes to the long-term care of the piece.

- The NFT Difference:

The blockchain network stores the work's full provenance and copyright information and the possibility to add a wealth of additional data that would be useful to historians and archivists. Standard contracts, such as ERC-721, are widely used by artists unsure about establishing their agreements. Should a disagreement over intellectual property emerge, an NFT's whole transaction history may be audited back to its creation, providing irrefutable "on-chain" evidence of which party's rights are valid?

GAMING, DIGITAL IDENTITY, LICENSING, CERTIFICATES, & FINE ART OF NFTS

Collectibles, art, games, and virtual worlds are the key categories of existing NFT use cases. However, other categories, such as sports, fashion, and real-world properties, are increasingly growing.

Terra Virtua is one of the world's first immersive digital collectible networks, with some of Hollywood's biggest names, including Topgun, The Godfather series, Pacific Rim, Sunset Boulevard Lost in Space. It also has a relationship with Paramount Pictures.

Antiques and collectibles

Collectibles are currently one of the most common applications of NFTs in terms of sales volume, accounting for about 23.6 percent of all sales in the former month. CryptoPunks, which debuted in June 2017 and has since sold for thousands of dollars, is one of the first collectible NFTs on Ethereum.

They were created before ERC-721 was launched, and a wrapper had to be designed to be traded on exchanges such as Opensea. CryptoKitties have become well-known collectibles, with sales reaching more than $38 million since their launch in November 2017,

Playing Video Games

Gamers, as formerly said, are an ideal target market for NFTs since they are already acquainted with virtual worlds and currencies. The gaming industry is booming thanks to NFTs, which enable in-game objects to be tokenized and easily transferred or traded using peer-to-peer trading and marketplaces.

On the other hand, traditional games forbid the selling or transferring in-game objects such as uncommon weapons and skins.

Since players have complete control of their digital properties, NFTs make the gaming experience more tangible and satisfying. They're also spawning a new economy, as players can now benefit from their in-game properties by constructing and improving them.

Artpiece

One of the most challenging problems for digital artists is copyright infringement, but NFTs are a remedy because they provide evidence of ownership, authenticity and eliminate counterfeiting and fraud concerns.

As museums and galleries close due to COVID-19, many artists have switched to NFTs and online showrooms, according to a Coindesk post, and "just as Bitcoin paved the way for peer-to-peer transactions by establishing a public events ledger, cryptoart has provenance built-in."

In July, "Picasso's Bull" set a new record for the NFT highest-valued art auction sale, selling for more than $55,000. "These ventures can also boost and streamline artists' income by linking them directly to customers via blockchain-based payment and exchange solutions," according to Cointelegraph.

Interactive Universes

Digital worlds are another application for NFTs. Users can build, own and monetize virtual land parcels and other in-game NFT products on decentralized virtual reality platforms, including Decentraland, The Sandbox, and Cryptovoxels.

Decentraland's LAND is permanently owned by the group, giving players complete ownership of their virtual properties and creations. Given Gen Z's experience with virtual worlds and how their understanding of valuable assets varies from that of former generations, virtual world assets provide them with the versatility and option that they value: "

Properties And Documentation From The Real World

Real-world properties such as property and bonds, and documents such as credentials, licenses, medical records, birth and death certificates, can be tokenized.

However, this category is still in its early stages of growth, with few applications. As the crypto world and NFTs grow and expand, who's to say you won't be able to own a vineyard in another country thousands of miles away one day (perhaps soon)? Your digital wallet can soon contain proof of every certificate, license, and asset you own, for all we know.

PROJECTS CONSTRUCTING A STRONG FOUNDATION BENEATH THE MARRIAGE OF DEFI AND NFTS

Digital collectibles on blockchains are operating the retail mania for crypto higher right now because they are calm and in part. After all, the market seems to have finally reached this consensus: Provable ownership of digital items can accrue real value.

When there is actual worth, there is finance. These collectibles also comprehended as non-fungible tokens (NFTs), have been verified recently to have very high importance. "NFTs are a foundational structure block of the emerging virtual economy," Stephen Young, the creator, and CEO of NFTfi, stated in a press release.

The most delinquent data point in the continuing story of the union of NFTs and decentralized finance (DeFi) is the latest funding for NFTfi. This project allows borrowers to post-digital items as collateral. NFTfi announced an $890,000 investment round from backers including CoinFund, 1kx, The LAO, and Dapper Labs CEO Roham Gharegozlou, among others.

NFT is one of several companies making it a lot easier to get money in, earn yield and bring it back out of the digital collectible space.

How It Operates

NFTfi is primarily like DeFi giants Compound and Aave, both money markets, but those two use fungible collateral, like ETH or various stable coins. NFTs are non-fungible, and they are demands with less liquidity, making price discovery more challenging.

That's transforming fast with more and more products coming onto the market, making it more manageable for liquidity to flow through the many outcomes. And recall, this is crypto: Switching fast means a wildly diverse thing in this enterprise than in the pokey ancient world of mobile phones and social networks. "As NFTs re-imagined how we create and define the right of digital content online, we'll also, in turn, start to re-imagine a whole new category of financial services established on these new building alliances," Lasse Clausen, a partner at the experience firm 1kx, said in a press release.

Beyond NFTfi, here are ten more projects that are making the NFT market almost as complex, flexible, and liquid as the remainder of crypto:

NIFTEX

The startup, whose outlet makes fractional ownership of NFTs possible, is working on a new version with many new features. For example, it will allow creators to earn royalties on trades of fractions, governance over the underlying NFTs for holders of a bit, and other tools that permit more fine-grained ownership. Also, a decentralized independent organization (DAO) is coming to manage the whole application. "Fractional ownership of songs, books, other scope is a no-brainer. One edition, lots of proprietors, individuality is king," co-founder Joel Hubert told CoinDesk in an email.

Ark Gallery

This company made a DAO that built wrapped CryptoPunks, making Larva Labs' pioneering NFTs more fungible. Ark has afterward created additional tools to enhance liquidity for the original non-fungible token, and probably merits some recognition for today's white-hot CryptoPunks market. It is presently working on Blank. Art. "We will launch NFT projects that are commandeering financial ideas and themes for artistic purposes," Ark's Roberto Ceresia told CoinDesk in an email.

Mintbase

Mintbase is an outlet that makes it leisurely to mint non-fungible tokens. It had an investment round lately led by Sino Global. It mainly enables users to mint on Ethereum, but the NEAR blockchain has gone out of its way to be consistent with the original smart-contract chain. Right now, Mintbase is establishing a characteristic on NEAR that allows royalties on sales to be shared with up to 1,000 people. "That is the fractional ownership part evis talking about," COO Carolin Wend told CoinDesk.

NFTX

This one allows community-owned index funds so that one token defines right in many NFTs. It has tokens for specific varieties of NFTs and others representing a scope of the market. "There are, however, numerous people out there that don't have the time or understanding to sell individual NFTs but would like disclosure to NFT markets. These are the NFTX mark users," the firm composed in January.

Charged Particles

This protocol aims to help any NFT encode or embed with an ERC-20 token. So just in point, there was any doubt an NFT had value, a user could cover it with interest-earning tokens, and it would contain been worth it beyond any doubt. That is the same as what the upcoming

Aavegotchi game is doing. What will it mean for non-fungible and fungible assets to become roommates? Time will tell.

Zora Protocol

According to its white paper, "Zora provides a cryptographically enforced registry of media independent of any platform." One of Zora's creators, Jacob Horne, told CoinDesk in an email, "We've directly built the market into the NFT, and we've created a net new auction model specific to NFTs. Zora auctions are perpetual; anyone can bid in any currency, the owner can accept any bid." If that sounds head-scratching, check out this new genre of poetry built with the help of the Zora team.

Unifty

"Unifty is an NFT management system. Think of it as 'the WordPress of NFTs,'" Markus Medinger of the Unifty team told CoinDesk in an email. Unifty has a marketplace with new features around copyright management and value drops, among others. The platform is somewhat unique in that it essentially performs off Ethereum. "We already help xDai, BSC [Binance Smart Chain], Polygon [née Matic], Celo, and Moonbeam Alpha. Multi-chain aid is one of our expertise," Medinger added.

Upshot

That is an as-yet-unrroject for crowdsourcing NFT appraisals. "The next step for financialization is cracking the NFT price discovery problem in a capital-efficient way," CoinFund's Jake Brukhman told CoinDesk.

NFT Trader

A peer-to-peer trading task for NFTs, still in beta. Be alert!

Polyient Games

This company is all over NFT financialization, from investing in the sector to more robust construction tools. It operates a decentralized exchange for NFTs, has its approach to fractional ownership, and has products built for NFT protection. The company is mocking a game now that vows to make DeFi more game-like. "Polyient Games is our decentralized ecosystem created to drive forward NFT invention, both internally and through third-party participation," Craig Russo, the co-founders, informed CoinDesk in an email.

State Of The Market

The initial DeFi players have not instantly made a lot of noise around NFTs yet. Scott Lewis of DeFi Pulse is entangled with NFTX and Aave supported in the video game that uses its tokens, Aavegotchi. "Aave community has an enormous interest," Stani Kulechov, CEO of the money market Aave, told CoinDesk in an email.

Usually, this is the portion of the post where we'd tell readers just learning about NFTs and DeFi that they should take a minimal amount of ETH or stable coins and buy some little things and play around. None of this stuff makes sense until a person tries it. Unfortunately, right now, most people can't spend a negligible amount of money on DeFi because transaction fees ("gas," in Ethereum parlance) make everything costly.

Layer 2 platforms are those that pose atop Ethereum and other blockchains, taking benefit of the underlying blockchain's protection while also allowing cheaper, faster transactions. NIFTEX's Huber told CoinDesk he foresees layer two solutions fundamental to this sector. Still, too little liquidity has moved onto anyone layer 2 to make it worthwhile for an app like his to move there yet. As made it hard to enjoy the DeFi playground on ETH mainnet," Marguerite deCourcelle of Blockade Games told CoinDesk. The blockade is in the middle of moving its users to layer 2, now comprehended as Polygon. "I think we're about to witness a lot of additional users and developers on L2," she said.

Nfts & Defi: A Good Combination?

If you want to understand what non-fungible tokens (NFT) are, why they are evolving increasingly famous in the crypto scene. What they have to accomplish with decentralized finance (DeFi), we must first dig the idea of "value" in depth.

What Is Value?

Value is the natural quality of a thing that makes it desirable to a certain extent. This value can be related to several tangible and intangible characteristics, mainly rarity.

Therefore, the economic value of something depends on its quality and scarcity.

Why Is Value So Significant To Nfts?

Non-fungible tokens (NFTs) are cryptographic tokens that are not backed by a traditional asset and instead are representative of something else, such as an artwork, an event, or a digital item. Thus, many people mistakenly jump to the conclusion that NFTs do not have value.

However, non-fungible tokens are indeed valuable. NFTs represent unique assets and are rare and cryptographically secure. They are not interchangeable and thus introduce scarcity to the digital world. Each of these tokens acquires value due to this scarcity. That occurs following the customary law of supply and demand — partakers are willing to pay more for a specific and rare NFT.

NFTs are thus optimally fitted for decentralized applications (dApps) to create and own special digital items and collectibles.

NFTs can be traded at businesses that connect buyers with sellers. In these exchanges, every NFT is individual and therefore gets its worth.

What Accomplish Nfts Have To Do With Blockchain?

It all began in 2016 when Bitcoin-based trading cards were issued as some of the first NFTs. In 2017, these early NFTs were printed on the Ethereum blockchain using CryptoPunks, a platform offering NFTs describing the artwork. However, the natural buildup started in December 2017 with the deployment of the blockchain-based game CryptoKitties, which uses NFTs to convey ownership of digital cats on its platform. Today, more than 131 million USD is wrapped in these two projects in Ether.

In the years since this initial NFT advertisement, hundreds of other NFT iterations have become known on the market.

Since the origins of using NFTs on the blockchain, various standards have been created to promote the issuance of NFTs. The most popular of these is ERC-721, a standard for the distribution and trading of non-fungible assets on the Ethereum blockchain. A more recent, improved average is ERC-1155, enabling a single contract to contain fungible and non-fungible tokens.

This standardization of NFTs allows a more high degree of interoperability, suggesting that unique assets can be transmitted between applications with relative ease, ushering in additional use cases.

What Are The Potential Areas Of Application?

It is clear that NFTs offer an increased status of interoperability and act as terms of non-traditional assets.

That means that NFTs can be used in many areas. That includes video games, digital originality, licensing, certificates, or fine arts. These tokens can and even allow for the fractional right of objects.

That is precisely where DeFi comes into play.

In all fields they are applied to, NFTs represent some worth. These values can be managed entirely in the blockchain via smart contracts. That perfectly fits the definition of a DeFi project: a financial tool operating along with the blockchain.

Present Defi Nft Offerings:

Current developments in this area are already diverse.

For example, DeFi projects represent themselves as a decentralized trade for NFTs. One of the best comprehended in this area is Rarible.

Another instance of NFTs and DeFi is Aavegotchi, an entirely decentralized collection game.

Likewise, Tinlake combines NFTs and Defi by offering a service that forms a bridge between real-world assets and DeFi. Its goal is to access bankless liquidity.

POTENTIAL CONCERNS OVER INTELLECTUAL PROPERTY

The controversies that surround this issue revolve around the definition of ownership and copyright. While NFTs are generally considered a strong representation of ownership over the digital art that it is linked to, there are some concerns regarding the ownership and copyrights associated with NFTs that will be addressed. Does owning an NFT mean that you own its copyright as well? The responses to these questions will have to be clearly defined within the budding NFT scene so as allow all stakeholders to grasp the legalities they are dealing with.

What Does Digital Ownership Truly Mean?

When you own an NFT, what does it indeed mean? There is a common misconception that when NFTs are minted, the digital files linked to them are also stored on the blockchain. Unfortunately, this is not the case. Digital media are often too large to be held on the blockchain. Instead, these digital files will be stored somewhere else on the web. When NFTs are created, the token will then be permanently linked cryptographically to the location of the digital file. The information stored on the blockchain is thus equivalent to directions that will point you towards the establishment at which the file is stored.

Files stored online are always at risk of being deleted or being moved. That means that NFTs may become worthless if the digital file it points to gets removed. To protect NFT owners from losing ownership of their digital assets, the Interplanetary File System (IPFS) was created. IPFS is a decentralized digital file storage solution whereby storage capabilities are distributed globally across multiple networks. The files uploaded and stored on the IPFS are permanent, and the location of files on the system will be suitable for being linked to an NFT.

In a nutshell, the purchase of an NFT represents your ownership of a digital file stored in a location recorded on the blockchain. That is the extent to which digital license means, which has thus far proven to be a sufficient representation of ownership.

Copyright Conundrum

Traditionally, there were only two forms of media. They had clear property distinctions, which led to different copyright laws imposed on physical and digital media.

The First Sale Doctrine Of Physical Items

The "first sale" doctrine was introduced to cover all physical items. The principle states that all material items bought can be then resold in a secondary market without the original creator having any control over the terms of the secondary sales. Royalties cannot be imposed on physical items, which is why we have items such as paintings, trading cards, and vinyl records being resold between individuals where the seller can keep the total proceeds from the transaction. The first sale doctrine was introduced because owners of a physical item cannot derive value from the work's copyright. It would thus be unfeasible to protect the physical object from any copyright law.

Rejection Of A "Digital First Sale" Doctrine

As the world became increasingly digitalized, it soon became apparent that a digital-first sale doctrine would be disastrous for digital content distribution. That is because digital files can be easily reproduced and copied. It is not easy to replicate a physical item completely, so the first sale doctrine makes sense. Under the original first sale doctrine, purchasers of digital files can make unlimited copies of the file and distribute it at a profit. That would be unjust to the creators of that file as the sellers would benefit directly from the work's copyright. For this reason, American legislators blocked the first sale doctrine from applying to digital files under copyright laws.

Differences Between Nfts And Traditional Digital Files

Up till the time before NFTs were created, all digital files could effectively be considered to be fungible since copied files are essentially the same, and none of them can be regarded as a unique digital asset. The non-fungibility of tokenized assets parallels physical items because no two material things can be identical. Two bicycles of the same model produced by the same company may have minor differences, no matter how small. This non-fungible quality of physical items has allowed the first sale doctrine to work out so well for physical works.

The advent of NFT technology then challenged the fungibility of traditional digital files. To take the example of Cryptopunks, they were algorithmically produced back in 2017. Its current value can be attributed to its legacy status and history. Another NFT linked to a copy of an image of a Cryptopunk would not be valued anywhere near what the original versions would be worth today. While the copied NFT may be linked to an identical piece of artwork, the apparent differences in their unique identifiers recorded on the blockchain have created a massive distinction between the copied NFT and the original Cryptopunk NFT. The success of NFT is primarily attributed to how it was able to assign a non-fungible attribute onto digital files effectively. That is where the problem comes in. NFTs are digital assets while also being non-fungible. Which copyright law shall it be covered under then? It becomes clear that none of the existing laws can be applied to NFTs, and a new set of rules will be needed to define the legal boundaries of NFTs.

Relationship Between Copyrights And Nft Ownership

What exactly does ownership of an NFT entail in terms of copyrights? When you purchase an NFT, you are not purchasing the copyright for that work. Copyrights for the job will still belong to the creator of the work. Distribution or printing the digital files without getting permission from its copyright owners can thus be considered to be copyright infringement. In this case, the rightsholder will be entitled to sell and distribute copies of the original NFT to the public. That can be seen in how NFT minting services allow for the creation of multiple NFTs that are linked to the same digital file. In summary, purchasing an NFT from the marketplace does not come with the copyrights associated with the work. Buyers should be made fully aware of this information to understand the full scope of what they are paying for.

However, there are cases where the copyrights to a digital file can be sold alongside its ownership. That can be facilitated by creating a smart contract that transfers the associated rights along with the digital asset to the new owner during a transaction. To illustrate how the smart contract can be used to generate specific terms involving the rights of a digital file, we can take a look at the $69 million Beeple NFT as a case study. The artist who created the artwork has included certain display rights in the image, enforced through a smart contract. However, the original artist retained the copyrights to the idea. In the case of NBA's Top Shot collectibles program, purchasers of the NFTs that the organization issued obtained a limited license that allows them to use, copy, and display the digital files for non-commercial and personal usage. Through these examples, we can see how artists can selectively confer rights to buyers to fit the desired terms of their NFT transaction. Creators may thus also choose to add full rights to their work to enhance the value delivered to the buyer of the NFT.

Controversies Surrounding Nft Creation

The default case for all digital works is that no NFTs exist before an entity chooses to mint that NFT. That creates a huge problem surrounding how copyrights can be proven before an NFT is minted. Unfortunately, anyone can take a screenshot or upload a digital file to mint an NFT. That means that while you may have created an art piece, someone else can take the file that you have uploaded and mint an NFT linked to it. In this case, even when you are the rightful owner and creator of the work, it appears as if another person owns your digital file and may even profit from the sale of that NFT.

The unauthorized creation of NFTs based on another person's work is evil and is an apparent infringement of copyrights. However, there is still a high risk of it happening to your work, and it essentially becomes a race for creators to "register" their work before anyone else steals the opportunity to do so. In some ways, it is equivalent to how patents work. The reason why the unauthorized minting of NFTs is occurring on a large scale is simply that it is too lucrative. Infringers are taking advantage of the information asymmetry to make a profit, and this occurrence has necessitated the creation of protocols designed to protect creators from copyright infringement.

To prevent unauthorized NFTs from being created and sold, marketplaces have instituted DMCA processes to identify and remove NFTs created from stolen content. Some of these marketplaces have also taken a stronger stance against copyright infringement and thus only allow verified works to be put up for sale. As the NFT market continues to grow and mature, we can expect stricter legislation to be imposed on the scene in a continued effort to protect stakeholders.

Technical Challenges Of Transacting Nfts

With the long list of legal obligations that may be tied to the smart contract of each NFT, there is the consideration of what level of liability sellers will have to hold in terms of fully representing the terms of rights to the buyer. It can be argued that all times of the sale are listed in the smart contract on the blockchain, and all of this information is fully accessible by the buyer. The seller would then not be responsible for clearly representing the information to the buyer before the transaction as the responsibility falls to the buyer. On the other hand, given the technical complexity of how the blockchain and smart contracts work, buyers may not get a complete picture of the terms of the sale, even after evaluationing the intelligent contract. In this case, it can also be argued that the seller should be responsible for explaining the full details of the upcoming transaction.

In cases where NFTs have royalty-based smart contracts encoded into them, the legality of how each NFT is represented also comes into play. For instance, the creator of a digital piece of art may sell the NFT linked to it to a seller while clearly stating that the creator retains all copyrights. The buyer may then inaccurately represent this information during a resale, where the buyer promises to provide all copyrights related to the work. That would naturally increase the valuation of the NFT. During the transaction, the owner of the NFT may then take a 10% cut as part of the intelligent royalty contract. There are grounds for the secondary seller to be accused of fraud in this case. As the original creator benefits from this instance of deceptiveness, to what extent would he be held responsible?

The technical challenges involved with understanding the terms of a sale will have to be overcome by creating strong guidelines regarding the sale of NFTs. In the most optimal scenario, each NFT transaction that takes place should have to be done with the provision of a comprehensive and straightforward description of its smart contract and sale terms.

AVOIDING SCAMS AND HOW TO SPOT THEM

Here are some of the most prevailing scams that occur in NFT, as well as tips on how to prevent them:

Nofraud.Org

In this case, the site utilizes catchy names and perks to get visitors to sign up for free trials, which ultimately results in them having to pay money.

Email

The con artists will provide them with a link to a website that seems genuine (but is not), or they will lead them to sign up for something on an actual website by transferring their email address to the con artists. Threats of legal action generally follow that if they do not sign up right away.

Nigerian Money Scam

That is the point at which you'll be requested for your bank account information so that they may transfer monies into your account, but this never occurs, resulting in you losing all of the money you've supplied them with and having no method of recovering it.

Phishing

In phishing, you are urged to do something by clicking on an email, a website, or even a phone call, and in exchange, you get something in return. Following that, you'll most likely be taken to another page or invited to download a file to your computer. This attachment may contain malicious software.

Surveys

Some websites may ask you to participate in a survey before allowing you to proceed with your purchase – but be aware that these surveys are paid by the company itself, which then uses the information to enhance their goods and services to meet your requirements better.

Fake Evaluations

Fake evaluations may be very damaging to brands and businesses developing new goods and services. If someone lures you in by writing a positive evaluation about a product, it would be easy to believe that the product will live up to those expectations, and even if that were to occur, they would introduce more competition to the market, which would be detrimental to the brand's business or product (as well as yours)

No Shipping Charges

When you purchase goods, you may be charged a delivery cost or be required to pay extra shipping charges that were not disclosed before buying the product.

Lack Of Trust

You're often urged to believe what others say about a product on the internet, but it's essential to read between the lines and understand that not every evaluation you read will be candid! One of the most productive ways to stop falling victim to this scam is to thoroughly study the critiques and ensure that they are authentic!

Refunds

If you are ever requested a refund, don't comply. There might be various reasons you need a refund, such as the product not lasting long enough or the product's appearance on your body not being what you expected it to be.

Fake Shipping Charges

That occurs when you are charged more for shipping than what was stated or when there is no tracking information provided for any products being shipped to your home - both of these are scams that can cause significant problems if they are not discovered until after the packages have been sent to the destination address.

Sales

Certain websites are quite deceptive in the manner they conduct sales. After purchasing a product at a low price, you'll see that the price has been raised later on. However, you won't be capable of withdrawing your purchase since it has already been sent.

Catch Up Scams

These are situations where you are offered membership or a subscription for a certain amount of money. They are required to pay them again every month if you want to continue using the service - this might wind up being far more costly than if you had paid once!

A LIST OF NFT PROJECTS I'M GOING TO INVEST IN 2022

NFTs—an emerging technology that uses crypto platforms to authenticate ownership of digital files. During the final crypto boom, the region—home to some of the most affordable power in the U.S.—was beset with a new energy-hungry home industry: basements and sheds loaded with racks of computers churning through advanced mathematical calculations to "mine" valuable crypto coins like Bitcoin and Ethereum. But even small crypto mines can overload local grids, making them a problem for energy companies. Far larger cryptocurrency mines have been set up from Texas to Iran to China's Inner Mongolia.

That may surprise artists and other NFT fans who are far removed from the technology's environmental toll. "You don't see your money is moving to a miner who's going to pay for fossil-fuel-based energy with it," says Alex de Vries, a financial economist.

Some in the crypto world are operating on solutions. Ethereum's developers promise to launch a less energy-intensive approach by 2022. But cryptocurrencies are popular partly because they're decentralized, attracting people who distrust governments. That means there's no single leader who could force a change.

Nft Topmost Projects

NFT-focused projects and products have improved in tandem with the rapid development of the NFT subspace. The top four NFT projects are listed below.

- OpenSea: This is the best place to buy and sell NFT collectibles and art. The marketplace accepts a variety of virtual currencies, including ETH. Virtual pets, ENS, and land plots are among the items listed. Notably, the marketplace agrees with various virtual currencies, including DAI and ETH.
- Async.Art: Async is another marketplace for non-fungible tokens where you can purchase, sell, and create non-fungible tokens. The platform has several programming features that will enable artists to define the appearance and actions of their work quickly. It also allows customers to buy and change "layers" of an artwork. In reality, it will enable customers to customize parts or "layers" of a piece of artwork that they bought.
- CryptoKitties: This project deserves to be at the top of the list of NFT projects because it brought the NFT game to the forefront. Even though we've already covered this project, it

still needs to be included in our top NFT projects list since it launched the entire NFT industry.

- The Ethereum Name Service (ENS): This is a design for a domain name service released in mid-2017. ETH domain names are non-fungible tokens (NFTs) that use Ethereum's ERC-721 formats and can be traded in the NFT market. The . ETH domain names are non-fungible tokens (NFTs) that follow Ethereum's ERC-721 specifications and can be sold on NFT exchanges.

- Decentraland: is a top NFT project that focuses on a distributed virtual environment. Participants can purchase virtual land here. In addition, each "inhabitant" has a unique digital passport that identifies them.

What Is Causing The Current Rise In Nfts?

The recent explosion of blockchain-based collectibles, particularly on the Ethereum blockchain, has created a new class of assets that anyone can own in the world and which has been dubbed Crypto Collectibles.

While this sounds exciting to many people, there is still a lot of confusion about what a crypto collectible is and how it differs from other crypto assets such as cryptocurrencies.

Is There A Market Bubble For Nfts?

Going back to the basics of a bubble, there is an extreme spike in the value of non-fungible tokens. But, how long will this bubble last? That is an inquiry that only time can answer. It is possible that NFTs are in a drop and that the bubble will pop, but we won't know for sure until the market adjusts to a new price.

Speculation

The crypto market is full of speculators and people who believe that they can predict the future. These people have been buying NFTs, hoping that the value will continue to rise. This type of behavior isn't necessarily a bad thing, but it can create a bit of volatility. Some people get hurt when the market fluctuates, and others make money. The goal is to make money, but many people cannot predict how high or low the price will go.

Media Attention

Many of the top NFTs are being used in games and virtual worlds. Some crypto art projects are making it big in the media and social circles. When something gets this much attention, it is easy for speculators to jump on board and buy NFTs at a higher price. When there is more demand for NFTs, the price will increase.

Limited Supply

A limited number of NFTs are being created each year for each project. The amount of tokens available at any given time is being reduced because of the projects creating new tokens. Some people believe that this reduction in supply will lead to a higher price, but it isn't necessarily true. A higher price will only happen if there is more demand for the tokens.

The Rise In Popularity Of Decentralized Games And Virtual Worlds

The popularity of decentralized games and virtual worlds is on the rise. Many projects are creating new games and virtual worlds that will utilize NFTs. Some of these projects have been victorious, while others have failed. When a project fails, it could mean that the value of the NFTs associated with that project will decrease.

Before launching yourself head-first into the world of NFTs, there are some common mistakes that you really must avoid. Although the creation and selling of NFTs have not been going on for too long, it is noticeable that some people are making the same mistakes repeatedly.

These mistakes can be catastrophic for your success in the NFT world. You will probably make other small mistakes when you are just starting, and that's OK. As long as you learn from these, it is OK. It would help if you avoided these vast mistakes that can mean the difference between success and failure.

NFT MISTAKES THAT YOU MUST AVOID

Thinking Too Short-Term

Yes, some NFTs have sold for millions over the last year. But that doesn't mean that you can create NFTs or invest in them and make a substantial amount of money the first time around. If you try to make too much money too fast with NFTs, then it is very likely that you will fail and give up on the whole idea.

There is no doubt that the NFT journey can be an exciting one. This doesn't mean that you will be a millionaire by this time next week, though. You are highly likely to fail if you go into NFTs with a "get rich quick" attitude.

The best way to succeed with NFTs is to provide value. You will also need a reasonable degree of patience as you may not sell your NFTs right away. Be consistent with your marketing efforts and take the time to form collaborations and partnerships that will serve you well in the future. If you are serious about the NFT game, then commit to it for the longer term.

You Are Not Promoting Your Nfts Enough.

It is just not enough to create your NFTs and list them on OpenSea, and expect the money to start rolling in. There are already millions of NFTs listening on OpenSea, and most of these are struggling to find buyers.

Forget about the "build it, and they will come" concept. It is not going to happen. You need to create a marketing plan and then stick to it. Identify your target audience and then find out where they hang out.

Use social platforms to leverage your NFT promotions. Use Discord forums, Clubhouse and Reddit to your advantage as well. Do whatever you can to obtain the word out about your NFTs and the talents that you have.

Some people might get lucky with their NFTs. They may list them on OpenSea, sell them quickly, and have people begging for more. Instances like this are sporadic. You cannot count on this kind of luck, so be sure to have a promotional plan and follow through with it.

Choosing The Wrong Marketplace For Your Nfts

This is another classic mistake that we see over and over again. NFT creators cannot do the necessary research, and they opt for OpenSea because it is the biggest platform. Yes, OpenSea does get a lot of visitors (nearly 40 million a month and growing), but this does not indicate that it is the best platform for your NFTs.

It would be best to find out several things about an NFT marketplace before you use it. The essential thing is knowing whether your target audience uses the marketplace or not. You need to consider if the NFTs you want to create are a good fit for the ethos of the market.

With several new NFT marketplaces emerging all of the time, you need to ascertain whether the market you are considering using is safe. The size of the community in the market is essential, but more important is whether the community is responsive and helpful.

Unfortunately, there are scam NFT websites already in existence. For example, these people will collect fees from you to pay Ethereum, and you will never sell anything. To avoid these scam NFT websites, use the Dapp Radar website to check for legitimacy.

I Am Doing Nfts On The Cheap.

The more that you can invest in your NFT venture, the better. Many people make the mistake of thinking that the world of NFTs is a free one and that they can do everything on the cheap. While platforms do not have fees for listings, most of the best quality ones do, so you need to factor this into your NFT budget.

In this guide, we have told you several times that the Ethereum blockchain network is by far and away from the most popular for NFTs. If you want to use the Ethereum network, you will have to pay gas fees.

You need to put some money after your NFT marketing as well. Unless you have a massive following on social media, you will need to use social media ads to showcase your NFTs. That is a reasonably inexpensive way to achieve results pretty fast.

While gas fees and listing fees may come down as NFTs become even more popular, this cannot be guaranteed, and you cannot rely on this happening. If costs come down in price, use the money you saved for more marketing. You need to take your NFT journey seriously and be prepared to invest in it for the maximum chance of success.

It does not understand how NFTs work.

We have seen so many people make costly mistakes because they didn't understand the basics of blockchain and crypto.

It would be best to have a good overview of how NFTs work and blockchain.

INVESTING AND FLIPPING OF NFT'S

If you are not aware of the term "flipping," you buy something at a low price and then sell it at a more elevated price. There are many examples of this in life, such as purchasing a real estate property for a low price and trading it for a higher price. You can apply flipping to things like comic books, services, and much more.

Investing in NFTs and flipping them for profits is something you can do. Not everyone is artistic and cut out for creating and selling their own NFTs. NFT trading is growing considerably, and investing in NFTs right now can be a brilliant move.

Benefits Of Flipping Nfts

Today, the NFT market is relatively new, and the competition is not that great. There is a lot of room for growth in this market. People are already making profits from flipping NFTs, and there are a lot of opportunities to do this if you know what you are looking for.

As an example of the profit potential in buying and selling NFTs, a token was sold in 2017 called CryptoPunks. This NFT sold for $456, worth around $26,000. There are a growing number of NFT collectors, so you should see these opportunities available for quite some time.

The people involved in NFT flipping right now realize profits from 10% to 50% in just a few days. They are building NFT portfolios, and some of the investors hang on to their investors longer-term to make even greater profits.

People Are Buying Nfts

You know from reading this guide and external sources that NFTs are very popular today. There is no doubt that blockchain technology is here to stay. Many businesses and organizations worldwide are looking at how blockchain technology can improve what they do, and some have implemented it already.

When you have major blockchain networks such as Ethereum allowing the tokenization of digital art, video clips, music, in-game items, and more, there is a massive appeal for owning NFTs.

The central selling point for an NFT is uniqueness and provenance. Many things are copied in the digital world, but there can only be one proven owner of an NFT. People are interested in purchasing different NFTs, and they vary in value.

Nft Flipping Opportunities

No form of investing is guaranteed, and this applies to NFTs. There are certainly opportunities for NFT flipping profits, but you have to know how to spot the best options. Flipping NFTs has already been confirmed to be a simple and relatively quick way to make good money.

There are no hidden secrets for finding NFTs that are good flipping opportunities. It comes down to 2 things:

The Nft Is Currently Undervalued

The NFT is expected to increase in value

Because there are NFTs in many different niches, it can be tempting to try and find opportunities in all of these. But this is not the best approach to use. You need to find a profitable NFT niche and learn everything about it. It is not likely to be an expert in every NFT niche. The more you know about an NFT niche, the higher the chances of good flipping projects.

We recommend that you do not go for more than 2 NFT niches. Start with one and then really dig into the community around it. Find forums and subreddits around this NFT niche, watch YouTube videos about it, listen to podcasts, and chat with people in the community.

It will take time for you to become knowledgeable about an NFT niche, so you need to be committed to this. You can never do enough research, so commit to learning about your chosen NFT niche(s) every day.

An NFT niche could be a popular game. The Decentraland game has a virtual real estate theme. An NFT investor made a profit of over $83,000 in just one year with this game. He purchased parcels of land from the game at a low price and sold them for a higher price. This guy knew the market and was able to capitalize on his knowledge.

Find Nft Flipping Opportunities On Marketplaces

You can go to popular NFT marketplaces such as OpenSea and Rarible to find flipping opportunities. We would liken these sites to garage sales, where you can find undervalued items. OpenSea, in particular, is a great marketplace to find hidden gems because there are a lot of crypto artists finding their way with the platform.

There are NFT flipping opportunities in the collectibles market as well. Here we are talking about niche opportunities at sites like NBA Top Shot, CryptoKitties, Atomic Assets, and Decentraland.

If you have some experience buying and selling trading cards for a profit, the Atomic Assets marketplace is ideal for you to start. This site keeps up with trends, and many collectors use it to find the NFTs that they want.

There is considerable interest in the NBA, and the Top Shot marketplace has NFTs available valued at more than $600 million. Creators drop new NFTs all the time on this outlet, and it is a very active marketplace. If sports memorabilia appeals to you, this is a great place to start. The bottom line is that you need to know and follow your niche.

For crypto art, the best sites are Nifty Gateway and Known Origin. The best way to profit from these marketplaces is to look for emerging artists and any high-quality art that you believe to be undervalued. Finally, you will see the entire market at SuperRare and Christies.

Use Nft Buying Strategies

Several successful NFT investors seek out bulk buys. That is one of the best ways to make a healthy profit from NFT flipping. Bulk buys are more common in the collectible and trading cards markets. Some of these bulk buys can be on a large scale, as many NFT sellers are happy to sell in a bundle because they do not want the hassle of trading individual tokens.

You can haggle the price on an NFT with sellers. The best way to do this is to connect with NFT sellers in the communities for your niche using private communication methods (instant messaging etc.). A lot of NFT investors make their most considerable profits through haggling.

Be prepared to network within the communities of your NFT niche. Constantly maintain an eye on the market and look for different trends. The more you are on top of your NFT niche, the more profit you are likely to make.

FUTURE OF NON-FUNGIBLE TOKENS

Since the beginning of NFT, the favor of NFT games has skyrocketed. NFT projects have been created by several prominent organizations, including the video game producer NBA and Ubisoft. As of January 2019, Dapper Labs, the organization that made CryptoKitties, has started collaborating with other NFT providers to facilitate interoperability between game platforms. That means that a native NFT can now be used on another platform without modification.

In current years, the potential for NFTs has expanded dramatically beyond the gaming industry. Organizations and organizations are investigating the possibility of non-fungible tokens as a means of establishing identity and certification, ticketing, and fractional right of both digital and physical assets. Any condition in which there is a requirement for traceability and explicit license falls under the purview of NFT use issues.

The fate of NFTs will heavily depend on the progress of the Ethereum network and broader blockchain technology.

It's secure to assume that as blockchain technology persists to grow, NFTs will mind – whether it's on the Ethereum blockchain, another broad network, or a remote web.

Crowdfunding A Non-Fungible Token

Non-fungible tokens are still moderately new, and most game developers have had to find out how they can be made as they go. Many NFTs are built using living smart contracts or making their protocol. In some circumstances, the founders of an NFT will also create a game to showcase its features and utility. That allows users to purchase the game and give it a level of credibility.

The Nft Approach To Crowdfunding

Allocation for a new company by using crowdfunding is a moderately new idea. NFTs (Non-Fungible Tokens) have been available on the Ethereum network since 2015. But they are still somewhat obscure among game creators and a broader audience. That means that many developers may not have the tools or resources to create an NFT. That is one of the reasons that the NFT Approach to Crowdfunding was made. This approach allows NFTs to be designed, hosted, and spread on any outlet (including mobile gadgets and web browsers). In expansion, game developers can also build crowdfunding campaigns using the "NFT-Crowdfund" standard. It supplies developers with the tools and resources they need to create their own NFT. That allows them to make their ERC-721 token; an NFT used as a crowdfunding campaign.

Constructing Nft-Crowdfund

Here is how you can potentially construct your NFT-Crowdfund:

- Make your colored token for crowdfunding on a platform (Ethereum Wallet, Metamask, etc.) or via a command-line interface (console).

- Use the NFT-Crowdfund protocol for creating and distributing the NFT.

- Use ERC 721 to convey your game items.

- Use ERC – 684 for constructing pre-order items with a deal. These will not be fungible behind the Crowdfund ends. Unsold pre-order things are burned.

- Rename your NFT if required to remember the marketplace name.

- Document your rare item(s) on a marketplace for selling post-crowdfunding using the NFT registry, or create your marketplace. All pre-order items must be re-categorized to fit your new marketplace category.

Buildup Art Nft Marketplace

Finally, I wanted to present you with this revolutionary project named Hype Art. I am creating with a team of art and cryptocurrency lovers.

Non-For-Profit (NFP) projects started to gain widespread notice. Although crypto was going through a downturn, the industry saw significant growth.

The most accustomed marketplaces for NFT (Superrare, Niftigataway, Rarible) present their platforms more to Amazon and eBay than to a craftwork gallery: collectors don't feel any creative venture when scanning these outlets.

The Artist is not in the middle of the discussion. No space is given to the idea and the thought behind its work.

What Do We Desire To Create?

We think the creative vision of the NFT creator needs to be placed at the center of the narrative. Each Artist will share the creative idea behind their work through a live interview (hosted by Koinsquare) jointly with a curated definition of the work presented.

We strive to create a 3d virtual gallery that allows the collector to repeat the same feeling of visiting works displayed in a real gallery.

We want to encourage the community of our collectors by using gamification; therefore, auctions will be completed in parallel to airdrops to our followers.

Where?

Hype. Art will utilize Opensea (ETH blockchain) and FAN (Tron blockchain) as venues where the Auction will carry place to access a bigger market.

Hype. Art will instead promote the community's artistic promotion and a structured team to allow artists to customize their "online exhibitions."

Key Players

There are three key players: the Zulu Republic, Koinsquare, and Satoshygallery.

The Zulu Republic is a location on the blockchain where people, businesses, and organizations can thrive on their representations. Our objective is to help promote the development of decentralized technology, which is likely to have an enormous effect on the advancement of human rights and empowerment throughout the world and mitigate the digital gap.

Koinsquare is a project that strives to promote and disseminate knowledge and knowledge in blockchain and cryptocurrency technology.

With our commitment, passion, and professional approach, we present and analyze different topics such as Cryptocurrencies, Smart Contracts, centralized/decentralized Exchanges, ICOs, the Fintech Industry, Market values of the significant crypto assets, Mining systems, and much more.

Satoshi Gallery was born in a very early stage of cryptocurrency history. Since 2013, it has been using iconography and art to fill the opening between technology developers and the general public and spread the crypto culture to a larger audience. Satoshigallery has provided art paintings to various private collectors worldwide, illustrated books for Andreas Antonopoulos, and drew some of the most iconic logos in the crypto space (Bitfinex, Tether, etc.).

When Will The Project Launch?

- March 2021: Hype. art was born

- April 2021: Platform and artistic development

- May 2021: Marketing development

- September 2021: Launch of platform for public

Do You Want To Participate In Airdrop?

Art. The art exhibition will include thousands of Airdrops and a premium Auction, ready to scream out the first Artist with the launch of Hype. You have been one of the first to get an invitation to view the Exhibition and bid in the Auction. We will be providing a date announcement to the subscriber as soon as possible.

HAS THE BUBBLE ALREADY BURST?

Even as some people remain optimistic about the future of non-fungible tokens, others believe that the bubble has indeed burst, and the statistics are there to prove it. Ethers, for example, lost over 50 percent of their value between the spring and fall of 2021, including a five-day, $1,000 devaluation in September. That was accompanied by an almost $10,000 drop-in Bitcoin, leading many to believe it was more of a market correction for cryptocurrencies. Still, other statistics show that adjustments are happening in the non-fungible token world.

At its peak, collectibles like CryptoPunks were leading the way to total sales. Their grasp on the market was staggering, outselling all other forms of non-fungible tokens by a wide margin. In August of 2021, total collectibles sales reached almost USD 165 million over seven days. Within a month, that had dropped to a mere $9 million. Similar drops were seen in art, gaming, sports, utility, metaverse, and Defi purchases.

Most charts showed a roller coaster-like rise and fall while others, namely sports, flatlined. Much of the buzz around sports non-fungible tokens is tempered by the fact that, unlike collectibles and art, they are limited as to which wallet can hold them and how they are sold. Dapper Labs has its wallet for non-fungible tokens traded on the NBA's Top Shot marketplace, which some collectors do not like. Major League Baseball's Champions series, non-fungible receipts of baseball players in the bobblehead style, are rising in price, mainly because the world's biggest baseball league ended their partnership with creators Lucid Sight, making the non-fungible tokens rare commodities.

But others believe the most robust future lies with businesses like NBA's Top Shot and other sports-related digital memorabilia, at least from a collectible point of view. The cartoonish CryptoKitties and CryptoPunks may have set the bar, but in a sports-obsessed world, non-fungible tokens of real-world athletes and sports teams could take things to the next level. Ethernity Chain, armed with its own crypto Erns, is banking on just this. They have entered into exclusive non-fungible token production of current athletes like Dallas Cowboys running back Ezekiel Elliot, former athletes like soccer's Péle, and athletes who have passed on, such as boxing icon Muhammed Ali.

"With the non-fungible token boom we have seen in recent months, it is clear in my mind that authenticated non-fungible tokens from actual real-world sports and entertainment statistics are the only real future for non-fungible token collectibles," said Ethernity CEO Nick Rose Ntertsas.

"When we launch a drop with Tony Hawk, Muhammad Ali, or the legendary footballer Pelé, these are all authentic, endorsed, and backed by these people, thus creating an actual underlying value for them."

Ethernity has taken collectibles to another level, adding a particular twist to their NFTs featuring Dallas Cowboys quarterback Dak Prescott. His digital collectible cards will change their look depending on how Prescott performs during the football season. They are linked to his quarterback rating, a mathematical formula that rates a player's performance based on his game statistics. A bad game and the card goes grey, with lightning strikes in the background; a good game, he's blue, and excellent performance will see him red, as in red hot, hoisted on the shoulders of his teammates.

Looking further down the road, Althea Artificial Intelligence has developed what they are calling intelligent non-fungible tokens. Through their technology, non-fungible tokens will become animated, allowing owners to interact and even converse with their digital art. In doing so, they have created a sub-category for non-fungible tokens, intelligent-non-fungible tokens (NFTs). Still, in the developmental stages, the company raised $16 million in capital through a private token sale in August 2021. They see iNFTs as the cornerstone of future, interactive metaverse technology.

As exciting as this is, it is still all speculation.

The Tulip Lesson

History is rife with economic bubble bursts, and the one drawing a lot of comparisons to the non-fungible token market is the Tulip Bubble of the mid-1600 in Holland. Economics moved a lot slower in those days, so it took longer to play out, but the similarities are glaring. Early in the Century, tulips arrived from Asia, brought by traders along what was known as the Silk Road. Europeans loved the unusual-looking flower, and it soon became a luxury item for the rich to have in their gardens. Like so many fads, people looked down on people who did not have tulips in their garden.

Unlike modern tulips, many of which can handle the harshest winters only to pop up in the spring, the tulips of the 17th Century were fragile and needed extra care and cultivation. That further elevated their status as a sign of prosperity. While tulip seeds could take over ten years to start flowering, the bulbs would bloom annually, so people scrambled to get the bulbs. When a mutant strain created striped tulips as opposed to those with a single color, an even greater status symbol was born; and the wealthy were willing to pay whatever it took to get the flowers into their gardens.

Like the non-fungible token market, people looked for ways to get in on the tulip action. Farms outside of the cities went from food production to tulip production, and the price of a bulb rose to the modern equivalent of $10,000 to USD 50,000. By 1636 tulips were being traded in the Dutch stock exchanges. It seemed nobody wanted to miss out, so people began borrowing against equity to buy bulbs. At one point, a tulip bulb cost more than a house along Amsterdam's Grand canal. Much of the cause of the price rise was that producers could not keep up with the demand due to the long time it takes for a tulip seed to reach maturity.

With so many bulbs bought on credit, panic set in when the price began to drop. Not wanting to be stuck with debt, buyers became sellers, and the price plummeted. By 1638 tulip bulbs were back at their regular prices. Stories emerged of investors who lost everything and were forced to eat the tulip bulbs they once prized. It is questionable whether "tulip mania" devastated the economy as much as history likes to believe, but it did explain why investing is risky.

With the significant drop in price and sales, it is not hard to see why some financial analysts believe there has indeed been a burst. That is not to say that non-fungible tokens are going away. Their usage is becoming more streamlined, but making a quick profit through buying or selling might not be as leisurely as it existed in early 2021. While the collectible market may be down, other markets like sports are up. Still, others believe that the gaming industry is the most bankable future for non-fungible tokens.

Already a 100 billion-dollar-a-year industry, the next step could be the convergence of non-fungible tokens and DeFi in gaming. The idea is somewhere along the lines of a rental shop for gamers. Investors could buy game pieces like a specialized weapon or armor, then rent them to a gamer for a small fee. This way, a gamer could profit from the game as they play. Swedish game developers Vorto are going hard at this concept with their game Hash Rush. Even in 2021, with the game not set to debut until 2022, Vorto is selling game pieces, and eager gamers are already scooping them up.

Fraud

For all the exciting and sometimes baffling news surrounding non-fungible tokens, there is an equally ugly side that could scare a lot of people away if it does not get better. If one thing can bring down a market, it is bad press. Even as marketplaces scramble for better security procedures, stories keep emerging about scams and hustles designed to exploit the unprepared.

Earlier, we consider the Russian men posing as women selling the Famed Lady Squad non-fungible tokens and an employee at OpenSea engaging in insider trading. Are there other scams or manipulations you should be concerned with? The answer is yes. Crooks are descending on the non-fungible token world, knowing there are a bunch of unsavvy buyers and sellers ripe for the picking. The one item they desire more than anything is your passkey.

If you recall, the key is the set of 12 words that secure your wallet. Scammers have become very creative in their attempts to get your key, including setting up fake sites that look and feel like a popular non-fungible token marketplace but with a subtle difference; they are listed as not .oi. The unsuspecting victim logs on but has problems accessing their wallet, usually connected to the site. They try and try, but the problem continues. The scammers hope that eventually, they will access tech support. When they do, the scam begins.

It usually starts; they ask the usual questions to make the victim feel at ease. The scammers can work in pairs, bringing in a second "technician" to help fix the problem. That can go on for hours, and it usually does by design. They are trying to wear you down so that eventually, you slip up. You reveal your keycode or the QR code that allows access to your wallet. Once they have that, everything ends. When the victim goes back and checks their wallet, everything, non-fungible tokens, and crypto alike, is gone.

Because the technology is so fresh and it draws in so many buyers unfamiliar with how things work, there are plenty of easy victims for the scammers to attack. But these guys are so good that collectors well versed in the non-fungible token community are also falling victim. To alleviate the problem, OpenSea closed their customer service segment of their website and moved it to Discord, a Voice Over Internet Protocol, instant messaging, and digital distribution application that has become the central hub for the non-fungible token community. Even then, the scammers followed (author's note: After purchasing some non-fungible tokens and joining Discord, I was asked about my wallet within two posts). So bold are these scammers that they even pretended to be OpenSea's customer support lead and their head of product by using their names. In one instance, respected digital artist Jeff Nicholas lost USD 480,000.

Impersonators

Scammers have also taken to impersonating artists and selling bogus non-fungible tokens. This sucker job is pulled by setting up a marketplace page that looks exactly like the actual artist's page but with subtle differences. The YouTube site Non-fungible Token Times illustrated these differences with a Bored Ape scam page listed as the "official" BAYC page. What was missing, and it is easy to forget, was that the page was not verified even though it had the verification checkmark next to the page's profile picture. Everything else looked legitimate, including links to the BAYC webpage and different social media accounts. The scammers hope that you miss the small details and take their bait.

HOW TO DISCOVER AND ANALYZE PROJECTS

At the outset of my foray into the world of non-fungible tokens (also known as digital assets), I had no clue where to begin or figure out which of the projects would be the best fit for my particular situation. After spending over a year in space and gathering a large number of NFTs, I think I have established a reliable method for selecting the most appropriate project for you and your long-term financial objectives.

The following three basic guidelines must be followed when selecting the finest NFT to purchase for yourself and retain for the long term:

Invest In Non-Financial Companies That You Are Interested In.

First and foremost, you should only invest in non-financial companies that pique your interest. After all, what's the purpose of spending money on something you're not going to use or enjoy? Consider looking for the "next greatest" NFT rather than the "next best" NFT corresponding to your specific interests.

There is no way for everyone to have the same interests and no way for everyone to make the same informed decision about anyone NFT project since we all have different degrees of comprehension of the category we have chosen to invest in.

For example, suppose you truly appreciate soccer and know a lot about the players and teams. In that case, it's fair to assume that a soccer NFT project would be an excellent topic to start your study on while developing your NFT project. Alternatively, if you are a true admirer of modern art, you should be delving further into the works of contemporary artists and their NFTs.

Carry Out Your Investigation

Who doesn't like a good bit of research? Once you've identified an NFT that you're interested in, it's time to get your hands dirty and understand all you can about that particular NFT. The process of researching NFTs isn't quite as simple as browsing the "evaluations" area of a website and reading all that other customers have to say, but it's close.

When you sit down to investigate any NFT, the following are the topics I urge you to attempt to collect as much information on as you possibly can:

- The creator(s)

- The community

- The project (brand)

The creator(s)

In my opinion, it is critical to identify that when you buy in a non-fungible token, you are genuinely investing in the person who is driving the project forward. As with betting on your favorite sports team, you place your wager on the player's ability to perform rather than on a random group of individuals.

When evaluating a project's originator, there are a few aspects that I look for, including their prior success and ability to execute, their social position, and their capacity to develop brand recognition within their target audience.

The community

Don't forget about the people in your community! A successful NFT initiative will have a thriving community due to their efforts. The presence of a generally pleasant attitude, helpful individuals, and a high level of communication from the project manager are all indicators of a thriving community. It is expected that this communication will include project updates, notifications and help with any difficulties that community members may be experiencing.

Okay, so now you're likely wondering where you can learn more about a project's community; the answer is simple: everywhere you go online and look for it.

The project (brand)

Finally, we get to the most critical component of the puzzle: the actual project. In my opinion, the projector, as I like to refer to it, the brand—is unquestionably one of the most significant parts of the NFT jigsaw. The brand attracts customers and maintains a high demand for its assets.

Don't Fund More Money Than You Can Afford To Lose.

The last piece of the puzzle in determining the ideal NFT for your position and goals should not just be regarded as a rule but an essential must! Do not put more money into an investment than you can afford to lose. There should, in my view, be no exceptions to this general norm.

Putting all of your funds into a project with no money to fall back on may place yourself and your family in a difficult financial situation. It's awful if you wind up losing all of your hard-earned cash on an NFT project that finally turns out to be of less value than you had anticipated.

I try to get into any endeavor with the mindset that the project might fail and be refunded. I understand that no one likes to consider the possibility that the initiative they have invested in may fail, but that is just the reality of the market.

NFTS AND DEFI

Both the NFT and DeFi (Decentralized Finance) ecosystems have collaborated in a variety of ways, including the following:

Nft-Backed Loans:

Some DeFi apps are available that allow you to borrow money by pledging collateral.

When a person wants one bitcoin, they must first provide 25 or 26 ETH as collateral. A person can acquire the loan he needs, and the lender can take the collateral if the borrower defaults on the loan. However, not everyone would have the necessary quantity of cryptocurrencies on hand to obtain the loan they require.

Some prospective projects are beginning to investigate the strategies for employing NFTs as collateral to assist such persons. As an example, suppose you purchased a rare NFT a few days ago that is now worth $63,000 at today's pricing. You can get a loan for 26 ETH if you hold this as collateral. If you can't pay back the ETH, the lender will take your rare NFT as collateral. Anything that can be tokenized as an NFT could be used in this way.

Because both the DeFi and NFT worlds employ Ethereum's blockchain technology, this will be a simple operation.

Fractional Ownership: In addition, creators can create shares for their specific NFT. That allows investors and fans to own a portion of an NFT without purchasing the entire asset. Miners and collectors of NFTs will have access to an increasing number of chances due to this.

The NFT marketplace and Decentralized Exchanges (DEXs) like Uniswap would be used to trade such fractions of NFTs.

There would be significant growth in the number of buyers and sellers.

The fractions of an NFT can be used to calculate its overall price. You will have a window of opportunity to possess and earn from goods that are important to you. It would be terrible if you desperately desired something but couldn't afford it.

To put it another way, this would be like owning a piece of Picasso art. You'd own a bit of a Picasso NFT, which means you'd also be a part-owner and have to say over things like income sharing. It's likely that having a piece of an NFT will enable you to form a decentralized autonomous organization (DAO) to administer that asset shortly.

DAOs are Ethereum-based institutions that allow anonymous people, such as global asset shareholders, to interact securely without trusting the rest of the globe. Even a single cent cannot be spent without the consent of all of the group's members.

As formerly stated, the space of NFTs, DAOs, and fractional tokens are all evolving at different rates.

Nonetheless, because they are all part of the same network, Ethereum, all their infrastructures may exist and work together.

Nfts And Ethereum

Ethereum enables NFTs to work smoothly in various ways, some of which are listed below: Token transaction history and information are open to the public and may be verified by anybody. As a result, proving ownership with the use of NFTs is simple.

It is impossible to change existing data after successfully verifying a transaction, which means the ownership status cannot be stolen.

NFT trades might be made directly, eliminating the need for platforms that often take a percentage of the money as compensation.

The technology used in Ethereum's goods is the same as that used in Bitcoin. As a result, even if you have an NFT on one platform, you can sell it on another as long as it is Ethereum.

Creators can list several properties simultaneously, and all of those items will have the most up-to-date information.

Because Ethereum is available 24 hours a day, 7 days a week, you can sell your NFTs whenever you choose.

Minting An Nft

The following steps are taken to create an NFT.

- The existence of the NFT as a blockchain asset should be proven.

- The creator's account balance should be adjusted to reflect the asset's inclusion. It can be ensured that the person owns the help in this way.

- The transactions, as mentioned earlier, will be confirmed and appended to a block on the blockchain, making them permanent (immortalized).

- It should be verified as valid by others in the network before recognizing that the NFT is on the web and belongs to the originator.

Anyone can check it because it is recorded on the public ledger. Finally, the creators' income potential would be raised due to this.

The duties, as mentioned earlier, are typically carried out with the assistance of miners. Miners inform other network members about these NFTs and who owns them. If the process isn't demanding enough, anyone can claim the NFT by claiming bogus ownership. There are numerous incentives in place to encourage miners to work honestly.

While data blocks are being added to the Ethereum blockchain, they must be created consistently. As a result, a data block will be added to the blockchain every 12 seconds. Nobody, however, will be able to change the data that is being uploaded to the blockchain. For example, suppose a hacker attempts to change the data of an NFT in block #200. When he tries to do so, the data on the other blocks will alter, and any Ethereum blockchain miner will be able to spot it and prevent it from happening.

Every day and NFT transactions are both added to the blockchain in the same way, so a block with no NFT transactions is the same as a block with NFT transactions. As a result, the computational power needed is the same. As a result, rather than being caused by NFTs, the environmental damage is caused by the blockchain or Ethereum.

Drawbacks

We've gone over most of the benefits and characteristics of NFTs, and a few things stand out. However, NFTs have some disadvantages listed below: Is it a bubble?

Ethereum, like the majority of other profitable cryptocurrencies, may be subject to additional scrutiny. If all governments agree to prohibit cryptos and everything linked with them, you will lose all of your priceless NFTs. As a result, the future implementation of cryptocurrencies is unknown.

Cryptocurrencies and related activities have been outlawed in Bolivia, China, Algeria, and Morocco. Furthermore, governments like India are attempting to enforce a ban on cryptocurrencies, and progress is being made.

So, if something seems too fine to be true, it probably is, and the same may be said of cryptocurrencies and NFTs.

Theft:

Assume someone put forth a lot of effort and created digital art. Someone else could steal it and make it his NFT before he could mint it as an NFT. There is no precise regulation in place to restrict such behavior.

Partiality:

People who have become renowned and have established a reputation may amass a large fan following and earn a lot of money, whether from music sales, art sales, or other means. So, what about up-and-coming musicians who are seeking to build a fan base? They are unlikely to make much money because most people prefer to buy anything from celebrities. As a result, it may benefit aspiring artists and innovators at the start of their careers.

Environmental Damage:

The most significant downside of NFTs is that they are based on Ethereum, which requires mining to add data blocks to its blockchain.

That is true not only for Ethereum but for most cryptos, particularly 'Bitcoin.' Using a Proof-of-Work (PoW) consensus mechanism to mine would necessitate a massive amount of computing power. High-tech computers and a lot of electricity would be required. The amount of energy consumed for Bitcoin mining is more significant than Argentina's total energy consumption. That would be harmful to the environment, and the carbon emissions might be substantial.

NFTs got a lot of publicity and popularity after Bitcoin, and there will be a rise in activity relating to them. As an outcome, there is a probability that NFTs may become the second most significant source of carbon emissions and environmental damage among all cryptos in the cryptocurrency ecosystem.

Data Hosting:

The digital asset and NFT are maintained separately, which means the NFT is on the blockchain while also containing the digital asset's location. A link is frequently used to connect the digital asset to the NFT. The association would stop working if the digital asset was destroyed from where it was stored or if the server that hosts the NFT encountered any technical difficulties.

As a result, the NFT will lose its value. If such a circumstance arises, there is no way to restore the NFT.

However, as formerly stated, Ethereum intends to migrate to Proof-of-Stake (PoS) from Proof-of-Work (PoW) (PoW). They can increase significantly less environmental damage because they will not require highly advanced computers or a significant quantity of electricity.

THE MOST FAMOUS TYPE OF SMART CONTRACT IS NFTS

In principle, an NFT is precisely the opposite of a cryptocurrency. By definition, all cryptocurrencies are fungible. Said differently, your bitcoin and my bitcoin are worth the same amount of fiat currency, which means we can easily trade one for another. NFTs are non-fungible. In principle, each NFT is unique, so you cannot change one for another as each has a market value of its own. In the physical world, most of the things we own are non-fungible. Your car and my car are both cars, but they cannot be exchanged for one another. That is also true of houses, most clothing, and most jewelry.

The two most widely-used NFT standards are smart contracts written and stored on the Ethereum blockchain:

ERC-721: A standard interface for non-fungible tokens, also known as deeds.

ERC-1155: A standard interface for contracts that manage multiple token types. A single deployed contract may include any combination of fungible tokens, non-fungible tokens, or other configurations (e.g., semi-fungible tokens).

NFTs are made ("minted") when a unique, standardized token and associated smart contract are registered on a blockchain. In theory, NFTs are non-fungible. Said differently, the NFT of Nyan Cat (sold at auction for roughly $560,000) is special and not interchangeable with other versions of the same file. Find a list of popular sites where you can mint your own NFTs here.

Using Nfts For Fan Or Audience Development

People have begun using the term "NFT" interchangeably with "digital collectible." That is unfortunate because while most of the digital collectibles in the news are NFTs, the technology can create value in many additional ways. When thinking about fan or audience development, which we define as a collection of purpose-built tools designed to grow communities of interest, perhaps the most obvious use for an NFT is a ticket to an event. Letâ€™s evaluation some of the benefits you might expect from combining a ticket, some unique digital assets, and a smart contract.

Nfts Are Smart Contracts

All NFTs are smart contracts. A smart contract is like an old-fashioned verbal or paper contract, except with a smart contract, the contract executes automatically when the conditions are met (digitally). Immutable, self-executing agreements coupled with the automatic exchange of funds (or tokens) open up a world of possibilities for ticketing.

The Elimination Of Duplicate Or Fraudulent Tickets

Every NFT is unique, and ownership is written on a public distributed ledger (blockchain) which anyone can read. If your request for an NFT has been validated, a quick matching of public and private keys (using something as familiar as a barcode reader) would instantly verify that the person with the NFT in their digital wallet was the authentic owner of the ticket.

Revenue From Secondary Markets

If someone sells their NFT ticket, that transaction can trigger royalty payments to the issuer as well as any other stakeholder â€ "artists, sports leagues, athletes, sponsors, promoters, a charity, or anyone with a digital wallet. These business rules can be hard-coded into each NFT, and like all smart contracts, when a transaction occurs, and the conditions are met, funds automatically change hands.

Visibility Into Transactions

Bots, scalpers, bad actors, criminals, and 2nd-party sales on eBay or other auction sites. NFT tickets offer an easy way to gather actionable business intelligence about how and where your tickets are being sold and resold. You can find the exact moment of the transaction, the same address of the digital wallets in use, the amount of the transaction, and much, much more. Contrary to popular mythology, NFT transactions are not anonymous. Several commercial firms such as Chainalysis and CipherTrace offer blockchain BI tools.

Reduced Ticketing Costs

NFTs are not mined; they are minted. That is a non-trivial technical distinction. Today, you can coin NFT tickets for less than 10 cents apiece ", and the price of NFT ticket production will continue to drop.

New Revenue

You can, of course, mint NFT tickets as stand-alone digital collectibles. But you can also use NFT keys to allow fans access to an auction where they might bid on NFTs containing more valuable exclusive content. Because of the NFT's ability to collect 1st party data, they can also augment loyalty programs. The marketing techniques will need to be tested, but the technology is built-in.

Data-Driven Marketing Opportunities

Today, if you purchase six tickets to a sporting event and bring five family members or friends, the ticket seller has a business relationship with you but has no information about the other five people in your party. NFTs have the power to change that. If each attendee were required to present an NFT for entrance, the NFT would need to be transferred to their digital wallets. Depending upon how you wrote the business logic and what data you asked for as a condition of the ticket sale, the NFTs could collect a wealth of actionable first-party data.

Defi Opportunities

NFTs can be bought, sold, traded, swapped, or used as collateral, borrowed, or lent. In other words, your ability to financially engineer to create additional value is only limited by your creativity and your audience's willingness to participate. The blockchain's ability to democratize finance is part of what makes the technology super-exciting, super-dangerous, super-volatile, and fabulous! It is also why the world of crypto and DeFi (decentralized finance), writ large, has the attention of governments and regulators worldwide.

Next-Level Marketing

Whether your audience is a community of interest, a community of practice, or a community of passion, next-level marketers will have the opportunity to let their imaginations run free. What does your audience value the most? How can you empower them to participate? What additional value can you help them obtain? What is the next generation of loyalty programs? How much "access" to the star attraction can they achieve? Smart contracts will give smart marketers the tools they need to design new kinds of marketing programs with ongoing, automated value-creation components built-in.

What's Next

Traditional ticketing software has been a race to the bottom. Most of the systems are old and tired. Not surprisingly, almost every major ticketing company has announced that they are planning or already working on or about to launch a new NFT ticketing product. This is great. While there will be way too many different approaches, some will emerge as better than others. Consumers will vote with their wallets (as they always do), and this new tech will evolve.

Notably, some of the most exciting blockchain projects are poly chains or multichain, built to aggregate disparate blockchains. These new blockchains will empower Web 3.0 and certainly play some role in the evolution of NFT ticketing. In the meantime, I hope some of these ideas resonate with you and get you thinking about new ways to create value for your business.

SOME BRANDS ARE ALREADY INTO NFTS

Nike

Nike is now including a digital version of your next pair of kicks in the box.

Nike is a household name, and the legendary shoe and sportswear brand has begun to use NFTs to guarantee the authenticity of a pair of sneakers. Under the Crypto kick project, purchasing a couple of the brand's sneakers will now upload a digital merchandise replica to your 'virtual locker.' Given the burgeoning youth culture of acquiring, selling, and reselling shoes, adding a digital stamp of legitimacy to the token's physical counterpart elevates it to new heights and levels. Given that this is a digital collectible related to a tangible item, it is a unique method for NFTs. Still, it can also be utilized for cartoon characters or online sneaker communities, demonstrating that digital fashion is a purpose for NFTs far beyond more "traditional" aesthetic use as presumed by many.

Team Gb Nfts For 2021 Olympics Games

The NFT project initiated by Team GB after this summer's very unique Olympic Games, which will go down in the history books for its lack of worldwide fans and supporters, is another excellent example of NFT. The British Olympic Committee formed an NFT shop where fans could buy NFTs for restricted collectibles like murals by artist Ben Mosley or one-on-one encounters with Team GB gold medalists. It was a fantastic project to assist and compensate supporters who could not go to stadiums to cheer on their national side while recognizing their accomplishments and raising donations for the British Olympic Association.

The Nba And 'Digitally Owning' Moments

The NBA has designed a method that may very well be the game-changer of this field. The National Basketball Association (BNA) has launched 'NBA Top Shot,' a novel online marketplace of registered digital collectibles where enthusiasts can buy moments from their favorite sports teams, players, or games and obtain a certificate as well as an original clip, to broaden its attractiveness to Western audiences and switch its attention to more virtual and efficient service delivery. Buying and selling collectible cards is one of the sports' earliest extra revenue schemes, and the NBA has developed a system that could very well be the future of this field. With NFTs, the future is bright for NBA.

Taco Bell

Yum Brands, the parent firm of some of the world's largest most well-known fast-food franchises like Pizza Hut, KFC, and Taco Bell, has also developed an NFT approach. Taco Bell made and sold a set of NFT gifs on the specialist online market Rarible in February 2021, with all of them sold out in less than 30 minutes. The ad demonstrates that NFTs are not just suitable for artworks worth hundreds of thousands of dollars but also for $1 gag buys to fundraise for a Taco Bell-affiliated scholarship scheme. Some of these pieces have a resale value of $3,000 or more.

Coca-Cola Participates In The Nft Movement By Holding A Nonprofit Auction.

For International Friendship Day in 2021, the Coca-Cola Company held an NFT bidding, releasing the first-ever variety of electronic collectibles that "re-imagine a few of Coca-famous Cola's trademarks for the metaverse, with each NFT driven by shared experiences of friendship. A future recreation of the legendary Coca-Cola delivery jacket, virtually usable on Centralland, a distributed 3D virtual reality environment, was among the one-of-a-kind objects up for auction. Special Olympics International, the world's most prominent institution for impaired athletes, received 100% of the funds from this promotion.

Asics: Sunrise Red

Asics was one of the first to jump on the NFT bandwagon, releasing its debut collection in August 2021. It was a test for the brand and the recreational vertical as a whole to bridge the print and virtual divide for brands.

Asics, Joe Pace, leader of business development, stated that Digital experiences are part of the daily routine; he said he finds it difficult to envision a tomorrow without digital items prevalent in most people's lives. He explained that Asics decision to be part of it was part of being inventive, ahead, and having an idea for what the tomorrow might seem like from a business development perspective, or more importantly, from an invention development one. The sportswear company is establishing an artist-in-residence program, with earnings from the NFT auction supporting digital artists.

WHAT ARE NFTS ROYALTY SHARES?

Even after selling their NFTs, artists and content creators find that these tokens can be very advantageous since NFTs are in the glare of publicity. This feature is principally thought-provoking; they're called NFT royalties. You may want to know what NFT royalties are if you are new to this field. Let's find out!

What Are Nft Royalties?

All those times when you can sell your NFT creations on a marketplace, you will get a portion of the sale price; this is due to NFT royalties. Smart contracts automatically execute ongoing royalty NFT payments. You can choose your royalty percentage in most marketplaces. A standard royalty is about 5-10%.

There are numerous differences between NFTs and other traditional royalty payments.

When an author makes resales, some incentive is given back, known as the royalty payout. Royalty payouts are recorded into the smart contract on a blockchain. Whenever a resale happens, the smart contract ensures that the NFT set terms are achieved. In royalty specifications, a certain amount of money is sent over to the original artist from the revenue generated from the resale.

Every NFT does not yield royalties; this should be kept in mind. If you wish to receive royalties from your NFTs, you have to mention that in the terms and conditions. Those terms and conditions are recorded in the Ethereum blockchain network, and the rest of the process is all done automatically. It is not necessary to have intermediaries, and also it does not depend upon the wishes and demands of the person who is transacting. That is great for digital content, gaming accessories, physical items, etc. NFT royalties are a never-before-opportunity to increase the revenue generated by the artists and content creators. That is a benefit for the artists they get from these NFTs after creating or repeatedly producing something. As more and more these artists become popular, they may increase the returns that they receive from their work.

That is an excellent scheme that the NFTs offer. That makes the artists and digital content creators work with more motivation and enthusiasm. This is also motivating them to become a part of the NFT industry. The system of royalties may be different for each of the marketplaces. Many new marketplaces are developing other techniques and ways to help artists receive enough money for their production.

The artists would not be paid enough before the royalties' concept began on the NFT marketplaces. They would only be paid for the time they sold their work as an NFT on the marketplaces. After selling their work online, the artists would not track other subsequent transactions that occurred after that. The only time they made a profit was for selling it the first time, and then the buyer would gain profit after reselling. That was not something that motivated and inspired these artists and digital creators.

The people who would buy their work would wait for the right time and then sell that at excellent prices. This system only benefitted the buyer and not the artist who created the art initially. The artist got no penny from his artwork, and all that profit would go to the pockets of those who bought. Hence the familiar concept of artists as penurious or the starving artist.

NFTs have changed this whole concept from the grass-root level. Artists will be given a justified share every time their creations are sold. This will be forever.

How Do Nft Royalties Work?

Here, the question arises that how does the royalty system work? So basically, what happens is that at the time of minting the NFT for an original piece of artwork, the artist can decide over a certain amount that he would get after any other subsequent sales made by the buyer. Whenever the buyer sold an artist's painting, he would get the pre-determined amount of money from the revenue the buyer would generate from the sales. All the marketplaces do not allow you to have royalties claimed while minting the NFT However, Rarible does give you the option of royalties at the time of minting the NFT.

For example, you have an NFT artwork created on Rarible. Somebody buys that NFT for, let supposes, 8 ETH. That means that you have earned 8 ETH from your artwork. While minting your NFT, you have clearly stated that you would get a 10% revenue generated anytime this artwork is sold again. That means whenever the buyer sells that painting, you will get 10% of the money generated.

Now let suppose the buyer waits for the right time for a resale. Your popularity has grown by now, and the buyer sells your artwork for guessing 200 ETH. But as you have stated in the terms and conditions already, you would get a 10%incentive, which means you would get 20 ETH from the sale that was just made. That means that the buyer made a lot of money, whereas you, the original creator, could not earn that much.

Now let's imagine that the new owner might also sell your artwork; you would get 10% proceeds from that sale. That means that every time your painting is sold, you will get some revenue out of it. You will repeatedly be paid for your sold artwork. With the NFT royalties, you are at an advantage. That is an excellent way for the authors and original creators of the art to get paid for as long as their artwork is sold.

That means that no artist will have to suffer now. No content creator will struggle financially. There will be no fake or counterfeit products available in the market. Even if they are, they would not be worth the original product—identification of what is authentic and what is not has undoubtedly become easy.

All these great things are a result of blockchain technology. Blockchain technology works on a distributed ledger that records all the transactions that happen over the blockchain network. That makes the whole transaction process transparent and decentralized.

This digital ledger which records the data of transactions, makes the work more authentic. Whatever conditions are set in the smart contract are to be fulfilled at all costs, and that is possible due to the automated protocols of the network. You do not need an intermediary to process any transaction or dealing. All that is done automatically with excellent transparency.

Who Gains From An Nft Royalty?

Musicians creators, content creators, and artists gain from NFTs royalties. That is not again for the artists only but also the buyer. The buyer cannot be cheated as he would know what is authentic and what a replica is. He would not be fooled to buy something that is not original. That lets the buyers show off their digital collectibles and purchased assets and can resell them at higher prices. It's a win-win situation for both parties!

NON-FUNGIBLE TOKENS – RISKS AND CHALLENGES

I n 2021, NFTs have made quite a stir, especially following the $69.3 million in March NFT sales. Many people are wondering how long the NFT trend will continue. As a result, it's critical to consider the most significant NFT risks and problems. Non-fungible tokens, or NFTs, are one-of-a-kind digital assets. They have specific qualities, and exchanging them for other assets is difficult.

Non-fungible tokens have found their way into various industries, including music, domain names, art, and real estate. While NFTs have the potential to increase in the future, it is prudent to consider the potential NFT hazards. The next meeting will provide you with a thorough overview of the risks and issues associated with NFT so that you can better understand them.

Challenges And Risks With Nfts

Non-fungible tokens, or NFTs, are an entirely new sort of digital asset, meaning that the NFT ecosystem is prone to extreme swings and unpredictability.

The following are examples of frequent NFT challenges:

- Legal and regulatory challenges
- Evaluation challenges
- Intellectual Property or IP rights
- Cybersecurity and fraud risks
- Anti-money laundering (AML) and CFT challenges
- Smart contract risks and NFT maintenance
- Consideration of NFTs as securities
- Environmental Social Governance (ESG) challenges

Let's look at these NFT dangers and obstacles to see how they affect NFTs.

1. Legal and Regulatory Challenges

NFT lacks a clear definition and may be used to describe a wide range of assets, relying solely on specific characteristics. NFTs, for example, are one-of-a-kind, not interchangeable, and not fungible. However, there are several regulatory approaches to NFTs that are worth mentioning. In Europe, the proposed Markets in Crypto-assets (MICA) Regulation by the European Commission might establish a regulatory framework for NFTs.

Existing legislative suggestions suggest that the management of NFTs in the EU and the UK regulatory regimes may differ in the future. The European Union's proposal for Markets in Crypto Assets Regulation, released in September 2020, can serve as a platform for regulating specific NFT-related market activity. The current regulatory precedents in the UK, on the other hand, are most likely to exclude NFTs. However, a case-by-case analysis of how to sell or market NFTs and derive value from them might aid in deciding if NFTs would be subject to regulatory precedents. Surprisingly, NFTs are included in MICA's definition of "crypto-assets." Furthermore, the current draft of MICA's description of "crypto-assets" does not indicate that NFT issuers must publish a whitepaper.

According to the FCA rules, NFTs might be exempted from the UK promotion regime due to the idea of qualified crypto assets. NFTs may qualify as e-money, security, or unregulated tokens in these regulatory settings, depending on their qualities.

In Singapore, NFTs do not qualify as legal tender. NFTs are excluded primarily because they are non-fungible and may only be exchanged for particular items. Additionally, they might fall under the category of "limited purpose digital payment tokens," which would exclude them from PSA restrictions.

For the Payment Services Act of Japan, NFTs in Japan are classified according to their ability to fulfill an economic function, such as functioning as a payment method or being exchanged for cryptocurrencies. The Payment Services Act does not apply to NFTs with restricted activities, such as in-game products or trading cards, and no engagement in economic operations, such as payment instruments. Such NFTs should be thoroughly examined and evaluated in line with the functions and specifications of the NFT in question. In addition, the structure of the NFT platform or application and how the NFT is used should be taken into account.

The technical improvement in NFTs demonstrates the significance of considering legal and regulatory NFT issues. As NFTs continue to grow and extend into new use cases, laws and regulations should adjust. Many of the existing legislation relating to NFTs are now stalled on determining the best definition for NFTs. It's becoming more challenging to develop a strong foundation for NFT compliance as the type and quantity of NFTs grows.

2. Evaluation Challenges

The ambiguity in calculating the value of non-fungible tokens is another significant addition to the list of non-fungible token dangers and issues. The scarcity of NFTs, the perceptions of owners and purchasers, and the availability of distribution channels all have a role in their worth. It's incredibly impossible to predict who will be the next buyer of an NFT or what variables would influence their decision. As a result, the value of NFTs is primarily determined by how the buyer perceives their price, resulting in volatility.

3. Intellectual Property Rights

Intellectual property concerns are the following significant element in NFT risks and obstacles. It's crucial to evaluate an individual's rights to a certain NFT. It's critical to determine whether the vendor genuinely possesses the NFT before purchasing. There have been instances of someone photographing NFTs or minting reproductions of NFTs. As a result, when buying an NFT, you acquire the right to utilize it, not intellectual property rights. The metadata of the underlying smart contract contains the terms and conditions for owning an NFT.

However, all illusions about traditional law not applying to decentralized blockchain technology must be dispelled. The intellectual property risks and constraints associated with NFTs imply that buyers only have the right to exhibit NFTs and are the sole proprietors. The limitations on NFTs are also visible in the service standards that customers should adhere to when utilizing NFT markets. As a result, it's critical to examine fundamental IP rights such as copyrights, trademarks, patents, moral rights, and the right of publicity.

4. Cyber Security and Fraud Risks

The exponential surge in popularity of NFTs, along with the digital world's expansion, has resulted in significant cybersecurity and fraud issues. NFT is concerned about imitation stores that seem identical to legitimate NFT stores and use the same logo and content. Fake NFT stores are another significant difficulty linked with the hazards and challenges involved with NFTs in cybersecurity. Fake NFT retailers may sell NFTs that were never there in the first place. Buyers must also be aware of the risks associated with artist impersonation and counterfeit NFTs.

You should also be aware of the dangers of social media frauds that advertise NFTs. Some shady characters can mimic well-known NFT artists and sell counterfeit NFTs in their names. Copyright theft, copying of popular NFTs or false airdrops, and NFT giveaways are other major non-fungible tokens threats and issues regarding cybersecurity and fraud.

For example, some companies created NFTs from artworks in the digital collection of public domain paintings on exhibit at the Rijksmuseum in Amsterdam without the museum's permission. The instance of hackers taking NFTs from Nifty Gateway customers is one of the most recent examples of the NFT cybersecurity concern.

5. Smart Contract Risks and NFT Maintenance

One of the most significant worries in the NFT ecosystem is smart contract risk and NFT maintenance problems. Hackers recently targeted the renowned Defi protocol Poly Network, which features cross-chain interoperability. The NFT heist, which resulted in a loss of over $600 million, focuses on severe flaws in smart contract security.

For such large-scale assaults, hackers could take advantage of Poly Network's smart contract vulnerability. The poly network allows users to transfer tokens across multiple blockchain networks while collaborating. The hackers have returned about $300 million to the Poly Network as of writing.

6. Consideration of NFTs as Securities

One of the most significant non-fungible token dangers and concerns is the treatment of NFTs as securities. According to the Securities & Exchange Commission Chairman, most NFTs on the market are sold as securities. In contrast, the Supreme Court has linked NFTs to the idea of an investment contract. As a result, to demonstrate their eligibility as securities, NFTs must meet the Howey Test's unique requirements.

The following are some of the critical concepts of the Howey Test:

- determining whether or not the NFT is a security

- If the NFT is security, look to see if it was registered under the Securities Act of 1993.

- Check if participants are registered as securities broker-dealers if the NFT is about securities.

- Verify if platforms for security-like NFT transactions are registered as securities exchanges.

- Take into account the potential exposure for security NFT sellers under SEC Rule 10b-5 for the Use of Manipulative and Deceptive Practices.

7. AML and CFT Challenges

In July, the FATF published a study stating that distributed ledger technology poses risks. The paper focuses on NFT risks and problems, with a specific emphasis on AML/CFT. AML and CFT issues might arise due to decentralized blockchain transactions and allow for non-intermediary peer-to-peer transactions without any supervision. Furthermore, because there is no clear precedence for regulating NFTs, they are connected with jurisdictional problems.

As a result, it might put the traditional FATF rules, which focused on the regulation or oversight of intermediaries, to the test. In October 2020, the Office of Foreign Asset Control (OFAC) issued an advisory warning, identifying high-value artwork as the source of restricted people's access to the US market and financial system.

Bottom Line

The field of NFTs certainly faces a broad spectrum of dangers and problems. Because it is a new area, resolving non-fungible token risks and issues will aid its development. Identifying many dangers and problems with real-world consequences emphasizes the seriousness of each case.

Learn more about NFTs and how to deal with the problems and hazards they pose. As the globe becomes more accessible to NFTs, it's critical to have a consistent regulatory architecture, tailored AML and CFT norms, and safe platforms for NFT development and exchange. Furthermore, having a clear picture of the consequences of each risk and issue might aid in the discovery of alternative solutions.

BECOMING PART OF THE NFT COMMUNITY

The entire concept of decentralized finance, which includes cryptocurrency and NFTs, is a concept that came into public consciousness a little more than ten years ago. NFTs, in particular, have been around for less time than that. Thus, the field is still malleable and fluid, with everyone coming up with many different concepts and ideas. As an outcome, some of these ideas will fall by the wayside, and some of them will define the future of NFTs in both particular and decentralized finance.

A few early adopters and far-seekers are already seeing the potential in NFTs. They are preparing to be at the forefront of the evolution by seeking like-minded individuals to form a community, given that communities have a farther reach than an individual can ever have—even if the individual has the most modern gadgets or is the most experienced trader or businessperson.

There is a common misconception that creators and traders will shape the NFT space. While those people are undoubtedly crucial to developing the NFT space, they are not the only people who have significant roles to play. So, if you are a newbie coming into the NFT space, I'll advise you on finding a community to join. Once you have entered that community, you can then find other ways to contribute to the growth of your NFT community.

Blogging (Includes Podcasts, Youtube, Vlogs)

It is usually misconstrued that most of the jobs available for people in the NFTs world are for "artists" or "graphic designers" since NFTs are "artsy"; however, many people entering these fields are looking for information and regular updates along with guidance. This need is where sites and blogs come into the equation. There are now tons of people who don't even trade in NFTs and have never created a single NFT artwork, but who have made huge money by aggregating ideas from different people into helpful information newbies can use, along with more experienced creators and traders.

My point? Bloggers make tons of money from explicitly blogging about NFTs. If there are millions of people trading and performing different operations on NFT platforms, millions of people seek to acquire more knowledge about them. The truth is that most people in NFTs either have no time to do exhausting research of subjects in the field or are overwhelmed by the fluidity of the space. So, if you can harmonize seemingly disparate ideas, and break complex notions or ideas into more straightforward concepts, then blogging about NFTs might be helpful for you to break into the NFT space.

Community Managers

The ultimate determinant of whether a field will grow is the creation of communities. And the people who will be at the forefront of those communities and who will shape their futures are not just good at the technicalities of NFTs but are also good at bringing people together—not only across different spheres, but also across different states, countries, or even continents.

A space where community managers will prove crucial is in areas at a disadvantage because of their location—for example, people in technologically less-developed rooms like in sub-Saharan Africa, Asia, parts of Latin America, or even within the United States itself.

Thus, if you can bring people together and have the ability or the time to moderate a forum where everyone—regardless of race, gender, or location—can express their ideas without being intimidated or silenced, you can be part of the NFT community.

Researchers

Researchers collate data and process it to become information. A researcher aims to provide valuable details about improving a product or service. People and companies are beginning to get honest about the fact that not only have NFTs come to stay, but they are also the future. Therefore, researchers are constantly working on improving the platforms to improve blockchain's security. Researchers also conduct in-depth analyses about the NFT industry.

Most traders and creators have day jobs that might not do much research. Thus, researchers need to understand and predict the volatility of the NFTs market since it's all a business of risk. Researchers who can make a difference in volatility prediction have a front-row seat in the NFT world.

Web Developers

While it may sound like web developers do the same work as software engineers, they don't. Software engineers build and maintain NFT platforms and applications while web developers write and maintain code. With the plethora of NFT platforms and applications available now, there is no denying that web developers will look for jobs in that space. Usually, being qualified gets you a job, and in the NFT market, there seems to be a lot of emphasis on qualification and expertise. Therefore, web developers must have Python, Solidity, React, and JavaScript skills.

Writers

There is a need for writers who are not just bloggers but skilled at technical and academic writing. If history serves well, the first Bitcoin white paper was written by Satoshi Nakamoto.

Although Bitcoin did not boom upon its creation, Nakamoto's white paper kept hope alive for his dream. The white paper gave investors something to believe in, and they invested in it well enough to make it become the current boss of all NFTs platforms. As a result, the development of NFTs is moving beyond hobbyists and enthusiasts to include academic studies, so writers must document this development.

Without a doubt, the rapid expansion of NFTs will lead to more forms of NFTs aside from the ones we know now. Hence, there will be a need to write white papers for these NFT start-ups. Most founders do not do this job alone; they try to see who can help convey the purpose of their platforms in more readable terms as this will help fetch investors. And as we all know, investors make companies grow.

Business Representatives

In every company, there is a group of people whose sole job is to represent their interests wherever they find themselves, or more specifically, wherever the company sends them. For most of these business representatives, what works for them is conducting analytical research on the company they wish to work for. Thus, these employers are satisfied they don't have to worry about bringing them up to speed about the mission and vision of the company.

This situation also occurs for NFTs. With the pool of competition, there is a need for experienced people who can adeptly communicate the company's strengths and benefits to investors and the public. It is no longer news that today's world is becoming a world of propaganda where people believe what they are told to think, regardless of the source. Therefore, it is better to have people who communicate "the real thing" to the public. For NFT platforms, traders are willing to use which serves their interests most.

Many "big leagues" on Bitcoin discourage people from making Bitcoin their number-one choice. Business representatives can meet the need for other platforms that serve their interests.

Strategists

This list is incomplete without these people. As most people call them, strategists or financial analysts help people and companies make the right decisions when it comes to trading or investing in NFT platforms. In addition, these people constantly conduct analyses of NFT platforms, which gives them the authority to advise people on the market's volatility.

Strategists help tell traders and investors when it is wise to go long or short, when to trade, and when to retain. In addition, they enlighten their clients through online chain tool accounts and explain how to expand their trading ledgers realistically.

Much emphasis has been placed on the necessity of communities being incorporated into NFTs due to the latter's expansion. Software engineers are needed to build reliable NFT platforms and applications. AI engineers are required to program good algorithms for blockchain. Bloggers are required to offer up-to-date information and resources to people invested in NFTs. Researchers are needed to collate information and conduct an in-depth analysis of NFT growth for predictions. Writers are required to write white papers to woo investors and categorically state the mission of emerging NFT platforms. Yet, you should know these occupations are only a few of the roles available in the booming NFT world.

There is no doubt there will always be a place for human communities in NFTs. The NFT community has come to stay and will continue to grow. One should not misconstrue this situation as humans being a means to an end, but rather, the key to continuing forging the expected future for NFTs. It is also essential to cite that you do not have to be restricted to a single role; you can be fluid and perform different functions, just like NFTs. The most important thing is to continue growing and learning about the NFT space.

TOKENIZING

The concept of tokenizing is taking an object and assigning a digital token. That has always been done by attaching the token to the physical object itself in the past. Think of it as a coupon or a gift card. You can't take the value with you when you go, but you can use it in that store or restaurant. That works great for physical items, but what about digital?

NFTs allow us to attach that "coupon" to something digital. Your item is then represented on the blockchain and can be used by others as they see fit. That opens up a lot of potential in the digital world. We wouldn't usually take or store many items digitally, but now we can.

That is a new frontier for the digital world, and there is still much to learn and discover.

What Is Tokenization

Tokenization is the process of taking a digital object and turning it into a digital token. That is commonly done with collectibles. For example, if you have a rare item, like a Pikachu card or a pack of cards with one valuable card in it, you can tokenize it and take that value and turn it into something else. You can then sell the digital token to anyone in the world with crypto. In other words, Tokenization will allow you to take your items and make money out of them if you don't want them or need them anymore.

Minting An Nft

Minting is the process of taking an NFT and making it available to be sold. When a token is minted, it is created out of thin air, and you own that token. The token will show up in your wallet as a new asset when this happens. That can be done with any NFT with metadata attached to it.

There are two of the most common ways to mint an NFT. The first way is to take your item and scan it into a mobile application like Decentraland or CryptoKitties. Then you can send that item into their system, where they track all of the things in their ecosystem and assign them an ID number.

The second way is to upload the image file of your item into an online platform like Rare Bits or OPSkins. Once this has stood accomplished, you can go on either app and search or buy your item from yourself.

You will need to research which one is right for you. Rare Bits and OPSkins have both been around for a while and have done well, but Decentraland and CryptoKitties are sometimes considered up-and-comers. Decentraland, in particular, has a lot of hype around it, so it is worth looking into when you are researching Tokenization.

The Process Of Tokenizing

The process of tokenizing can be broken down into four steps: creating a token, the initial offering, the trading/trading pairing, and the final exchange.

Token Creation

The first step is creating a token. That is a way of assigning value to an item or object. You can do this by creating a new token with a fixed value. Then you can use that item or object as collateral for the token's value. That is the same concept as a gift card because it was created after it was bought.

Initial Offering

The next step is to offer that token for sale. That is done through an Initial Offering (IO). The IO involves creating a smart contract that will allow people to buy and sell your token on an exchange. When you conduct this sale, you take the value of your physical object and turn it into a digital deal. If you were to sell your physical object, you would be selling its monetary value and not its actual object. That's why this process is called Tokenization.

Trading Pairing/Listing

This part of the process involves pairing your new token with another crypto asset so people can buy it on an exchange. That is the process of pairing your token with tokens already on sale, so people can buy it using an existing crypto asset. For example, if you wanted to sell your Pikachu Pokeball token, you would need to pair it with BTC, ETH, or any other token already on an exchange. This pairing is done using the smart contract you created in the IO.

Final Exchange

This part of the process is to list your token on an exchange. Once your token has been paired with another crypto asset, you can list it on a deal for people to buy and sell it. That will give your new token an accurate market value that anyone in the world can take advantage of.

Tokenizing Guidelines

Now that you have a fundamental idea of Tokenization, here are some guidelines to consider. That will help you when it comes time to tokenize your items.

Value

First of all, the item should be valuable to a broad audience. That is a safety precaution and will ensure that your item will always have value. Think of a rare piece of art or a one-of-a-kind item from the past. Those are perfect uses for Tokenization. Digital collectibles are also a great idea since they can be created and destroyed at any time by the creator.

Authenticity

The digital token you create should be linked to a physical item or object. That can be a simple serial number or an item ID tied to the original piece. That will ensure that no one can fake your item and sell it as the real thing. It will also allow people to track the history of your item, ensuring that they can trust the history and value of your token.

Liquidity To Fiat Currency

Once you have created your token, make sure you know how to liquidate it back into fiat currency. That is important for two reasons:

You can get your money when you are finished with the item.

You can sell it to someone else and allow them to continue the life cycle of your item. If you are tokenizing a vintage baseball card, for example, the token should be sold back into fiat currency.

It should be able to be sold again as an NFT.

Trustless

Your NFT should also be trustless. That means that you don't have to trust the issuer to hold on to them to retain their value. That makes them much easier for people who are collecting or looking at items as investments since they don't have to worry about the issuer backing out on them or not being able to liquidate their tokens back into fiat currency.

Should Be A Digital Asset

The token created should be a digital asset. That means it will be stored on the Ethereum blockchain and won't have any value outside the blockchain. That will ensure that no one can do anything with the token that you wouldn't like, like sending it to an address they control or creating replicas of your item and selling it as accurate.

Transparency

You also want to ensure transparency about how your tokens work. Explain what they are for the public in a way that makes sense and how they can use them. Also, make sure you provide information on how to access them, who owns them, and what the contract is storing them on the blockchain if someone wants to get into your NFT details more deeply. Transparency will help create trust in your NFTs from your supporters and users across the industry. That will also ensure that people are confident in selling goods in the future that may be tokenized.

Have A Blockchain Labeled For Your Token

It would help to create a blockchain specifically designed for your token. You can do this by making your blockchain or using an existing one like Ethereum. That will ensure that your NFTs are easy to find and accessible across the internet in the future. It will also allow you to have specific functions written into the smart contracts that tokenize your item, so people can access only certain things about it, like how much it is worth or when it was created. You can even create a marketplace on your blockchain to sell items and offer rewards for doing so in exchange for tokens on your chain.

The Importance Of Certificates And The Basics Of Issuing A Tokenization Certificate

Tokenization Certificates are the first step to turning your physical item into a digital token. The Certificate is a document issued by a trustworthy third party that tells you that your own thing is now tokenized. This Certificate will contain information on what item it is, the date of issuance, an ID number for the tokenized asset, and your ownership. The Certificate will also have details on when you can sell your tokenized asset or whether you can only trade it with other people who have issued certificates, or if it can be switched on a digital exchange.

For example, let's say that you collect baseball cards and have 30 valuable baseball cards in your collection. To protect these cards from being lost or damaged, you decide to have them protected digitally through Tokenization. You go to an NFT Certifier and submit 60 baseball card cards to get them all tokenized at once. After some time has passed, you receive your Certificate, and now your baseball cards are officially tokenized.

The issuer of the Certificate may charge you for this service. That can be in the form of cash or NFTs that they own. For example, if you were to take your baseball cards to a certification agency like NFT Certifiers, they would issue you a Certificate for each card worth USD 0.25 Each. You can then take these certificates to another third party and exchange them for other NFTs on their platform or sell them on an exchange.

How To Issue Your Tokens/Certificates

There are different ways to issue your tokens/certificates depending on what asset you want to tokenize and how much trust you want in your business or brand.

One way is using a platform like NFT Certifiers, a neutral third-party forum that issues certificates for physical items and digital assets/NFTs. You could also set up your certificate issuer and have it act as a broker between you and the customer. You would have to make sure that the assets you issue are secure and cannot be copied or forged.

You can also issue your certificates through your digital wallets. That can be done by taking pictures of the physical objects you want to tokenize or scanning them with a camera, then adding them into an excel document with their names, descriptions, images, and ID numbers. You can then check this document into your digital wallet. Then when someone wants to buy one of these tokens, you will send them the token directly from your wallet, just like any other digital asset or NFT.

IS NFTS REALLY REVOLUTIONARY?

In many ways, NFTs have the potential to be revolutionary. They are an asset class that has formerly been nonexistent, and they have already shown themselves to be a significant disruptor in the world of gaming.

However, NFTs are not perfect. There are many challenges that developers will need to overcome if they want to make NFTs a reality for everyone. That is where things get tricky.

NFTs, by their very nature, cannot function without some form of blockchain technology or another similar technology. That presents a significant problem for most developers because the current blockchain space is relatively inaccessible for developers who don't have the proper technical knowledge or resources at their disposal. For this cause, there is a strong need for better developer tools and a more robust blockchain infrastructure if NFTs are going to achieve mainstream adoption anytime soon.

In addition to these challenges, it will take some time before players get used to having digital assets that can be traded freely on secondary markets and even longer before people start spending money on digital assets instead of spending money on traditional video games themselves. That being said, as long as progress is made on both of these fronts (developer tools and more robust infrastructure), it won't be long before NFTs become a reality for everyone.

NFTs are still in their infancy, but there is no denying that they have the potential to be revolutionary. They have already shown themselves to be major disruptors in the world of gaming. If developers continue to push forward with them, it won't be long before the mainstream population uses them. However, there are still many challenges that developers will need to overcome if they want to make NFTs a reality for everyone.

What Makes Nfts So Unique:

NFTs are a particular type of digital asset that has never existed before. These assets are very similar to traditional digital ones, but they can be far more valuable and exciting than conventional ones.

Traditional digital assets have existed for many years now, but they haven't changed much over the years. With NFTs, however, there is a possibility that they will change a lot in the coming years. They can vary by becoming more secure, getting more adoption from developers and gamers alike, and getting more widespread support from exchanges and other organizations.

Because of this, NFTs could become far more valuable than traditional digital assets. That is because of their potential to create actual ownership over in-game items and even other things such as land or even tangible goods such as cars or houses in the future.

Another reason why NFTs are so special is because they are genuinely open source for anyone who desires to use them in their games or on their platforms. Everything is already built into the NFT protocol, and everything is open source. Because of this, developers can create unique games and applications without worrying about copyright infringement or other legal issues that may arise when using NFTs with other technologies like blockchain technology or smart contracts.

However, there are still some challenges that developers will need to overcome if they want to make NFTs a reality for everyone. These challenges include that NFTs can only function with blockchain technology or another similar technology. That means that most developers don't have the proper technical knowledge or resources at their disposal to create NFTs for their games. That is why there is an emotional need for better developer tools and a more robust blockchain infrastructure if NFTs will achieve mainstream adoption anytime soon.

What Are The Conditions For Nfts To Go Mainstream?

It's an excellent question, but one that is difficult to answer. Theoretically, NFTs could be used in various applications and even have their currency that can be used to buy/sell items or pay for services.

However, the actual execution of this is not so simple. NFTs need to solve two main problems: scalability and interoperability. Let's research each of these in more detail.

Scalability

The NFT ecosystem has two problems that prevent it from being genuinely scalable: blockchain bloat and slow transactions.

To understand blockchain bloat, we must first understand the difference between State Channels and Off-Chain Transactions (OCT). A State Channel is a communication channel between parties in which transactions are conducted off-chain instead of on-chain (which most blockchains do). That means that transactions do not need to be broadcast across the entire network but only between the parties involved in the transaction itself. That saves time and computational power and reduces blockchain bloat by limiting transactions to just those relevant to a specific contract or innovative contract operation (in our case, an NFT transaction). To learn more about State Channels, click here.

OCT refers to transactions being conducted off-chain (in a State Channel) or on-chain. For example, Ethereum currently uses on-chain transactions, meaning that every transaction has to be processed by the entire network.

NFTs have their unique scalability issues due to the nature of NFTs themselves. The Ethereum blockchain is currently incapable of processing all on-chain transactions needed for an NFT ecosystem (e.g., all transactions related to auctions, commerce, and transfers). That is because it takes an extremely long time for Ethereum's Proof of Work (PoW) algorithm to process a transaction. And even then, it's not guaranteed that your transaction will be included in the next block (it could take hours or even days). That means that users are limited in how much they can transact within a certain period — if you try to transact too much at once, your transaction may never go through. It's just not scalable enough for mass adoption yet.

The solution? State Channels! Using State Channels can eliminate some of these issues by allowing users to conduct NFT transactions off-chain and limiting the number of transactions to only those relevant to the contract or intelligent contract operation. That permits quicker and more efficient transactions that don't have to be processed by the entire network.

But how can we do this with NFTs? Currently, State Channels are not compatible with NFTs. That is because an NFT transaction is essentially a simple "message" between two parties, meaning that it doesn't include any vital information about the transaction itself (e.g., "the sender transferred X amount of tokens to the receiver at address Y"). So how can we create a State Channel that works with NFTs?

We need a protocol that allows us to use State Channels with an NFT — one which gives us:

Privacy: State Channels allow users to conduct transactions off-chain without broadcasting them on-chain. That means that they are not visible to other users on the blockchain (or other blockchains). But for this to work, all parties involved in a transaction must see the details of the transaction. So how can we ensure privacy while using State Channels?

Fungibility: As mentioned above, a significant issue with NFTs is that each token has a unique identifier, meaning that each token is not interchangeable. That means that if I were to send you a token with an identifier that you don't recognize, you would reject it. That is because it is essentially useless to you — there's no way for you to determine whether or not the token was sent to me by mistake or if I am trying to scam you by sending you an unusable token. But what if we could eliminate this problem?

Uniqueness: State Channels only allow us to broadcast transactions on-chain in the case of an error or dispute (i.e., a conflict arises when the two parties involved in the transaction disagree on what happened).

State Channels are an excellent solution for scalability issues, but they cannot be used for NFTs without these three requirements above. So how can we solve these problems? Well, let's take a look at some solutions and their limitations:

Solution 1: NFTs Without State Channels (on-chain)

This possibility does not require any protocol changes. It simply requires that users use the Ethereum blockchain directly to conduct NFT transactions. In this case, all transactions are visible to everyone on the blockchain. That means that there is no privacy or fungibility issue. Still, it also means that the network would have to process many on-chain transactions (e.g., every transaction between every NFT owner).

Solution 2: Non-fungible Tokens (NFTs) With State Channels (off-chain)

This option requires protocol changes that allow for privacy and fungibility of NFTs while using State Channels. This solution is theoretically possible but difficult to implement. It would require some anonymization layer for each token so that two tokens with different identifiers can be used interchangeably within a single transaction (i.e., it allows you to send me an NFT even if I don't recognize its identifier). That can only be done if all NFTs are stored in a single address, meaning that all tokens are fungible and there is no privacy issue.

The problem with this solution is that it requires each NFT to be stored in a single address, meaning they are not genuinely non-fungible. For instance, let's say that you created a CryptoKitty and want to sell it for some ETH. If all NFTs are stored in a single address, then anyone can easily see the value of your CryptoKitty and buy it from you (or copy your CryptoKitty's identifier and make their copy). That means that you would lose ownership of your CryptoKitty without getting paid.

For this solution to work, we need to come up with some way to hide the value of each token while still allowing for privacy (so that no one can see which tokens are owned by which users). The most helpful way to do this would be through Ring Signatures — an advanced cryptographic method used for ring signatures (and often used in cryptocurrencies) that allows users to conceal their identities while sending transactions. But even then, there is still a risk of loss because if someone could copy your NFT's identifier, they could still copy your token. That is because Ring Signatures only allow you to conceal the transaction sender's identity, not the sender's address.

Solution 3: Non-fungible Tokens (NFTs) With State Channels (off-chain) and Protocol Changes

This option requires protocol changes that allow for privacy and fungibility of NFTs while using State Channels. The protocol changes necessary for this solution are similar to those needed for Solution 2 above, but with one significant difference: they require that all NFTs be stored in a single address — meaning that all tokens are fungible and there is no privacy issue.

But what if we could eliminate the possibility of copying an NFT's identifier? Well, we can! But first, we need to understand how Ethereum works with smart contracts. Currently, all smart contracts in Ethereum are stored on the blockchain. That means that any information within a smart contract is visible to everyone on the blockchain (i.e., all smart contracts are public). So how can we solve this problem? We need to store only an encrypted version of our smart contract on the blockchain instead of the entire agreement.

HOW IS A PIECE OF DIGITAL ART ONE OF A KIND THROUGH AN NFT?

When it comes to online copyrights, digital artists - or those who digitize their works - have had a hard time in history. It's easier to use non-fungible tokens with smart contracts to protect copyrights. That is because non-fungible tokens enable you to have detailed attributes like owner identity, metadata, and a safe connection.

Let's face it: paying for an abstract property of digital content hosted on the internet goes against the well-known mode of operation, in which you can download absolutely anything for free with just one click. And this essentially means the original copyright for a piece of work cannot be easily verified after many different copies go into circulation. The amount of art then loses its value, and there is no compensation for the original author of such art.

NFT experts agree that this technology can solve exactly that dilemma: the near-impossibility of leveraging digital works of art and assigning a monetary value to them. Since we know that "NFT is an individual digital asset passport that records the ownership," it makes sense that it can be leveraged. That can be done by simply attaching a unique identity to an original copy of digital art and its subsequent digitalized copies.

For example, you bought yourself a seat on the train. It is characterized by a unique combination of carriage and number. Even if you print out a thousand tickets and distribute them to everyone around you, the seat is yours only. Also, anyone can download a digital asset for themselves. Nevertheless, it is allocated to the owner in the same way as the seat on the train endorsed by the ticket. It turns out that NFTs are tokens that give rights to unique items.

Tokens can only have one official owner. A decentralized blockchain protects them - information is stored by thousands of nodes worldwide. Since they write every operation to the registry, it is nearly impossible to change or tamper with it. Moreover, the details about the owner are easy to verify. Also, NFTs can be easily bought, sold, or created, which is also a convenient way to transfer ownership.

Let's take this step by step. First,

What Is Cryptoart?

Any artwork tokenized using blockchain technology is referred to as crypto art. These are limited-edition multimedia artworks in pictures, videos, or GIFs with unique tokens. That enables collectors, artists, and enthusiasts to purchase, sell, and exchange digital goods as if they were physical goods. The certainty that a limited number of artist-authorized 'pieces' of the artwork encourages 'tradability' of the artwork at a value. As a result of stable blockchain technology, the digital signature on the file is indelible and non-fungible.

In simple language, crypto art is a digital art prized as physical since its ownership can be proved.

The authenticity of IK Aivazovsky's original work "The Ninth Wave" from the Russian Museum is checked by his signature on the raft, art critics' opinions, and scientific knowledge. Using NFT (Non-Fungible Token) technology, the cryptographic image's validity is checked in probably even more secure ways.

The ease of copying and redistributing digital art is a significant and ongoing problem. When something is freely reproduced and distributed, its value plummets, and the whole market perspective disintegrates. An object or service must be in short supply to be valuable.

By implementing the blockchain, digital artists can solve this dilemma. Simply put, blockchain has come as a solution to the long-standing problem of digital artists, and this is just by introducing the concept of "digital scarcity"; this means that the artist has only a limited copy of his art in the digital world, and each of this copies is linked to a unique propriety token.

The token is a digital certificate stored in the blockchain, a stable and decentralized ledger. It validates your right to anything unique. It can be attached to any image, including JPEG, GIF, MP4 files, and music. The blockchain stores this token, proving ownership of the "original" file.

"NFT is a type of intellectual property whose ownership is publicly verified on the blockchain."

Anyone can download and exchange your painting and even print and display it on their wall, but only you can own it. And you stand the only one who can sell this work of art. To put it another way, in the crypto world, the blockchain will be the "expert" verifying the validity or the originality of IK Aivazovsky's paintings.

A New Direction In Art

Digital art is part of our trendy culture and is something from our current cultural graphics. Technology is now allowing us to address authenticity in digital art, making digital art as it stands a potentially colossal investment. The advancement of blockchain technology and the concept of digital property have given artists the most significant technology recognition.

Digital art products offered through digital galleries like Superrare have grown significantly over the past few months. Most importantly, the stakes on these digital artworks have also increased considerably.

It is entirely unclear whether the value of these works will increase or decrease over time. In retrospect, we can only determine the actual value of each piece of art or the entire amount of skill.

One of the current problems with digital art is that it is difficult to display. A virtual reality world like Cryptovoxels can provide a way to present digital art to viewers. But there is also the requirement for a physical way to showcase digital art. Maybe a particular screen will be introduced. These unique displays will allow the owners/creators to display their favorite pieces stored on the blockchain in their digital currency package. Digital art can also have moving images, highlighting the importance of using a screen instead of a canvas.

Art's direction now follows a mode of operation that deviates from the conventional norm. Soon, it can almost be concluded with certainty that NFT will verify the identity of most artworks (even physical art). That then raises the question of how. How can NFT be used to confirm a piece of digital art or any other form of digital asset?

Confirming The Authenticity Of Digital Art

The record of transactions that indicates how an artwork passed from one owner to another, linking it back to the actual owner — the artist — is known as provenance. Many art galleries and auction houses use origin to determine the authenticity of a piece of art. To trace an artwork's history to its creator and show that it is authentic, auction records, exhibition records, gallery bills, shipping labels, or dealer stamps are commonly used. Sadly, provenance records are often forged or counterfeited despite all precautions, and fake artworks are sold as originals.

NFTs provide enhanced security and also the unique authentication of valuable assets. In doing business, one essential attribute is trust, and blockchain can defeat this trust and encourage trade and more commercial activity in markets that are deemed risky. Distributed Ledger Technology (DLT) (the blockchain network in this case) helps build trust in industries concerned with non-fungible assets where counterfeiting and tampering are common, such as art and memorabilia. According to a study carried out by Havocvscope, approximately about $480 million worth of art or even more is stolen annually in the UK. Technology can always recognize the originality and authenticity of the collectible (maybe a digital art); track it; create a legal and operational supply chain; and set documents on the ownership, control, and transfer of that collectible.

For example, artists are given a token after submitting a picture of the artwork or a URL of digital painting. They also offer a few basic details to companies that provide tokens, including title, measurements (size and dimension), and date. When the token is provided, the artwork will be added to the blockchain simultaneously. If an artist sells an artwork, the artist passes the token to the new owner along with the artwork, and this token exchange is digitally registered on the blockchain. When an artwork is sold, the change of ownership is written on the blockchain by generating a new block with the deal's data and a time stamp. Any sale is then added to the permanent transaction record.

Therefore, the owner of a piece of art will always remain as long as the blockchain network exists or the ownership token is not transferred to another address. That is very similar to how Bitcoin is monitored and tracked when a transaction takes place. The token is exchanged between two addresses. Depending on how innovators design the application for their intended use, this technology will also record the history of non-fungible assets; add timestamps of critical events, and provide auction prices and other confirmed information.

The blockchain, like provenance, is a ledger, a collection of transactions linked together by cryptography. However, unlike provenance, blockchain is a decentralized technology. A vast network of computers confirms and records transaction data any time a change of possession is recorded on the blockchain by solving complex mathematical algorithms. This history of transactions is nearly impossible to falsify.

Suppose one machine attempts to tamper with these documents. In that case, the rest of the network will notice and reject the modification, making the records nearly impossible to forge.

By tracking the artwork's blockchain URL, you can see how many times an artwork has changed hands since it was created and easily trace it back to the creator. Suppose the token for the artwork you want to purchase comes from the artist's wallet. In that case, you have irrefutable evidence that the artwork is genuine.

Additionally, blockchain technology and NFT are ideal for selling digital art multiples. Creators can sell limited edition digital art to several collectors by simply sending one token to each collector. An artist may authorize an entire series of works by obtaining 50 or 100 tokens as certificates of authenticity.

Printed in Great Britain
by Amazon

NFT
INVESTING

ISBN 9798798305650

9 798798 305650